Leo Hoodman-

W9-AUV-583

GOVERNORS STATE UNIVERSITY LIBRARY

3 1611 00073 8184

THE BANK DIRECTOR'S HANDBOOK

THE
BANK DIRECTOR'S
HANDBOOK

Second Edition

EDWIN B. COX
MARTIN L. ERNST
S. THEODORE GUILD
HOMER J. HAGEDORN
MAURICE D. S. JOHNSON
DONALD H. KORN
ROBERT E. MOLL
ROBERT K. MUELLER
ROBERT P. POPADIC
LEWIS M. RAMBO
GEORGE B. ROCKWELL
BLAIR C. SHICK

Staff of and consultants to Arthur D. Little, Inc.

with the participation of
CHARLES J. THAYER
Citizens Fidelity Corporation

GOVERNORS STATE UNIVERSITY
UNIVERSITY PARK
IL 60466

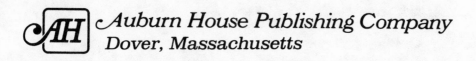

Auburn House Publishing Company
Dover, Massachusetts

HG 1615 .B34 1986

The Bank director's handbook

292183

Copyright © 1986 by Auburn House Publishing Company.

Previous edition copyright © 1981 by
Auburn House Publishing Company.

All rights reserved. No part of this publication may be reproduced,
translated, or transmitted in any form or by any means without
permission in writing from Auburn House Publishing Company.

Library of Congress Cataloging in Publication Data

The Bank director's handbook.

  Includes index.
  1. Bank management—Handbooks, manuals, etc.
2. Banks and banking—United States—Handbooks, manuals,
etc. I. Cox, Edwin Burk, 1930-   .
HG1615.B34   1986   332.1'068   86-3592
ISBN 0-86569-145-2

Printed in the United States of America

FOREWORD

In 1981, when the first edition of *The Bank Director's Handbook* was published, the banking industry was entering what would prove to be a period of significant change. Deregulation, reregulation, and expanding competition have dramatically altered the environment in which banks do business. This new edition addresses the impact of those changes on today's environment while it also looks ahead. It provides an invaluable guide to fundamental banking issues and areas of concern to both management and directors. Roles and responsibilities of the Board are clearly defined. A new chapter recognizes the importance of technology as both a tool and a catalyst in our rapidly changing industry.

As the banking industry has changed, it has become more vital than ever that directors understand the role banks play in today's society. Directors are instrumental in mapping the bank's strategic direction as it attempts to respond to the needs of a changing marketplace. They need to be able to integrate legal and human resource concerns into policy decisions. This book highlights the critical issues in a way which can enable the director to become a more effective partner with bank management.

For both new and experienced directors, this revised edition of *The Bank Director's Handbook* will be a welcome and useful pathfinder to the present as well as into the future.

WALTER J. CONNOLLY, JR.
Chairman
Bank of New England Corporation

FOREWORD

These are very exciting and risky times for bank directors and this handbook provides a basic overview of the responsibilities and the duties of the Bank and Bank holding company directors. The contents are current and relevant and should have broad applicability for both small and large bank directors.

In the past, a bank director's job may have been largely an honorary position but is now a big job and getting bigger. We are faced with a constant changing environment, new business opportunities, consolidation, interstate banking and the list goes on and on. To sort all these choices requires having a general background and knowledge of banking and this handbook fills an important need and should be required reading for all bank directors.

Areas covered that are of a great consequence include: banking functions and services, roles and responsibilities of the Board, asset/liability management, bank capital issues, measuring management's and bank performance, legal concerns of the Board, strategic planning and human resources management, technology and the banking environment of the future. These chapters are up-to-date, comprehensive, and written in simple, easy to understand terms.

The focus on the bank director's role has been greatly magnified in recent months because of bank failures and the litigious society in which we operate. This handbook will be helpful in getting the new director started and be useful to the more experienced director as well.

HAL SCONYERS
President, Modesto Banking Company

PREFACE

As the elected representatives of the shareholders, corporate directors have always been legally accountable for the financial soundness and moral integrity of the corporation. Today, however, the scope of their responsibilities has grown far beyond these traditional areas. In a world of ever-increasing complexity, directors have been forced to become more aware of their responsibility for relationships with employees, customers, and government and for the widening range of influence of the corporation's behavior on society at large. The increasing frequency of challenges to the actions of directors by shareholders testifies to the demise of the era in which a director could be a passive observer of management's decisions. To offset the growing burden of keeping informed about the activities of the business and its management, however, the modern director has the opportunity to play an active role in the work of the board and to exert constructive influence on the affairs of the corporation.

A commercial bank has powers and responsibilities which distinguish it from other corporations and which indeed increase the level of responsibility and the range of opportunity for service of its board of directors. Banks provide the modern lubricant which permits a highly organized, market-centered economy to operate—that is, credit. True, commercial banks offer an array of services that may not seem to embody credit-granting power—for example, accepting deposits, managing trust relationships, facilitating payments with checks and wire transfers, processing corporate payrolls, and providing traveler's checks and foreign currencies. However, all of these services are supplementary to the lifeblood of banking: the granting of credit to worthy borrowers. In the process, banks help businesses expand, families grow, markets develop, technologies mature, and communities prosper. It is the directors who are ultimately responsible for the continuation of the bank's soundness and integrity, so that credit—an essential ingredient of economic prosperity and growth—will continue to be available and used wisely in the community.

This book has been written to help bank directors understand and carry out their responsibilities at a particularly critical time in the evolution of our banking system. Banking executives have been put to severe tests in recent years, as inflation and deregulation combined to create unprecedented change in financial markets. No longer can banks, or their competitors in the thrift industry, expect to see funds deposited in low-interest-bearing savings accounts or in corporate checking accounts carrying high balances and low demands for service with little or no marketing effort. On the contrary, gathering funds has become an intensely competitive business, with interest rates being driven up by market forces and regulatory restraints on those rates rapidly disappearing. While depository institutions (banks, savings and loan associations, savings banks, and credit unions) have intensified their efforts to attract deposits and loans, old and new competitors for banking's traditional markets have risen on all sides, using technology and product innovation to fuel the competitive fires. Commercial paper, for instance, is a well-established competitor to the bank's lending activity, while money market funds have surged to prominence as a competitor for deposits. Changes in the law have brought thrift institutions into the trust, unsecured consumer lending, and credit card businesses. With new, innovative products, brokerage firms and life insurance companies are contending for not only the savings but also the transaction balances of consumers. In short, no area of the bank is left untouched by competitive pressures.

As consultants to commercial banks and to many of the financial institutions competing for the same business, the authors of this book are involved daily with the significant issues facing the directors and management of commercial banks in the United States. We have included coverage of the major areas of responsibility and described the challenge to directors and members of senior bank management. This new edition, written in the fall and winter of 1985, includes discussions of the major trends in banking likely to characterize the banking climate through the rest of the decade.

We believe that you will find much of value in these chapters. It is our hope that the book will contribute to your ability to be an effective director in your bank. Through you, our work can thereby contribute to improving the overall performance of your bank and of the entire banking system, so vital to the health and prosperity of our society.

EDWIN B. COX

ABOUT THE AUTHORS

EDWIN B. COX, a senior member of the Financial Industries Section of Arthur D. Little, Inc., is responsible for strategic, operational, and analytical assignments relating to financial services. Prior to joining Arthur D. Little he taught at Boston University and the University of Pennsylvania's Wharton School. He has authored books in finance and statistics and is editor of the *Bank Performance Annual*. Dr. Cox received his doctorate in economics from the University of Pennsylvania. His articles have appeared in the *Harvard Business Review, ABA Banking Journal*, and *The Bankers Magazine*.

MARTIN L. ERNST is a Vice President of Arthur D. Little, Inc. and a senior member of the corporate professional staff. His primary management responsibility is for company activities in the fields of communications and computer applications and in work concerning the use of technology in financial industries. He previously had served as Associate Director of the Operations Evaluation Group managed by Massachusetts Institute of Technology for the Chief of Naval Operations. Mr. Ernst, a graduate of MIT, is a past president of the Operations Research Society of America.

S. THEODORE GUILD, a senior member of the Financial Industries Group of Arthur D. Little, is concerned with the issues of risk administration and the implementation of strategic decisions, both in this country and abroad. He joined the company after many years as a commercial banking executive. Mr. Guild is a past president of the New England Chapter of Robert Morris Associates and served on the Investment Committee of a Small Business Investment Company. He received an MBA from the Graduate School of Business at Harvard University and is a graduate of Stonier School of Banking.

HOMER J. HAGEDORN is an organization practice leader within Arthur D. Little's Management Counseling Section. He concentrates on problems of organizational change, adaptation, planning, innovation, and policy formulation. He has consulted extensively with managements in business firms, governmental agencies, and non-profit associations and institutions. His focus is on the management of change and adapting the organization to carry out its strategies effectively. Dr. Hagedorn received his Ph.D. in history from Harvard University in 1955. A post-doctoral year at the London School of Economics was followed by work as Assistant Director of Professional Personnel at MIT Lincoln Laboratory. Subsequently, he became Assistant to the Director and a project leader at the Institute of Naval Studies. Dr. Hagedorn joined Arthur D. Little, Inc. in 1966.

MAURICE D. S. JOHNSON, a consultant to the Financial Industries Section of Arthur D. Little, Inc., was formerly chairman of Citizens Fidelity Bank and Trust Company of Louisville, Kentucky. His banking experience includes commercial lending, trust policy supervision, and general bank management, including the formation of a bank holding company. Mr. Johnson has served on the boards of numerous business institutions and non-profit organizations. He is a graduate of the University of Minnesota and received an Honorary LL.D. from Kansas State University.

DONALD H. KORN is principal of DHK Associates, a management and financial consulting firm. He was previously a senior vice president of Independence Investment Associates, Inc., the investment management subsidiary of John Hancock, and formerly a senior management consultant in the Financial Industries Section of Arthur D. Little, Inc. Earlier, Mr. Korn was on the securities research staff of State Street Research and Management Company in Boston. He received advanced degrees in engineering from Tulane University and Massachusetts Institute of Technology. A Chartered Financial Analyst, he is a member of the Boston Security Analysts Society and served on its Board of Directors. Mr. Korn is also co-author of or contributor to five other books and several journal articles in his fields of interest.

ROBERT E. MOLL is a senior member of the Financial Industries Group of Arthur D. Little, Inc., and Manager of the Operations and Technology business unit. His consulting activities are concerned principally with marketing, operations, and computer sciences as they relate to the savings and loan, mutual savings bank, and commercial banking industries. Prior to joining Arthur D. Little, Inc., Mr. Moll was President of Moll Associates, Inc., a subsidiary of Systems Development Corporation. Mr. Moll has received a Bachelor's Degree in Industrial Management and a Master's Degree in Business Administration from Northeastern University.

ROBERT K. MUELLER, former Chairman of Arthur D. Little, Inc., is Chairman of Arthur D. Little Enterprises, Inc., Chairman of the Board of Critical Fluid Systems, Inc., and a Director of Arthur D. Little International, Inc. His responsibilities include corporate governance and management aspects of various industries and financial organizations. Prior to joining Arthur D. Little, he was Vice President of Monsanto Company and a member of its Board of Directors and Executive Committee. Mr. Mueller is a Director of several financial institutions and a Vice Chancellor of the International Academy of Management. The author of numerous books and articles on management and board of director matters, he received a B.S. degree in chemical engineering from Washington University and an M.S. degree in chemistry from the University of Michigan.

ROBERT P. POPADIC, a senior member of the Financial Industries Section of Arthur D. Little, Inc., specializes in assignments in planning, marketing, finance, and management information, particularly as they relate to financial organizations. Prior to joining Arthur D. Little, Mr. Popadic was Vice President of Planning and a member of the Management Committee of State Street Boston Corporation. He received a B.S. in electrical engineering from the Massachusetts Institute of Technology and an MBA from Harvard Graduate School of Business Administration.

LEWIS M. RAMBO, Vice President—Personnel of Arthur D. Little, Inc. directs the full range of personnel activities for the company. He has consulted in the areas of executive compensation and long-term and deferred incentive packages, as well as on organizational analysis and human resource utilization planning and programming. Prior to joining Arthur D. Little, he was Manager, Organization and Manpower, in the Aircraft Engine Group of General Electric Company. Dr. Rambo received a B.A. degree from Southern University and M.A. and Ph.D. degrees from Wayne State University. He has also completed a postdoctoral program at Harvard's Graduate School of Education focusing on midlife career change and pre-retirement planning. He has authored numerous publications concerned with personnel management, training, organization development, and the education and employment of the disadvantaged, minorities, and women.

GEORGE B. ROCKWELL, Vice President of Arthur D. Little, Inc. and Director of the Financial Industries Section, specializes in operational and strategic plans to diversify business risk and optimize return for financial industries. Prior to his association with Arthur D. Little, Mr. Rockwell was Vice Chairman of the State Street Boston Financial Corporation, having formerly served as President and Chief Executive Officer of its major subsidiary, State Street Bank and Trust Company. Mr. Rockwell has served as a director of a number of diversified companies. He is a graduate of Harvard College and Harvard University's Graduate School of Business Administration Advanced Management Program.

BLAIR C. SHICK, a senior member of the Financial Industries Section of Arthur D. Little, Inc., specializes in the distribution and regulation of financial services. A graduate of Dickinson College and the University of Pennsylvania Law School, he is admitted to the practice of law in Florida and Pennsylvania. Mr. Shick was a member of the Consumer Advisory Council of the Board of Governors of the Federal Reserve System from 1977 to 1979 and has published several articles and books on the regulation of financial services.

CHARLES J. THAYER, Executive Vice President and Chief Financial Officer of Citizens Fidelity Bank and Trust Company of Louisville, is responsible for managing the company's accounting, control, financial analysis, corporate planning, and financial relations. His previous responsibilities included the corporate-wide coordination of asset/liability management and workflow management. Mr. Thayer is a graduate of the University of Kansas School of Business and has attended Financial Management Programs offered by Harvard University and Stanford University. He served as a member of the American Bankers Association's Task Force on Bank Accounting Principles from 1977 to 1981.

CONTENTS

CHAPTER 8
Strategy Development 193

Chapter 1

THE CHANGING ROLE OF BANKS IN THE FINANCIAL SERVICES INDUSTRY

by Edwin B. Cox

Introduction: Emergence of the Financial Services Industry

Sometime in the early 1980s, *financial services industry* became the expression widely used to describe all business organizations that offer services relating in some way to financial resources—cash, deposits, credit, payments, investments, taxes, and so forth. In the past, we had banks, life insurance companies, securities brokers, and finance companies. Each occupied a well-defined niche in the financial marketplace, provided a well-defined set of services, and could be expected to stay within its niche and field of service. Thus, we have always been comfortable with references to "the banking industry," the "insurance industry," or "the brokerage industry." Although these industries have not disappeared, they should be thought of as components of the larger financial services industry, a phrase that emphasizes the growing interconnectedness of firms in the previously separate categories.

As the director of a commercial bank, you will find it increasingly important to recognize the relationships of your bank to other types of financial service providers. Some of these relationships

1

may be competitive, while others may be cooperative, even to the extent of being affiliated with the same holding company. A growing number of financial service businesses are broadening their product line and/or becoming partners with other financial service providers through holding-company or franchise affiliations. The historic separations are crumbling as banks and others take advantage of opportunities provided by changes in law or regulation, new technology, and innovative financial products to diversify their product line and take on an ever-widening range of competitors in the marketplace.

Chapter 1 briefly profiles the participants in the financial services industry. It then offers a deeper look at the banking industry and how it is changing. The chapter closes with some consideration of the forces that are changing the role of banks as providers of financial services. Later chapters provide an in-depth look at the role and responsibilities of bank directors, what banks do and how, and the critical strategic issues that will face banks in the latter years of the 1980s.

Profile of the Financial Services Industry

The businesses active in the financial services industry are those that have traditionally been referred to as *financial intermediaries*—so named because they assist in the operation of financial markets by moving funds from providers (depositors, savers, investors) to users (borrowers, entrepreneurs). At the beginning of 1985, financial intermediaries held approximately $6 trillion in assets, with commercial banks accounting for about one-third of this amount (Table 1–1).

When thrift institutions (savings and loans, savings banks, and credit unions) are added to commercial banks and affiliates, we find that deposit-taking financial institutions hold more than half of the assets of financial intermediaries. These deposit-taking institutions differ from all other financial service organizations in one important respect: They hold deposits insured by government-backed organizations (Federal Deposit Insurance Corporation and Federal Savings and Loan Insurance Corporation). A few deposit-taking institutions remain outside the federal insurance structure, but the number is declining rapidly, and the share of deposits held in them

Table 1-1　Domestic Assets of Financial Intermediaries (December 31, 1984)

Financial Intermediaries	Assets	
	Billions of $	Percent of
Commercial banks and affiliates	2019	34
Savings and loans	990	17
Savings banks	205	3
Credit unions	115	2
Insurance companies		
Life	695	12
Property and casualty	240	4
Finance companies	283	5
Pension funds		
Private	623	10
State and local government	352	6
Money market mutual funds	210	3
Other mutual funds	161	3
Brokers and dealers	55	1
REIT	4	0
Total	5952	100

Source: Flow of Funds Accounts, Board of Governors of the Federal Reserve System.

Note: While these numbers may differ from those appearing in the text or subsequent tables due to definition and measurement methods, they are internally consistent and can therefore be used for comparison purposes.

is trivially small. Failures during 1985 of state-insured thrifts in Ohio and Maryland have speeded this process.

Funds flow into other financial organizations in a variety of ways, including the sale of stocks or bonds, the receipt of premiums, direct investment by owners, or the sale of shares in the case of mutual funds. Financial innovation—the invention of new financial products and services—has accelerated dramatically in recent years, as ingenious individuals and organizations respond to new needs and opportunities for service. Although the fundamental needs they serve, and therefore the functions they perform, have not changed dramatically, financial intermediaries offer a growing number of recently introduced services that demand greater levels of sophistication among users and providers and call forth new competitive responses, as well as regulatory and legislative responses. There is truly a new dynamism in the financial services industry that is challenging established managements, attracting new and talented young managers, and spawning an entire new generation of financial service-providing organizations.

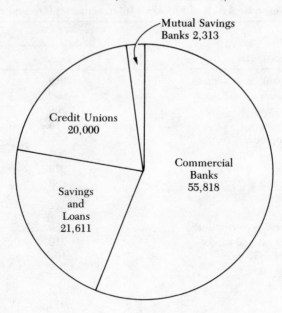

Locations (Total = 100 Thousand)

Mutual Savings
Banks 2,313

Credit Unions
20,000

Commercial
Banks
55,818

Savings
and
Loans
21,611

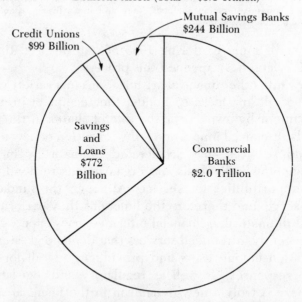

Domestic Assets (Total = $3.1 Trillion)

Credit Unions
$99 Billion

Mutual Savings Banks
$244 Billion

Savings
and
Loans
$772
Billion

Commercial
Banks
$2.0 Trillion

Figure 1–1 Commercial Banks Compared with Thrift Institutions (December 31, 1983). (*Source: Bankers Desk Reference,* 1985, Warren, Gorham, and Lamont.)

Commercial Banks

Commercial banks play a vital role in the life of every community and region of the United States, in that they provide essential services to governments, businesses, and consumers. Businesses, large and small, must have banking relationships to make and receive payments, to secure needed credit, and to benefit from a wide array of other banking services (international, corporate trust, stock transfer, cash management, and so on). Commercial banks provide retail services through branches and automated teller machines located conveniently in every neighborhood and commercial area, where they compete vigorously for the deposit and loan business of families and individuals. At the start of 1984, commercial banks operated nearly 56,000 banking offices throughout the country. Thrift institutions operated an additional 44,000 offices, so that, in total, the public had 100,000 offices of deposit-taking institutions serving their needs (Figure 1–1).

Commercial banks are an important source of credit for consumers; they provide nearly one-half of the consumer installment credit, and nearly one-fifth of mortgage credit (Figure 1–2). Other financial service providers play important roles in these markets, as well. Finance companies and credit unions provide over one-third of consumer installment credit, and about two-fifths of the mortgage lending is done by savings and loan associations, mutual savings banks, and life insurance companies.

Thrift Institutions

Commercial banks feel strong competitive pressure from many directions. The most direct competition is from thrift institutions, or "thrifts." These include about 600 savings banks, 3,400 savings and loans associations, and 19,000 credit unions. The thrift institutions are like commerical banks to the extent that they accept and hold deposits that can be withdrawn on demand by the customer. Thrifts have historically focused their services on the consumer market, where they have recently gained broader powers. Savings banks and savings and loan associations have also won new authority to provide services to business customers. Thrifts are chartered by the federal government or by a state government and are—with rare exceptions—members of a federal or state organization that

Shares of Consumer Installment Credit (Total = $460 Billion)

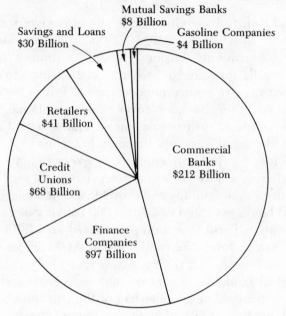

Mutual Savings Banks
$8 Billion

Savings and Loans
$30 Billion

Gasoline Companies
$4 Billion

Retailers
$41 Billion

Commercial
Banks
$212 Billion

Credit
Unions
$68 Billion

Finance
Companies
$97 Billion

Shares of Mortgage Debt (Total = $2,034 Billion)

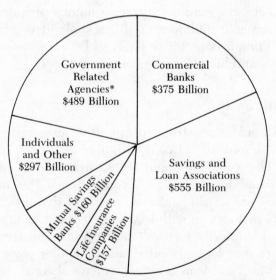

Government
Related
Agencies*
$489 Billion

Commercial
Banks
$375 Billion

Individuals
and Other
$297 Billion

Savings and
Loan Associations
$555 Billion

Mutual Savings
Banks $160 Billion

Life Insurance
Companies
$157 Billion

*Includes $332 billion in guaranteed-mortgage backed securities.

Figure 1–2   Importance of Banks and Their Competition in Supplying Credit.
(All values are as of the end of 1984.) (*Source*: Board of Governors
of the Federal Reserve System.)

insures their deposits. As can be seen in Figure 1–1, thrift institutions hold about a third of the assets of deposit-taking institutions and have about 45 percent of all the locations.

Recent federal legislation blurred the historic distinction between savings banks and savings and loan associations. In the past, savings banks were all state chartered and were concentrated heavily in the Northeast. A savings bank could be organized only as a mutual institution owned by depositors. Savings and loans have always had the choice to obtain a charter from the state or federal government. Federally chartered associations had to be organized on a mutual ownership basis, while state-chartered associations could be owned mutually, or organized as publicly held corporations. Since 1982, mutual savings banks have been free to convert to a federal charter and go public through a sale of stock. Similarly, federally chartered savings and loan associations have been free to sell stock to the public. As a result, no longer does the name of a thrift or the source of its charter necessarily identify the nature of its ownership or the services it offers.

Savings and loans have historically concentrated their assets in mortgage loans and mortgage-related securities, while savings banks have held slightly more diversified portfolios, including securities and consumer loans. At the beginning of 1984, mortgage-related investments represented three-fourths of the assets of savings and loans and 60 percent of the assets of savings banks.

Credit unions, the third type of thrift institution, outnumber all other deposit-taking institutions combined. An average credit union holds only $5 million in assets, and its scale of operation in comparison with any other form of deposit-taking institution is very small. Credit unions are formed by a group of individuals with a "common bond" such as employer or church or fraternal organization. The members decide to try to serve their own needs for a safe place for savings and low-cost small loans. Most credit unions are run by a small staff and a members' committee to review loan applications. The nation's 19,000 credit unions hold about 3 percent of the assets of all deposit-taking institutions; these assets are held almost entirely in the form of loans to members. In some local markets the credit union is a major competitive force for the business of individual customers, with the competition felt most keenly by other small institutions that rely on local presence and personal contact with the public.

Insurance Companies

Life insurance companies have begun to expand far beyond their historic product line, both through the introduction of new products and the acquisition of new subsidiaries and affiliate organizations. Whole life insurance has always had a savings aspect, but more recent introductions such as variable life have an investment as well as a savings feature. Life insurance companies have acquired as subsidiaries banks, thrifts, investment management companies, securities brokers, and financial planning organizations. Life insurance companies continue to compete with commercial banks in the lending area, as a major source of mortgage funds for residential and commercial borrowers, and in the trust area as providers of insured pension programs and annuities to retail and corporate customers.

Other insurance companies (health, property, and casualty) are less involved in new competition with other types of financial service providers, although some are owned by parents engaged in vigorous competitive initiatives (Sears, American Express, Travelers). Product introductions have been motivated less by deregulation or competitors' initiative and more by new market needs, particularly in the health and liability areas.

Securities Brokerage and Investment Banking

Securities brokers traditionally have been identified with marketable securities rather than the deposit of funds or provision of credit, which are traditional banking services. In recent years, however, brokers have innovated services that provide competition to commercial banks, especially for the business of upper-income individuals—an important and profitable market for commercial banks. Brokers provide services that combine the benefits of a checking account, a money market fund, a credit card, and a traditional securities trading account, including margin account services. The outstanding example of this is Merrill Lynch's "Cash Management Account," of which there are reportedly more than 1 million on the books.

Investment banking, the underwriting of securities when first offered in the public market, has been off limits to commercial banks for 50 years as the result of depression-era legislation (the Glass-Steagall Act). However, commercial banks are taking renewed interest in the investment banking business and are trying to reestablish their legal right to engage in securities underwriting.

Mutual Funds

Money market mutual funds continue to offer serious competition to banks for deposits. In the early 1980s, at the peak of interest rates, money market funds attracted $232 billion. After declining to a low of $163 billion at the end of 1983, they resumed their gradual increase, passing $200 billion once again at the end of 1984. The ability of money market funds to attract deposits away from banks in the period of extremely high rates prompted legislation giving deposit-taking institutions the authority to pay market rates on consumers' checking accounts. While this legislation allowed banks to compete on an equitable basis, it has substantially increased the average cost of consumer deposits in commercial banks and thrift institutions.

Mutual funds represent an attractive investment vehicle for individuals and institutions seeking diversification and professional management at a modest cost. As such, mutual funds compete with the services of brokers, bank trust departments, and insurance companies. The number of funds has grown from 564 in 1980 to 1,246 in 1984, as sponsoring investment management organizations appeal to the specialized needs of investors in particular market segments. The assets under management in equity, bond, and income funds (not including money market funds) have grown from $58 billion in 1980 to more than $137 billion at the end of 1984.

Finance Companies

Finance companies have long been a source of small consumer installment loans. With offices in communities of all sizes, they offer competition to the consumer loan activity of commercial banks and credit unions. Many consumer finance companies have been acquired by bank holding companies. In some markets, the competition for a bank may be coming from the consumer finance subsidiary of an out-of-state bank holding company. While some consumer finance companies are owned by bank holding companies, other consumer finance companies have acquired small commercial banks or thrifts to gain access to the payment system and provide the vehicle for holding deposits as well as supplying consumer credit.

Commercial finance companies provide business financing and thereby compete with the commercial lending activities of commercial banks. Bank holding companies have shown more interest in acquiring retail finance companies than commercial finance companies. This is because the retail finance company provides an instant network of retail locations, often in states where the bank could not branch. Commercial finance companies do not offer this attraction.

Mortgage Bankers

Mortgage bankers are special-purpose financial businesses that deal in residential and commercial real estate mortgage origination and servicing. They compete directly with commercial banks in these activities. Many bank holding companies have acquired mortgage banking companies as wholly owned subsidiaries, to extend the mortgage activities of the bank into geographic areas distant from the bank. A commercial bank may compete in its local market with a mortgage bank owned by an out-of-state bank holding company. Bank holding companies see mortgage company acquisitions as well as consumer finance company acquisitions as ways to penetrate out-of-state markets. The increasing variety of participants in the financial services industry is demonstrated by the 1981 acquisition of the nation's largest mortgage banking organization, Coldwell Banker, by Sears Roebuck and Company.

Retailers

Sears Roebuck and Company is not truly a recent entry into the financial services business, since Sears has owned Allstate Insurance for decades. However, other retailers are taking on new importance as competitors in the financial services business. Sears and J. C. Penney both own commercial banks. K Mart provides space for branches of several different deposit-taking institutions in its stores.

While retailers take on new roles in the financial services business, they also hold the view that banks are newcomers in competing with them for their traditional business. Retail merchants have long offered credit to their customers to encourage purchases in their stores. In the late 1960s, banks created the bank credit card to provide the same form of credit on a multistore basis. Many smaller retailers dropped their individual credit programs completely and have replaced them with the bank credit card. Some large retailers continue their own program and accept the bank credit card in addition. A few large regional and national department store chains still do not accept the bank card, but rather rely on their own credit program. The bank credit card emerged because the banks entered a market to compete with retailers who were already established providers of credit. Sears Roebuck and Company sponsors a multimerchant card, the "Discover Card," in direct competition with bank cards. Thus, retailers are seen as competitors by banks, while banks are seen as competitors by retailers.

Foreign Banks

Foreign banks have become a major competitive force in the large money centers of the United States—New York, Chicago, San Francisco, Los Angeles, and, most recently, Miami. The traditional role of foreign banks in the United States has been to serve in an agency capacity, assisting firms based in their home country in their dealings with U.S. businesses and vice versa. They are now taking a more aggressive role by establishing full service banks in this country, either opening a new bank or acquiring an established U.S. bank. In the last 10 years, 7 of the 50 largest banks in the United States (including the 11th and the 13th largest) have been acquired by foreign owners, expanding the financial capacity of the acquired bank and giving it immediate relationships with other components of the acquiring banking organization around the world.

These developments are generally believed to be in the best interests of the U.S. businesses using the services of foreign-owned banks, but some concern has been raised about the size of the position in the U.S. banking system gained by foreign interests. U.S. banks, of course, have held a major position within the banking systems of a number of foreign countries for many years. Under the circumstances it would be unwise to curb too tightly the foreign banking interests here. To date their activities have been

Number of Commercial Banks, 1984 (Total = 16,153)

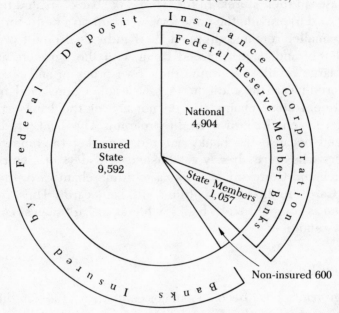

Non-insured 600

Domestic Assets ($Billions) (Total = 2,515)

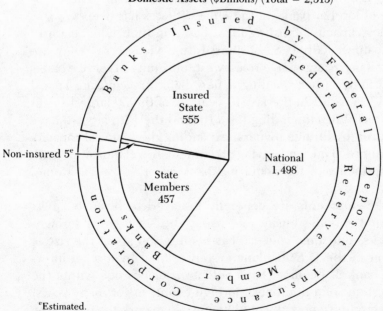

Non-insured 5ᵉ

ᵉEstimated.

Figure 1–3   Commercial Banking in the United States. (*Source:* Federal Deposit Insurance Corporation.)

restricted to major financial centers, and it seems unlikely they will have much impact on banks in smaller communities or on small banks anywhere.

Profile of the Banking Industry

As the director of a commercial bank, your responsibilities will include assuring that the bank is managed in compliance with relevant law and regulation, and managed so that optimum performance on behalf of the shareholders is secured. These objectives must be realized by the strategies set by the bank's management and approved by the board, taking into account the highly competitive nature of the banking industry itself, as well as the broader financial services industry. In this brief profile, we will preview a number of the subjects taken up in detail in later chapters. This overview will help develop your understanding of some of the characteristics of your bank, and how it is similar to, or different from, other banks.

Charter and Insurance Options

The United States has more than 14,500 insured commercial banks, all of which are corporations organized for profit. Nearly one-third are chartered by the federal government and the rest by the states (Figure 1–3).

A state-chartered bank may choose to be a member of the Federal Reserve System, a choice that had greater significance in the past than it has today. Legislation passed in 1980 requires all banks and other organizations holding deposits in checking or similar accounts to hold reserves against those deposits at levels prescribed by the Federal Reserve Board. This condition is the most expensive of those imposed on Federal Reserve members. Avoiding membership no longer avoids this cost. Nonmembers tend to be small banks, in comparison to members. Among state banks, members of the Federal Reserve System have assets averaging $432 million, while nonmembers' assets average only $65 million.

The Federal Deposit Insurance Corporation (FDIC) was created by Congress in 1933 to insure deposits in financial institutions and to prevent the kind of losses suffered by many depositors when banks failed in the early days of the Great Depression. The level of insurance was raised to $100,000 per account in 1980. Fewer than 4 percent of commercial banks have chosen to remain outside the FDIC's insurance program, and they hold less than 1 percent of all assets. The noninsured banks are rare, and such status should require compelling justification by the board of such a noninsured bank.

Branching Environment

One of the most controversial issues in commercial banking is the nature of the branching environment in the state where the bank is headquartered. This remains the most important area of a bank's policy that is subject to limitation by the law of the state. The state law governs the branching behavior of national banks because of the provisions of the McFadden Act, a federal law that has come under severe criticism in recent years. Table 1–2 shows the branching restrictions existing in each state as of September 1985.

Nationwide, at the beginning of 1984, the 15,000 commercial banks had 41,000 branches in addition to their headquarter locations, so the industry had 56,000 locations to serve the public. In the unit banking states, the 5,700 banks had 2,300 "branches" in spite of the apparent prohibition of branches in those states. Some of these are the result of acquisitions, some existed before the law was enacted, and others are "facilities" that are allowable under the laws of the state. The banks in states that allow branching have an average of five locations each (including their home office). However, this figure is heavily influenced by the banks with the largest branching systems, with between 200 and 1,000 branches in each. The 808 banks in California and New York had nearly 8,700 locations in their home states. Both states allow a bank to branch anywhere in the state.

Financial and Operating Characteristics

Banks differ greatly in size, from less than $1 million in assets to more than $100 billion. They also differ in financial performance, and the larger do not always fare as well as the smaller. Each bank operates in its own market under a unique set of operating conditions. These conditions, and management's response to them, produce the financial results for the individual bank.

Table 1–2 Geographic Restrictions on Branch Banking in the States (September 1985)

Statewide Branch Banking Prevalent	*Limited Branch Banking Prevalent*	*Unit Banking Prevalent*
Alabama	Arkansas	Colorado
Alaska	Georgia	Illinois
Arizona	Indiana	Kansas
California	Iowa	Missouri
Connecticut	Kentucky	Montana
Delaware	Louisiana	North Dakota
Florida	Michigan	Texas
Hawaii	Minnesota	Wyoming
Idaho	Mississippi	
Maine	Nebraska	
Maryland	New Hampshire	
Massachusetts	New Mexico	
Nevada	Ohio	
New Jersey	Oklahoma	
New York	Pennsylvania	
North Carolina	Tennessee	
Oregon	Virginia	
Rhode Island	West Virginia	
South Carolina	Wisconsin	
South Dakota		
Utah		
Vermont		
Washington		

Source: Conference of State Bank Supervisors, *A Profile of State-Chartered Banking* (Washington, D.C.: Conference of State Supervisors, 1986).

Bank Size. Most banks are small (Figure 1–4). At the close of 1983, nearly 9,600 of the nation's insured commercial banks held assets of less than $50 million. This group, representing two-thirds of the nation's insured commercial banks, held less than 11 percent of the domestic assets of commercial banks, an indication of the heavy concentration of assets in larger banks.

Financial Performance. The financial performance of a bank is generally measured by comparing net income (after income taxes and securities gains or losses) to total assets and to total equity capital. For the industry in 1983, 65 cents of net income was produced for each $100 of total assets, and $10.81 of net income was produced per $100 of equity capital. These figures have to be considered carefully in light of the size of the bank (Table 1–3). In return on assets (ROA), banks with between $10 and $500 million

Share of All Commercial Banks

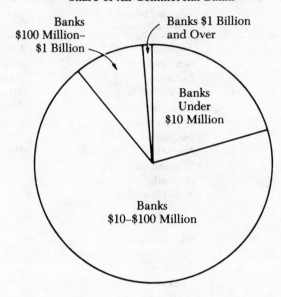

Share of All Commercial Bank Assets

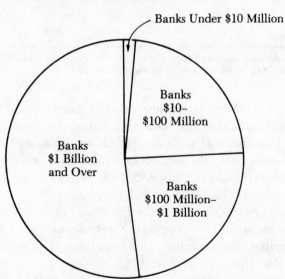

Figure 1–4 Banks and Bank Assets (December 1983). Banks are grouped by asset size, using domestic assets only. (*Source*: Federal Deposit Insurance Corporation.)

Table 1–3   Financial Performance of Banks in Similar Asset Size Groups (1984)

Assets ($ millions)	1984 Return per $100 of:	
	Total Assets	Equity Capital
Less than 5-24.9	.89	9.42
25-49.9	1.01	11.72
50-99.9	1.03	12.85
100-299.9	1.01	13.62
300-499.9	1.00	14.41
500-999.9	.94	13.93
1,000-2,999.9	.93	14.96
3,000-9,999.9	.87	13.79
10,000 and over	.56	12.50
All banks	.97	11.63

Source: Federal Deposit Insurance Corporation.

in assets outperformed either smaller or larger banks. When net income is expressed as a return on equity capital (ROE), the big banks look better because of their higher leverage (ratio of total assets to total equity capital). Banks with assets between $25 million and $5 billion averaged above $11 in ROE. The very largest banks, with assets of $5 billion and more, performed well below the industry average on both measures, reflecting a variety of upward pressures on costs and downward pressures on income.

Bank Holding Companies

If a bank is owned by another corporation, the parent corporation is said to be a bank holding company (BHC). A BHC owning one bank is a one-bank holding company; if it owns more than one bank, it is a multibank holding company. Congress enacted the first legislation relating to holding companies in 1956; the Bank Holding Company Act made the Federal Reserve Board responsible for regulating multibank holding companies. At the time there were 53 BHCs, which owned 428 banks with only 7.5 percent of all domestic bank deposits. By 1970 121 BHCs controlled 895 banks with 16 percent of domestic bank deposits (Figure 1–5).

Growth of Bank Holding Companies. Growth during the 1960s was largely in one-bank BHCs, which were not subject to Federal Reserve regulation with regard to their nonbank activities

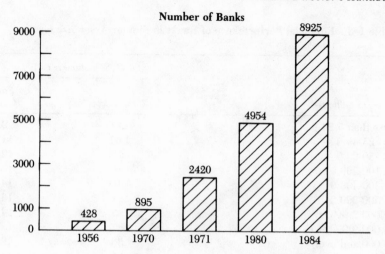

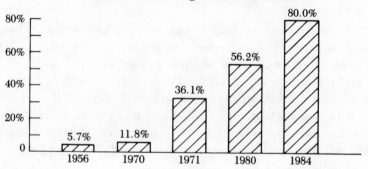

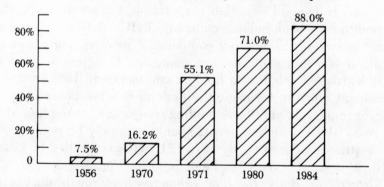

Figure 1–5   The Growing Importance of Bank Holding Companies. (*Source*: Association of Bank Holding Companies.)

due to an oversight in the 1956 Act. As the one-bank holding companies became active in a wide variety of financial and nonfinancial activities, they created some concern over the danger to the financial soundness of the bank arising from the risks being taken in the nonbank activities of the BHC. The 1970 amendments to the Bank Holding Company Act brought one-bank holding companies under the jurisdiction of the Federal Reserve Board and required the board to specify and approve activities in BHCs as being "related to banking." BHCs were required to divest by the end of 1980 any activities not permissible under the 1970 amendments. At the end of 1984 the number of BHCs had reached 6,300; they controlled 8,925 banks with 88 percent of the nation's domestic bank deposits.

Rapid growth in BHCs began in 1970 and has continued, largely due to the creation by individual banks of a parent BHC to which the bank's stock is transferred so that nonbank activities can be launched through new subsidiary companies of the BHC without changing the actual ownership of the bank. The Federal Reserve's list of activities "related to banking" allows for such activities as mortgage banking, consumer finance, credit-related insurance, financially related bookkeeping and data processing, community development finance, investment or financial advice, discount brokerage, loan servicing, and trust banking. Other areas of activity are shown in Table 1–4.

Bank holding companies continue to grow through the acquisition of individual banks. Holding companies are seen as a substitute for statewide branching in some states that permit multibank holding companies but that still restrict branching. As state laws are changed, multibank holding companies fold the separate banks into a single statewide bank and convert all of the locations to branches of a single bank.

Role of Director in a Holding Company Bank. In a bank that is part of a BHC, the relationship of a bank director to the management and board of the BHC must be clearly defined. The major decisions regarding the bank may be closely concentrated in the board and management of the BHC, with limited discretion allowed to the affiliated bank's board. However, the directors of a bank continue to maintain legal responsibilities, so they must monitor the financial soundness of the bank, the quality of the bank's loan portfolio, and the performance of the bank's management.

Table 1–4   Permissible Nonbank Activities for Bank Holding Companies under Section 4(c)8 of Regulation Y (November 1984)

Activities Permitted by Regulation	*Activities Permitted by Order*	*Activities Denied by the Board*
1. Extensions of credit[2] Mortgage banking Finance companies: consumer, sales, and commercial Credit cards Factoring	1. Issuance and sale of travelers checks[2, 6]	1. Insurance premium funding (combined sales of mutual funds and insurance)
2. Industrial bank, Morris Plan banks, industrial loan company	2. Buying and selling gold and silver bullion and silver coin[2, 4]	2. Underwriting life insurance not related to credit extension
3. Servicing loans and other extensions of credit[2]	3. Issuing money orders and general-purpose variable denominated payment instruments[1, 2, 4]	3. Sale of level-term credit life
4. Trust company[2]	4. Futures commission merchant to cover gold and silver bullion and coins[1, 2]	4. Real estate brokerage (residential)
5. Investment or financial advising[2]	5. Underwriting certain federal, state, and municipal securities[1, 2]	5. Armored car
6. Full-payout leasing of personal or real property[2]	6. Check verification[1, 2, 4]	6. Land development
7. Investments in community welfare projects[2]	7. Financial advice to consumers[1, 2]	7. Real estate syndication
8. Providing book-keeping or data processing services[2]	8. Issuance of small denomination debt instruments[1]	8. General management consulting
9. Acting as insurance agent or broker primarily in connection with credit extensions[2]	9. Arranging for equity financing of real estate	9. Property management
10. Underwriting credit life, accident, and health insurance	10. Acting as futures commissions merchant	10. Computer output microfilm services
11. Providing courier services[2]	11. Discount brokerage	11. Underwriting mortgage guaranty insurance[3]
12. Management consulting to all depository institutions	12. Operating a distressed savings and loan association	12. Operating a savings and loan association[1, 5]
	13. Operating an Article XII Investment Company	13. Operating a travel agency[1, 2]
		14. Underwriting property and casualty insurance[1]
		15. Underwriting home loan life mortgage insurance[1]
		16. Investment note issue with transactional characteristics

13. Sale at retail of money orders with a face value of not more than $1000, travelers checks, and savings bonds[1, 2, 7]

14. Performing appraisals of real estate[1]

15. Issuance and sale of travelers checks

16. Arranging commercial real estate equity financing

17. Securities brokerage

18. Underwriting and dealing in government obligations and money market instruments

19. Foreign exchange advisory and transactional services

20. Futures commission merchant

21. Options on financial futures

22. Advice on options on bullion and foreign exchange

14. Executing foreign banking unsolicited purchases and sales of securities

15. Engaging in commercial banking activities abroad through a limited purpose Delaware bank

16. Performing appraisal of real estate and real estate advisor and real estate brokerage on nonresidential properties

17. Operating a Pool Reserve Plan for loss reserves of banks for loans to small businesses

18. Operating a thrift institution in Rhode Island

19. Operating a guarantee savings bank in New Hampshire

20. Offering information advice and transactional services for foreign exchange services

17. Real estate advisory services

Source: Federal Reserve Board.

[1]Added to list since January 1, 1975.

[2]Activities permissible to national banks.

[3]Board orders found these activities closely related to banking but denied proposed acquisitions as part of its "go slow" policy.

[4]To be decided on a case-by-case basis.

[5]Operating a thrift institution has been permitted by order in Rhode Island, Ohio, New Hampshire, and California.

[6]Subsequently permitted by regulation.

[7]The amount subsequently was changed to $10,000.

In a BHC the movement of capital between the bank, the BHC, and other subsidiaries of the BHC is of particular importance. Capital is essential to the financial health and soundness of the bank. However, the desire of the BHC to enlarge nonbank activities may tempt the BHC management to reduce the capital of the bank—that is, "upstream" capital to the BHC. It is the responsibility of the board to be sure the affiliated bank can afford the diminishing of its capital in this way. Adequate capital must be maintained in the bank.

Correspondent Banking

By developing relationships with larger banks, small banks are able to gain access to specialized services and to assist their customers in arranging loans larger than would be possible with their own resources. This cooperative relationship between commercial banks is the essence of "correspondent banking" and is important to a full understanding of the working of the U.S. banking industry.

Every bank has relationships with other banks in the form of accounts, check-clearing arrangements, and syndicates for handling very large loans. The larger the bank, the more likely it is to provide services to smaller banks through correspondent arrangements. These services include helping the small bank with such day-to-day operational and financial management problems as processing checks received by the smaller bank that must be collected from distant banks, providing international services for the smaller bank and its customers, and helping supply amounts of credit larger than the smaller bank is allowed to loan to a single customer. The smaller bank pays for these services in the form of balances left on deposit with the larger bank, fees paid for particular services received, or a mix of the two.

The larger bank is almost always a member of the Federal Reserve System and historically has provided the small bank access to some of the services of the Federal Reserve, which prior to 1980 were available only to members. Federal Reserve services are now available to all banks at a price. Depending on whether the larger banks can be competitive with the Federal Reserve in providing services, a smaller bank may continue to work through correspondents or deal directly with the Federal Reserve. A bank director should understand the workings of the correspondent relationships in which the bank participates. A periodic review of the costs and benefits of each relationship should be provided to the board by management.

Banking Markets

The idea of a "market" is easy to comprehend when there is only one bank in town, and even easier if the town is a small rural community 30 miles from the next town (Figure 1–6). Typically, such a bank handles the needs of everyone living within a 15-mile radius. Many banks meet this description. Their customers are the business people in the community and the farmers and ranchers in the surrounding area. Customers' needs are for both deposit services and loans to finance construction, equipment purchases, and seasonal credit needs. Employed workers in the area also use the bank for checking and savings services and credit for home mortgages, auto loans, and so on.

Larger communities may have several banks, some of which may be branches of banks headquartered in the community or elsewhere. The meaning of market must be broadened here to include the larger community and the presence of competition in it. One by-product of competition may be some degree of specialization, with a bank choosing to stress its ability and competitive advantages in one area of service or in meeting needs of one type of customer. For example, one bank may stress its orientation to the needs of small, independent businesses, another to customers in need of personal banking services, and still another to relationships with large business customers. In general, any bank is willing to handle the needs of any customer, but a bank's position in one area of service may be stressed to gain an advantage over competitors.

Competition and Bank Size. The larger the community, the greater the number of banks, and, generally speaking, the more intense the competition. For individual customers, the location of a bank is the most important consideration in choosing a bank. As electronic banking spreads, however, location may decline in importance compared with a bank's flexibility and quality of service. Business customers are more willing to choose a bank on the basis of service and price, with less concern for location. In large metropolitan areas, the usual pattern is for major downtown banks to attract the business of the large corporate customers in the area. Smaller downtown banks serve medium-size businesses. Banks

Small Communities: Pure Geographic Markets

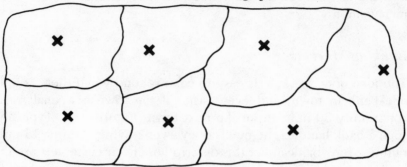

Larger Community (No Branching): Overlapping Markets

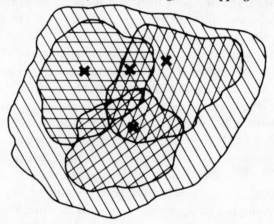

Metropolis (Unlimited Branching): Each Bank Covers Market

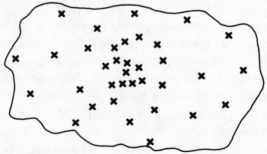

Figure 1–6   Simplified Geography of Markets.

with headquarters farther from downtown—which tend to be smaller—serve smaller businesses in outlying areas.

This pattern in large part is due to the legal limits on the amount that a bank can lend a customer, based on the bank's assets. The larger the business, the larger the bank it wants to deal with because a large bank will be needed to accommodate its credit needs. Typically, as a company grows, it moves from smaller banks to larger banks, which generally means from neighborhood to downtown. At some point, a growing company may have to develop relationships with banks in New York or one of the other major national financial centers such as Chicago, Los Angeles, or San Francisco, to serve its full range of needs, particularly international banking needs.

A bank's market is determined by the size of the community in which it is located, the extent of the branching system it has developed, the area of service it has chosen to emphasize, and the market segments—customers—to which it has chosen to appeal. Finally, the size of the bank will be the most important consideration in determining the market the bank serves or can consider serving.

Trends in Bank Size and Concentration. Following a trend that persisted through 1980, large banks grew at the expense of smaller banks. Since 1955, the share of commercial bank deposits in the 10 largest banks rose from 20 percent to nearly 30 percent, and the share of the 100 largest from 46 percent to more than 50 percent. The share in the largest 300 had held steady at slightly more than 60 percent (Figure 1–7). Since 1980, there has been a reduction in the concentration, as shown in Figure 1–7, reversing the 25-year trend. This is partly the result of banks in the top 10 not being able to grow as rapidly as banks just below them in size, for many reasons, including population shifts, branching restrictions (in Illinois), capital limits, and changes in financial markets (growth of the commercial paper market).

The existence of more than 12,000 banks, each with less than $100 million in assets at the beginning of 1985, shows convincingly that there is room for smaller institutions to survive by meeting the needs of local markets. Some of these banks are affiliates of holding companies and derive strength from the holding company relationship. Many others remain independent but are able to satisfy the growing needs of their customers by relying on services provided by large correspondent banks in the financial centers. These

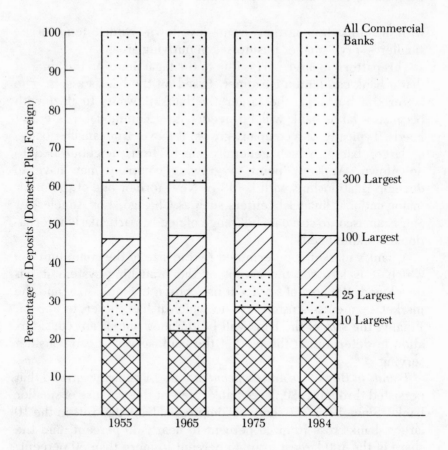

Figure 1–7 Concentration of Deposits in Large Commercial Banks. (*Source*: Federal Deposit Insurance Corporation.)

arrangements through holding companies and correspondent relationships are part of the genius of our banking system and allow small, locally managed institutions to bring sophisticated, capital-intensive services into local markets.

Mergers and Acquisitions

The number of commercial banks has remained almost constant for the past ten years. Each year, several hundred new banks have been formed, while about as many have ceased to exist as independent institutions when they were acquired by larger banks and became branches of the acquiring institutions. The future is likely to see a change in the traditional pattern resulting from intra- and interstate mergers. States that have recently authorized the start-up of statewide branching, or the formation of statewide holding companies, have been the scene of the coalescing of many previously separate banks into larger new banks or multibank holding companies. This pattern has been repeated in Pennsylvania, Ohio, Virginia, and Florida.

The Supreme Court endorsed the principle of regional interstate banking compacts in 1985, in effect upholding laws in Florida and Massachusetts that have set the pattern for regions throughout the country. States have joined together to sanction interstate mergers in New England, the Southeast, the Midwest, and the Far West. It is too early to foresee the outcome of this process, but as geographic barriers come down, the outlook for small independent institutions will inevitably dim. The number of such institutions will decline, not precipitously but gradually.

The directors of every bank must begin to give serious attention to the potential for their bank, both as an acquiring institution and an acquired institution. Some recent mergers have been characterized as "mergers of equals," suggesting the intent to maintain equal roles for the philosophies, traditions, and strategies of the banks joining in the merger. While this may be feasible in a limited number of situations, the more general outcome of a merger, as well as an acquisition, will be the emergence and ultimate survival of a single institution bearing the characteristics of the larger and/or dominant partner in the original pairing. While the larger will usually be dominant, there may be exceptions to this traditional pattern. Directors in both institutions must recognize and accept their responsibilities to investors, employees, and customers of the bank to insure equitable treatment of their interests as the institutions are combined.

Capital Requirements

In recent years increasing emphasis has been directed to the question of the appropriate level of capital in a commercial bank. Historically, the ratio of capital to assets has declined in commercial banking, particularly in large banks where ratios of under 5 percent have not been unusual in recent years. In 1983 Congress enacted legislation that directs the federal banking regulators to "cause banking institutions to achieve and maintain adequate capital by establishing minimal levels of capital for such banking institutions and by such other methods as the appropriate Federal Banking Agency deems appropriate." In 1985 regulators approved final rules raising the capital requirements for banks to a minimum of 6 percent of total capital to total assets, and a minimum of 5.5 percent of primary capital to total assets. Primary capital consists of common stock, perpetual preferred stock, capital surplus, undivided profits, reserves for contingencies and other capital reserves, mandatory convertible instruments, and the allowance for possible loan losses. When the requirement was finalized, it was estimated that banks would have to raise an additional $6.3 billion in capital to be in compliance. An alternative to raising additional capital is to reduce assets, an unusual strategy to be sure, but one that would significantly improve the financial soundness of the bank and, quite probably, the quality of its earnings.

Directors must give continuing close attention to this matter. It will be discussed in more detail in a later chapter.

Forces Changing the Role of Banks

The environment in which banks operate is changing constantly, and rapidly, in response to a variety of forces. Banks and their directors must understand how these forces are affecting each bank and the role of banks in the financial services industry.

Deregulation and Reregulation

The legal framework in which banks function, derived from law, regulation, and the decisions of courts, has been enlarging the freedom of banks and other financial institutions with respect to both pricing and the nature of services provided. The most dramatic change in the last five years for commercial banks has been the total deregulation of interest rates payable on deposits, formerly governed by Regulation Q of the Federal Reserve Board. While deregulation has increased the ability of banks to compete for deposits, particularly with money market mutual funds, it has raised the cost of funds significantly. In the same time frame, thrift institutions were granted broader asset and liability powers, enabling them to compete directly with banks for consumer business and commercial business.

With the end of Regulation Q restrictions on rates that banks can pay on deposits, banks have been forced to reevaluate their pricing practices. Consumer reaction to increasing fees has been strong, leading to attempts to bring state and federal legislation that would require banks to offer "lifeline"—that is, basic—banking services. The contention behind demands for such legislation is that banks provide essential services, in the manner of public utilities, and that these services must be available to all consumers at or, if necessary, below cost. Complex issues regarding pricing, service features, eligibility, and source of the subsidy (if any) must be resolved to put this theory into practice, and legislators may find resolution difficult.

A record-setting 120 commercial banks failed in 1985. The dramatic upsurge in the number of failures among deposit-taking institutions and the financial drain placed on the Federal Deposit Insurance Corporation and the Federal Savings and Loan Insurance Corporation have raised concern about the soundness of the insurance programs and brought demands for closer regulation of the behavior of the insured institutions. As deposit-taking institutions found their costs of funds rising, it was inevitable that they would seek more risky assets, thereby placing their institution at greater risk of loss or, eventually, failure. Closer supervision of asset quality, as well as capital adequacy, by regulators is likely to result from this growing concern over the financial soundness of institutions holding federally insured deposits while competing in an increasingly deregulated industry.

Nonbank Competition

As depository institutions compete among themselves for consumer business, they are being joined by an array of competitors, some familiar and some wholly new to the market. On the liability (deposit) side, thrifts, brokerage firms, and insurance companies are all offering serious competition, with retailers beginning to enter via their own bank or thrift subsidiaries. On the asset (credit) side, finance companies, mortgage companies, retailers, insurance companies, and especially thrifts have increased the pressure on banks to secure pieces of the market for credit cards, residential mortgages, auto loans, and, most recently, second mortgages.

The commercial lending area, once enjoyed almost exclusively by commercial banks, has seen the growth of the commercial paper market, and increased competition from commercial mortgage and finance lenders, insurance companies, and foreign banks.

Geographic Expansion

Although banks have historically lived with highly restrictive laws covering their geographic expansion, their competition has seldom had such a problem. The 1980s will be remembered as the decade in which commercial banks, and bank holding companies, were freed of most of the geographic limitations so that they could match their competition in geographic coverage. State laws restricting branching or holding company activity are being liberalized at a rapid rate, while interstate activity is moving ahead at a slower, but steady, pace. Interstate banking, on a regional basis, appears to be the pattern through which eventual full nationwide banking will emerge. While this total freedom will provide tremendous opportunity to large institutions with capital and expertise equal to the challenge, it will unquestionably mark the end of the road for many smaller institutions. If the process is managed well, the owners of the smaller institutions that do not survive need not suffer, and their customers will continue to receive high-quality banking services.

Technology

Technology presents an opportunity, and a threat, to commercial banks. If commercial banks understand and use the potential of technology properly, they can build on their strong image and reputation with retail and corporate customers by introducing technology-based services for customers that improve on traditional services in quality, features, price, and convenience. By using the increased power over storing, manipulating, and moving information, banks can offer entirely new services that will enlarge the range of their relationships with customers. The opportunity to improve service, while reducing costs, is perhaps the greatest potential that technology offers to commercial banks.

While technology holds out this range of opportunities to commercial banks, it also offers corresponding opportunities to other financial service providers, and many nonfinancial organizations, to give bank customers new advantages that may reduce their dependence on commercial banks. One of the traditional advantages of commercial banks as financial intermediaries has been their position in financial markets—serving funds providers on one side and funds users on the other. The microcomputer is proliferating among funds users and funds providers, particularly the more active and sophisticated participants on both sides of this market, giving them the ability to communicate among themselves. This is threatening the traditional role of intermediaries throughout the financial markets, including all types of brokers, agents, and other middlemen. Economists refer to this trend as improving efficiency in the market, with information of better quality, quantity, and timeliness available to participants. Technology is also a factor in the increasing rate of introduction of innovative financial services, to be discussed later in this chapter.

The net effect of these contrasting impacts of technology on the role of commercial banks has yet to be seen. Directors, working with management, must monitor developments in the technological area and their banks' use of technological opportunities.

Shifting User Characteristics and Demands

The manufacturer and distributor of any consumer product learns to pay close attention to early signs of changes in the market. Banks have too long taken for granted the need for banking services, believing that the public and business users will always need and want the same thing from a bank. As lifestyles change, the age pattern of the U.S. population moves upward, and consumers' expectations for quality and tailored service offerings grow, banks are being forced to come to terms with new realities in the market. Consumers will be served, and whether their needs are met by commercial banks or other financial institutions or nonfinancial organizations is seldom very important so long as their needs are met. Commercial customers have shown their ability to become independent of banks by developing the commercial paper market and devising means of conducting many of their financial activities outside the commercial banking environment.

Banks can no longer take the customer, or the market, for granted. In service design and delivery, as well as in the structuring of the terms of financial agreements (rates, repayment sched-

ules, handling of overdrafts, funds availability schedules, etc.),
banks must be market driven in their strategic planning and in the
conduct of day-to-day business.

Financial Innovation

Beginning not long after World War II, and gaining momentum in
the 1970s, a tide of innovation has swept through the financial
services industry. In fact, it is fair to say that the very idea of a
financial services industry is the result of this tide as it swept away
traditional thinking about markets and traditional lines of separation among financial service providers. Innovation has been
spurred by dramatic increases in the level and variability of
inflation, opportunities for new technology-based services and
delivery systems, and the rising level of sophistication and demands expressed by individual and business customers. As financial institutions have created new services and means for delivering them, regulators have responded, sometimes by easing
regulations and occasionally by tightening them. The initiative-
response-initiative cycle has continued without interruption for 40
years and is not likely to abate for some time to come.

Innovation has affected financial instruments, the means of
accessing and delivering financial services, and institutional structures. It has also generated wholly new markets for old and new
financial instruments. Although banks have sometimes benefited
from innovation, more often they have been the losers, as competing financial or nonfinancial organizations have displaced them as
providers of old, and often new, services. While the board may be
the origin of an innovative idea from time to time, the directors'
responsibility lies in insisting that management be continually
alert to the opportunity to gain through innovation and to minimize harmful effects on the bank from competitors' innovations.

Conclusion

Banks are changing in dramatic ways as they strive to maintain
their leadership role in the emerging financial services industry.
Change presents opportunity, and risk, to an organization. Bank
management, continually observed and counseled by the board of
directors, is responsible for steering the bank through this time of

challenge and for applying ·the institution's resources—human, physical, financial, and reputation—to optimize the value of the shareholders' investment consistent with legal, moral, and professional responsibilities to the bank's employees, customers, and community.

Chapter 2

BANKING FUNCTIONS
AND SERVICES

by Robert P. Popadic

Introduction

The services a bank offers and how it is organized to deliver them
are influenced by the changing structure of banking in the United
States, the location and characteristics of the individual institution,
and specific decisions made by management and directors. Over
time the U.S. banking system has evolved to provide increasingly
convenient banking as the number of service offices in relationship
to population has increased. Deregulation has weakened the distinction between banks and nonbanks and has broken down the
distinction between thrift and commercial banking institutions.
Regional banking has emerged as a major force affecting the
concentration of banking assets. Restrictions on branching have
also been relaxed in many states. These changes have led to
increased competition, the merging of weaker institutions into
stronger ones, and increased specialization. Some institutions have
increased specialization in order to differentiate their service,
reduce service delivery costs, command a premium price, or just
stay in business. In addition to other regulated institutions, banking activities face competition from nonregulated or less regulated
industries.

The accelerated inflation rate of the 1970s and early 1980s
caused a breakdown in interest rate restrictions and thus changed

the relationship between financial institutions and their customers. Customers acquired a sensitivity to interest rates that has resulted not only in higher costs of deposits to institutions, but also in a reduction in customer loyalty. Most significantly affected were thrift institutions that historically had paid below-market rates to savers and in turn channeled that money back into the housing market. They accepted the risk of using relatively short-term liabilities to fund fixed-rate, long-term assets. The repercussions have included a substantial reduction in the number of thrift institutions, mergers of many institutions, and the emergence of a few institutions able to offer a wide range of financial services.

While changes occurring nationally will continue to have a significant impact on banking activities, market opportunities and constraints within local markets will also have considerable impact. Both sources of change are reviewed in the early portion of this chapter, while the latter portion is devoted to discussing the types of services and organizational forms typically found in banks. Also discussed are the possible implications of a changing environment.

Industry Structure

Both thrift institutions and commercial banks are a part of a regulated industry with a public franchise for dealing in the commodity of money. The unique nature of the franchise is a bank's ability to accept public deposits and thus have a customer who is both a borrower and consumer of funds and also, to some degree, a supplier of lendable funds. In most other industries there is very little overlap between customers and suppliers. Such an interrelationship adds to the complexity of managing bank marketing and customer service.

Since they are regulated, banks historically have been permitted to leverage their equity to a much greater degree than nonregulated financial institutions. Commercial banks on average have equity equal to only approximately 6 percent of total assets, while less regulated finance companies have 14 percent equity.

Regulation

The bank and its parent holding company (if one exists) are regulated by one or more federal or state agencies. These regulators include the Comptroller of the Currency, the Federal Reserve System, the state banking commission, and the Federal Deposit Insurance Corporation (FDIC). Federal and state laws define the products and services that may be offered to customers and to some degree interest rates and fee structures. In addition, through regular examinations, federal and state bodies influence the way that the bank is run.

Regulators will often compare the bank to other similar institutions or to the peer group averages (usually based on size). Institutions that differ from their peers either in the extent of services offered or in financial structure should expect the examiners to raise questions. Logical explanations are accepted, but the burden of proof is on the bank. Such a preoccupation with averages tends to insure that a new product or service is not new for very long; it is quickly copied in many institutions, often without full understanding of what is necessary for success. There are very few trade secrets in banking because of the commodity nature of money and because the regulatory process acclimates the banker to an environment of disclosure. The only possible exception may be in the application of technology to banking. That is not to say that bankers tell each other everything, but there is a great deal more communication among competitors than in most unregulated industries.

Money, a Commodity

While banks may offer a wide variety of services, in most institutions the majority of earnings come from the financial intermediary function of taking deposits and making loans. This continues to be true in spite of efforts generally to increase fee income. The banker who wishes to have return on assets and equity above that of peer institutions, without making riskier loans, is faced with the problem of how to differentiate in the customer's mind a lending product whose principal component is money—a commodity. This is usually done by developing some type of specialization in services offered, skill of personnel, or service locations. Specialization reduces the number of potential competitors and increases the likelihood of greater profit margins. A borrower may believe that a bank that understands a particular business very well may be more likely to provide financial support should the firm suffer a period of financial stress. Thus a specialist can attract customers and possibly also be paid a modest premium for its services. Since banking is a low-margin business, a modest premium in interest rate can cause a substantial increase in margin.

Commonality of Customers and Suppliers

In most industries the suppliers of raw materials and the purchasers of the product are different. This is generally not the case in banking, where the customer who is borrowing will probably also provide time and demand deposits. Some of the demand deposits may be a result of a compensating balance agreement in which the borrower—generally a commercial customer—agrees to keep on deposit a certain percentage of the line of credit granted or of the amount actually borrowed. One of the effects is to raise the net interest income to the lending institution. Other balances will be a result of deposits made by the customer to cover checks written but not yet presented for payment. However, commercial customers increasingly are aware of the delays between check issuance and presentation for collection and are consequently making deposits to cover checks in accordance with the expected date of presentation for payment rather than when the check is written. The result is fewer idle deposits in customer accounts.

Other deposits are there to pay for processing checks and other services. In the case of a commercial customer, these services might include cash management (the automatic investment in interest-bearing instruments of deposits in excess of those required to pay for specific services and/or the operation of a lock box to assist the customer in more rapid collection of payments receivable from others), data processing, international services (such as letters of credit and foreign exchange), and in some instances services received by the customers' employees (for example, the cashing of payroll checks at a branch near the customers' plant).

In addition to bank deposits made in the name of the customer, the bank may accept customer payments of federal social security and withholding taxes or state sales and withholding taxes. The bank would have use of these funds until the agency for whom they were collected withdraws them. In addition, the bank customer may generate escrow accounts on behalf of its own customers.

The fact that customers have multiple relationships with the bank has resulted in the past in the "double counting" of balances, a process in which a customer gets services in a number of areas in the bank without paying a fee because of the customer's substantial deposits. These deposits, while adequate to cover some services, may have been inadequate to pay for all services received. The practice has been reduced in many institutions with the introduction of customer profitability systems that accumulate in one place data concerning all loans, deposits, and fees paid, along with the cost associated with providing the services. Most banks give customers credit for both deposits that belong to the customer and related third-party deposits that exist because of the customer relationship.

Thus, a typical bank customer is a supplier of funds, a user of funds, and a user of other services that are paid for with fees or deposits. This means that a number of bank workers with different functional skills will be engaged in selling and servicing customers' needs. Consequently, a variety of organizational options exists, all of which require a flow of information between units and to some degree indirect reporting relationships.

Organizational Determinants

In banking, the structure of the industry, regulation, the commodity nature of its principal product (money), and customers who are both users and suppliers of funds tend to make the organizational relationships more complicated than in other businesses. Consequently, the sources of profitability are more difficult to determine. Within this broad framework, how a bank is organized is determined by its:

- Market focus
- Style
- Geographic franchise
- Size
- Location
- Organizational affiliation

Market Focus. Nearly all banks service both commercial and retail customers, but usually a bank specializes in one group or the other. Consumer or retail banking organizations tend to have many, often small, branches. They may compete aggressively with local thrift institutions for residential mortgages or consumer loans. Commercial or wholesale banks tend to have fewer, and larger, branches and are organized to make larger loans to business

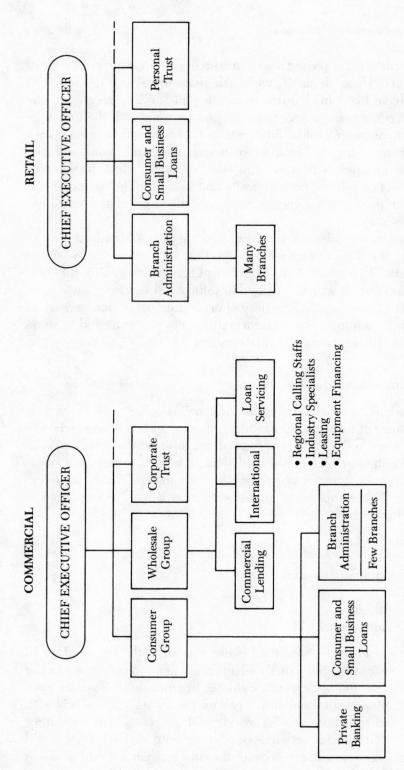

Figure 2–1 Market Focus: Commercial versus Retail Customers. The charts are for a medium-size bank, and only areas of significant differences are shown.

firms. In addition, they provide a broader range of services than might be available from a consumer-oriented bank (Figure 2–1). Banks may specialize in particular services, such as trust, may emphasize a particular type of loan, or may target a particular market segment. For most banks, increased specialization, particularly along market lines, is likely in the future.

Style. Some banks tend to be conservative or traditional in their approach to the marketplace, while others tend to be innovative. During the 1970s and early 1980s, many innovative institutions were on the leading edge of electronic banking, while others believed they could not afford to innovate but developed skills as early followers of successful innovations. The innovators often had larger data processing organizations reporting directly to top management.

Some institutions focused on traditional banking products, while others offered new services that were either developed internally or obtained through acquisition. These acquisitions consisted of, for example, consumer finance companies, leasing companies, mortgage bankers, and discount brokerage firms. However, increased competition from nonbanks and nonregulated financial organizations will likely cause increased market specialization by banks in the late 1980s.

Geographic Franchise. For both state and national banks, state law determines the geographic restrictions on branch location. State laws also determine the character and extent of regional banking by providing the ground rules, including specifying the domicile of out-of-state banking organizations that can operate in the state. In some states a bank can have branches throughout the state; in others, branches are restricted to a particular county or particular distance from the main office; in still others, only a unit banking (or single bank) location is permitted. The trend nationwide has been toward relaxing restrictions on branching. Large branch networks require a more extensive branch administration organization than smaller networks, and a unit bank requires none at all (Figure 2–2).

The high cost of branch locations has caused banks to consider other methods for increasing delivery of services to consumers: plastic credit cards, ATMs (automated teller machines), debit cards, point-of-sale devices (where customers use a debit card to transfer funds from their account to the merchant's account), bill paying by telephone, and other bank-at-home services. The regu-

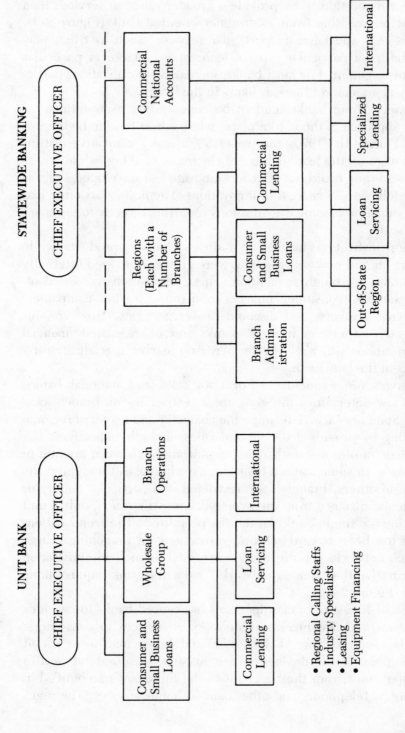

Figure 2–2 Geographical Franchise: Unit Bank versus Statewide Banking. The charts are for a medium-size bank, and only significant differences are shown.

lators are providing new rules that define by state how a bank may extend its reach beyond the branch. These rules vary by state as do branch rules. However, unlike branch rules, they are still emerging and often require the sharing of facilities among competitor institutions. Shared ATM networks now play a major role in most institutions' delivery systems.

Size. The size of a bank tends to dictate the complexity of the organization and the market serviced, with smaller institutions tending to focus on serving community needs. The relative size of the banks in a town can also affect the options available to a particular bank. Most of the 20 largest banks are "money center banks" with an international orientation, while slightly smaller banks have a regional focus. The money center banks are, with a few exceptions, located in New York City, Chicago, San Francisco, or Los Angeles. Many regional banks are quite large, but they do not offer the types of services or have the extensive presence outside of their region that characterizes a money center bank. Many regional banks have been involved in interstate mergers. The result has been both a concentration of banking assets and an increase in the number of organizations capable of operating a delivery system that covers a broad geographical area.

Location. A small bank in a less populous region may supply a broader range of services than the same size institution in a large metropolitan area where there are many larger banks. The smaller banks may develop skills for working with government agencies under loan guarantee programs or larger correspondents in order to provide services to customers whose credit needs exceed the bank's legal lending limit. Location determines for all but the largest banks (which can range nationwide or internationally) the industries that can be customers or the specialized functional units that might be set up. The type of industry in the banking region also determines the appropriateness of specialized functional units such as international, leasing, lending with accounts receivable as collateral, and factoring, which involves the actual purchase of a company's accounts receivable. The rate of economic growth and the regional style also influence the introduction of new services, their acceptance, and profitability.

Organizational Affiliation. Whether or not the bank is part of a holding company will affect organizational structure and services provided. A bank that is not part of a holding company does not have another organization to look to for specialized skills or finan-

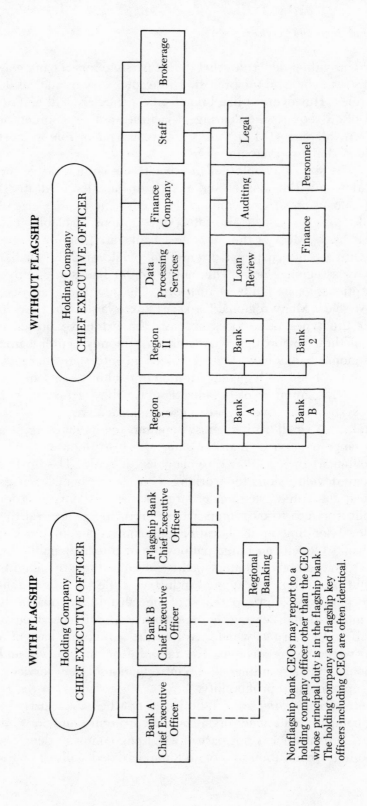

WITH FLAGSHIP

Holding Company
CHIEF EXECUTIVE OFFICER

Bank A
Chief Executive
Officer

Bank B
Chief Executive
Officer

Flagship Bank
Chief Executive
Officer

Regional
Banking

Nonflagship bank CEOs may report to a
holding company officer other than the CEO
whose principal duty is in the flagship bank.
The holding company and flagship key
officers including CEO are often identical.

WITHOUT FLAGSHIP

Holding Company
CHIEF EXECUTIVE OFFICER

Region I

Region II

Data Processing Services

Finance Company

Staff

Brokerage

Bank A

Bank B

Bank 1

Bank 2

Loan Review

Auditing

Legal

Finance

Personnel

Figure 2–3 The Influence of Flagship Banks on Organization. The charts are for a medium-size bank, and only areas of significant differences are shown.

cial support and therefore must stand on its own balance sheet and earnings. While bank regulators view each bank as a separate entity, they are aware that in times of stress certain services and resources are available to a bank that is part of a holding company, particularly to a small bank in a large holding company. Increasingly, bank holding companies must manage not only banks but a proliferation of nonbanking subsidiaries and deal with regulatory issues associated with their operation.

The organization of a bank that is part of a holding company may be influenced by whether the holding company has a flagship bank or is made up of banks of approximately equal size with no individual bank playing a dominant role (Figure 2–3). Regional banking has brought about a number of "mergers of equals" resulting in an increase in the number of large holding companies without a clear flagship bank. Where there is no flagship bank, holding company management tends to be independent of any individual bank. In a holding company with a dominant flagship bank, management of both the holding company and the flagship institution may be the same. Where a flagship exists, services and policies for smaller institutions in the group often tend to emanate from the flagship.

Functional or Market Organization

A pure functional organization would have departments that provide data processing, commercial lending, or cash management services to all classes of customers, while a pure market organization would have within the unit all the capabilities to both market and deliver all the services a particular market segment requires. For example, a large bank might have a thrift institution correspondent banking unit with the ability to lend money, provide data processing services, and provide consulting advice. Since most banks are not large enough to duplicate specialized units such as data processing, they often choose a hybrid form of organization in which the bulk of the back-office functions are performed centrally by functionally oriented units but in which the marketing of those services is handled by a marketing unit dedicated to a particular industry or group of customers. As stated earlier, many banks are increasing their market specialization in order to remain competitive. Directors must be aware of both the importance of specialization and the need to have the requisite resources, skills, and available market before deciding to specialize in a potential market.

In a functional organization, usually a designated unit is primarily responsible for the customer relationship. That unit often is determined by the key services a customer requires or by the particular type of customer the bank is trying to cultivate. Often, for a commercial customer, the lending area controls the decision. This unit may play a sales coordinator role and may largely determine what a customer pays for specific services. Units other than the designated unit may provide services to a customer, but often, rather than being paid directly by the customer, they receive either an internal transfer payment or a reimbursement of expenses from the designated unit. It is not uncommon for units to disagree over which should have principal customer responsibility.

In choosing a market organization, some functional skill and efficiency often is being given up in order to most effectively market a broad spectrum of services to a selected group of customers. Most banks find that customers who use a wide variety of services—services that are properly priced—tend to make the greatest profit contribution to the institution. Such a commercial customer might maintain a checking account having the bank handling the reconcilement, borrow under a line of credit, have a term loan or a lease to finance equipment, and use a lock box and cash management services to expedite the collection of payments and thus reduce the need to borrow. The customer's excess cash would be invested in bank certificates of deposit or in repurchase agreements. In a repurchase agreement the bank sells a portion of its portfolio to the customer and agrees to repurchase it at a specified time in the future at a predetermined price. The agreement generally runs for a much shorter period than the term of typical certificates of deposit. The net effect is the payment of interest on a collateralized deposit.

The bank may also handle the direct deposit of employees' pay to their accounts via the automated clearinghouse. Merchants may use the bank for processing bank card sales drafts, a source of coin and currency for change, and as a provider of point-of-sale banking (debit card). Exporters and importers would use the services of the bank's international department. The bank may also administer a company's pension plan or act as corporate stock transfer agent. Individuals might have savings and checking accounts, certificates of deposit, mortgage and personal loans, credit and debit cards, a brokerage account, and a safe deposit box. Individuals with greater net worth might also purchase large denomination (over $100,000) certificates of deposit as well as have a personal trust account.

One of the difficulties with a market organization is that it requires a certain critical mass of business in a particular market in order to justify a separate organizational unit. Thus, a smaller institution with a market focus must choose its specialized markets wisely since its size constrains the number of economically viable market-oriented units it can support.

Bank Services

The remainder of this chapter is devoted to describing the services that a bank offers and explaining how a typical medium-size bank might be organized to deliver them. The organization shown in Figure 2–4 is not that of any particular institution but reflects some of the common groupings of bank activities. The chart shows five groups: consumer, wholesale, trust, bank investments, and staff or services. Not all institutions would include the same components in each group. Units such as municipal services, correspondent banking, and automated customer services are often assigned to different groups, depending on the particular emphasis within the unit as well as its size. For example, if correspondent banking were a particularly important activity, it might exist at the group level. On the other hand, if correspondent banking activities were rather limited and primarily revolved around loan participations, the inclusion of correspondent as part of the wholesale group might be expected. If the automated customer services unit were small, it could be an extension of the bank's internal data processing division. If the automated customer services activities were primarily directed at servicing commercial customers, it could be part of the wholesale group. On the other hand, if the data processing services were directed at correspondent banks, this unit might be a subunit of correspondent banking.

A small bank would typically have fewer groups. Figure 2–5 shows a small bank with a consumer, wholesale, and staff or services group. This organization differs from the medium-size institution. It lacks a full-blown branch administration unit because the bank probably has only a headquarters and a branch or two. Many nontraditional banking services, such as insurance and dis-

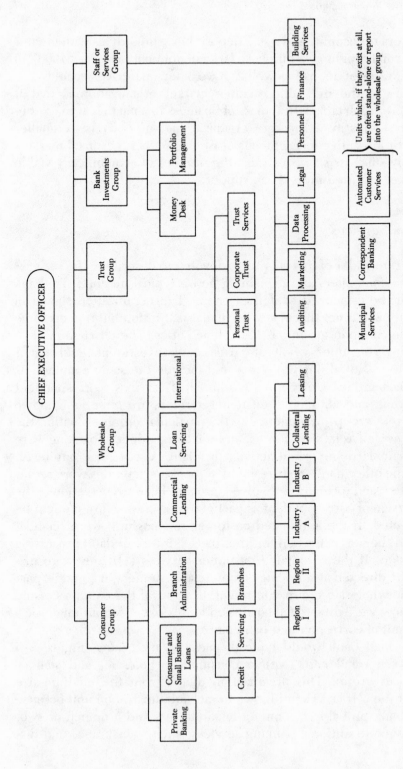

Figure 2–4   Organization of a Medium-Size Bank. In the wholesale group, either a geographic or industry organization is emphasized. Auditing reports results of audits directly to the board.

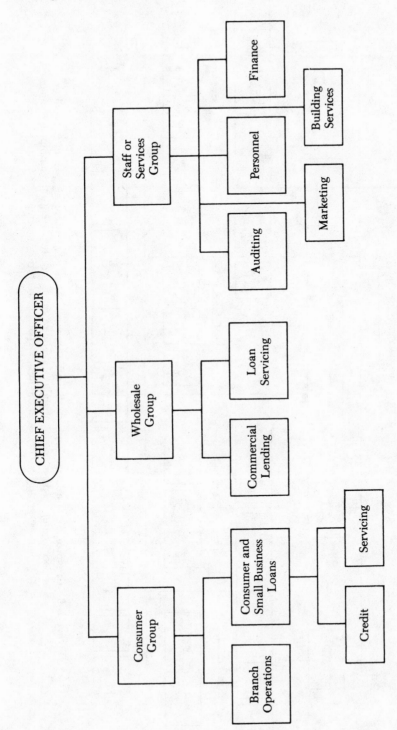

Figure 2–5 Organization of a Small Bank. Auditing reports results directly to the board.

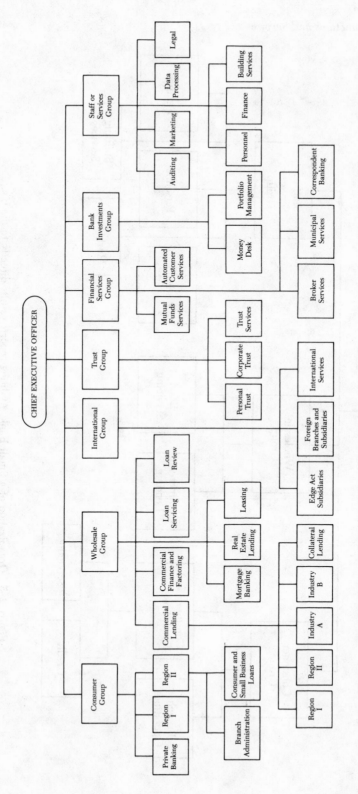

Figure 2-6 **Organization of a Large Bank.** Auditing Department, while administratively part of the staff or services group, reports results of audits directly to the board. Reporting relationships for some subsidiary corporations differ from the legal corporate structure.

count brokerage and more recently introduced electronic banking services, are obtained from third parties. The bank is a marketer or distributor rather than a producer of these services.

The wholesale group lacks an international capability and does not have within the commercial lending department any geographical or industry-oriented subunits. Specialized lending or leasing services are probably provided by a correspondent bank. A trust group may be lacking since small institutions often have difficulty getting enough money under management to justify the cost. The bank's investments function, which in all likelihood is limited to managing the bank's portfolio, is probably performed by the chief executive officer. The staff or services group performs many of the same functions as in a medium-size bank; however, they may be performed by individuals as collateral duties rather than by specialized units. Legal and data processing services are often contracted for from outside sources.

Larger institutions, while offering the same core services as a medium-size bank, also provide a wide range of more specialized services, although not every large institution offers every service. Larger institutions are more likely to produce the services they offer their own customers and to offer these same services to correspondent institutions as well. Specialized subsidiaries often exist for discount brokerage, mortgage banking, insurance, data and information processing, and investment banking.

The trust, bank investments, and staff or services group are similar to those of a medium-size institution (Figure 2–6). The consumer group will in all likelihood have the branches divided into regions. Each region may be semi-autonomous with the capability to process and service loans, and might even have personal trust capability. In addition to the regional organization, a separate unit may focus on the banking needs of high income/net worth individuals. That unit would work closely with the trust group, and in some organizations the private banking unit may reside in the trust group. In other banks where the target market is entrepreneurs with significant borrowing needs, private banking may be part of the wholesale group.

Certain activities in the wholesale group have increased in importance. For example, international is no longer just a service function of commercial lending, but is a group with foreign and domestic subsidiaries engaged in independent lending activities. Both industry and regional lending units can be justified, while in a smaller bank one emphasis or the other is usually chosen. Such activities as leasing, commercial financing, or factoring, which might be performed in a subsidiary corporation, would typically be more significant and would report at a higher level in the organization than in a medium-size institution. Real estate lending and mortgage banking might be emphasized as separate special activities. Because of the broader range of loan activities within the wholesale group, a loan review unit might exist to monitor adherence to bank policy.

Some larger banks have a financial services group that specializes in providing services to other financial institutions, such as mutual funds, brokers, municipalities, and correspondent banks. In smaller banks the financial service function is performed by the wholesale or trust groups. The automated customer services unit—if it focuses on financial institutions rather than nonfinancial industries—might be part of the financial services group. Figures 2–4, 2–5, and 2–6 are included to suggest some of the differences that can exist in bank organizations as a function of size. However, there is no truly standard form of organization—only common features. Each bank's organization should reflect its unique situation. A discussion of some possible bank service groups follows. The role of bank directors is included in the discussion of each group.

Consumer Group

This consumer group is usually responsible for branch administration; however, in larger institutions branches that handle primarily commercial business report to the wholesale group. The consumer group usually is responsible for noncomputer operations related to processing installment loans, credit cards, mortgages, and pay-by-phone transactions. If a bank's primary customers are professionals and executives, there may be a special unit to market to this subset of the consumer population. An alternate reporting location for a professional and executive unit is the commercial group, since very often such individuals have direct or indirect corporate relationships.

Through the delivery system of branches and electronic access devices the group markets and services individuals and local businesses. The branches accept savings deposits; issue certificates of deposit; grant consumer and small business loans; issue traveler's checks, money orders, and bank checks; provide foreign currency for travelers; and maintain safe deposit boxes. Branches also serve as a pickup point for other areas of the bank and perform banking floor activities for wholesale accounts, including provision of retail services to the employees of commercial customers. As the principal public contact point, the branches also refer customers to the trust and wholesale groups for pension and profit-sharing plans, personal trusts, larger business loans, leasing, and money desk, international, and automated customer services. Branches also provide customers with access to discount brokerage, financial planning, and other services. Increasingly under pressure to serve markets better and at the same time control costs, banks are moving to 24-hour service via electronic means, offering limited services through conveniently located mini-offices, and concentrating less frequently used services at regional hubs. This delivery system structure, often referred to as a hub and spoke, is predicated on the belief that customers will travel some distance to get less frequently used services from an institution that conveniently provides services needed on a frequent basis.

Typically, directors in all but the largest individual institutions are concerned with the opening and closing of branches, activities that require regulatory approval. Directors may be asked to act on policies relating to consumer loans, such as setting rate and risk policies, or determining the maximum size of installment, mortgage, and credit card loan portfolios.

During the late 1980s many banks will be considering investments in equipment and systems associated with the various forms of electronic banking. This could include the initial installation or upgrading of either on-line or off-line automated teller machines (ATMs). These devices are designed to dispense cash, accept deposits, and permit transfers between various accounts. With the proliferation of ATM networks, many banks are considering joining ATM networks to supplement or replace single institution proprietary ATMs. Services for authorizing the cashing of checks or for providing a point-of-sale capability may be considered. Other consumer services that may grow in acceptance during the late 1980s include pay-by-phone and bank-at-home. A pay-by-phone system allows the consumer to authorize payments in lieu of checks by using the telephone either to directly record instructions via a Touch-Tone phone or (only if necessary) speak to a live operator who keys the data into the computer. Bank-at-home is an evolving concept centered on using the telephone and a TV or TV-like screen to allow the customer to access banking records, make transfers between accounts, and possibly to perform accounting and financial analysis. Directors may be concerned with the location of the terminal devices associated with these programs as well as the funding of development efforts or the purchase of network services from correspondent banks or other providers.

Wholesale Group

The wholesale group, which markets chiefly to local, regional, and national institutional customers, is responsible primarily for lending functions. These include the granting of unsecured loans or lines of credit and the handling of loans secured by stocks, bonds, real estate, equipment, accounts receivable, or inventory. The group grants term loans and leases, as well as short-term working capital loans. In addition, it is involved with the industrial revenue bonds issued by its customers, even though these bonds may be purchased by another unit for the bank's portfolio. The group provides foreign exchange and international services to its customers in addition to accepting deposits.

The services provided to commercial accounts go beyond those available from the typical branch. In larger banks the group may be responsible for a number of predominantly commercial branches as well as for the commercial lending function. This commercial lending function would normally include the calling officers and the committee or individuals responsible for loan approval, loan servicing, and possibly loan review. The function of loan review is quality control: monitoring adherence to policy and procedures, periodically evaluating the loan portfolio to identify problem loans, and assessing overall risk and concentration within the portfolio. In some institutions loan review may report to the auditor or to some other independent group.

Account officers in the commercial lending area may be organized into special units focusing on individual industries. This is common in very large banks or in banks that serve only a small number of selected industries. Organization along geographical lines is more common, since it promotes efficiency in servicing customers. Often a separate unit is set up to handle real estate and construction lending because of its specialized nature. Banks large enough to have their own international or leasing function would have these units report into the wholesale group; otherwise these services are obtained from correspondent banks. In addition, quite often part of the commercial group includes cash management services that help customers collect receipts more rapidly through lock boxes, concentrate funds of secondary banks that are in excess of those required to compensate for services provided, and invest otherwise idle funds.

A number of specialized units may report to the wholesale group or may exist as separate units or groups, including the following:

- Correspondent banking: a unit in a larger bank that may deal with many smaller institutions purchasing federal funds, participating in loans, and providing data processing and other services that a correspondent bank may be unable to provide cost-effectively.
- Municipal services: a unit that services state and local governments by taking deposits and lending in anticipation of tax receipts, and in larger institutions arranging for the placement of tax-exempt bonds and notes.
- Automated customer services: a unit that provides data processing services such as payroll to commercial customers and accounting services to correspondent banks.

The organizational choice is often dictated by the size of the specialized unit and the degree of customer commonality with the wholesale group's other units.

A director will be regularly involved in the activities of the wholesale group since loans are reviewed by the board of directors and since lending activities not only are a primary source of earnings but also have the potential for substantial losses if loan charge-offs become too great. Banking is a low-margin business; even riskier loans priced at prime plus 3 or 4 percent need to have a high probability of repayment. Director concerns include not just the establishment of suitable policies but assuring that management complies with them. Policies should address not only the handling of individual loans but also the composition of the portfolio in order to avoid excess concentration in a single industry and the consequent risk of major losses.

On a policy level, directors may be concerned with setting acceptable levels of risk, lending limits (which, in all likelihood, will be lower than the maximum legal lending limit), the maximum term for which a loan can be written, and direction as to the industries to be emphasized in the loan portfolio. If an international department exists, directors may be concerned with setting country limits (the maximum amount that can be lent in a particular country) and the maximum foreign exchange position that traders can take. A director may also be asked to participate in business development activities.

In small institutions where directors have a closer involvement with a larger portion of the loan portfolio, bank policy may evolve by board action rather than through a specific written loan policy. In larger institutions with greater numbers of lending officers to be kept informed, the policy will probably be one written by the senior lending officer and reviewed with the board. In a multibank holding company, loan policy guidance may also be provided by the holding company board.

The policy addresses the principal risks involved: credit, interest rate, and liquidity. Credit risk is inability of the borrower to repay a loan as agreed, resulting in the loss of interest income and possibly principal. Interest rate risk results from granting term loans at fixed rates and funding them with short-term liabilities whose rates fluctuate with the market. The result at certain times can be a reduced or negative net interest income spread (interest income less interest expense) on the transaction. Liquidity risk is the inability to fund all of one's assets through normal means such as regular deposits, large certificates of deposit, repurchase agreements, federal funds, or other borrowings, with the result that the bank must borrow too frequently at the Federal Reserve Bank discount window or make excessive sales from its portfolio. The Fed is more willing to lend regularly, via the discount window, to a small institution than to a regional or money center bank that has alternative funding sources available. The risks are to some degree interrelated, since loan defaults and difficulties in raising liabilities are associated with periods of unusually high interest rates.

Risks can be reduced by diversifying the portfolio's industry composition as well as by focusing lending efforts in a few areas where real expertise can be developed. Industries come under earnings and cash flow pressures at different times and to varying degrees during the interest rate cycle. A bank that experiences significant deposit run-offs in certain periods during the interest cycle or times of the year may wish, if its markets permit, to emphasize lending to customers whose borrowing needs decline during similar periods, thus reducing liquidity risk. The policy can also emphasize anticipated growth industries and avoid industries thought to be in decline or heading for earnings problems. However, sometimes this isn't enough. Small banks that operate in limited geographical areas are often exposed to a systematic or common risk. For example, the difficulties many segments of American agriculture experienced during the mid 1980s have contributed to bank failures in rural parts of the country.

Limits on term loans address both liquidity and credit risks. The bank is locked into the term loan provided loan covenants are satisfied. If liability sources decline, the term loan remains and the bank must seek adjustments elsewhere in its portfolio. Demand loans provide greater flexibility but not as much as appears on the surface, since calling the loan of a borrower without funds or an alternate source of financing does not result in repayment. A term loan has greater credit risk because of the time period involved for repayment and the limitations on its activities the bank has as long as the covenants are satisfied. Thus the bank may be forced to wait until a problem fully develops rather than to take action when the first signs of the problem emerge.

The legal lending limit is determined differently for state and national banks, but the basis is a percentage of certain capital accounts. Thus large banks have higher limits and can attract larger customers with greater borrowing needs. Many banks set internal limits that are more restrictive than the legal limit, even for their best borrowers, and have declining limits as the degree of credit risk increases. The latter is an attempt to minimize the impact of a single customer's failure. Policies of this nature require some type of credit rating system. In the more formal systems the rating is a function of the customer's access to credit markets, industry stability, company financial condition, management quality, and so forth. Smaller institutions will be limited to regional or local credits that tend to be weaker than the best national customers. Consequently, loan limits are often set below the maximum, and the bank is not leveraged as highly as a large institution would be.

Country limits for international loans reflect the assessed political risk in a country, because very often the type of loans all but the largest institutions make are to governments, quasi-government agencies, or banks, or are guaranteed by the local government. All creditors are subject to the stability of the government and potential monetary restrictions. Countries are also grouped together on the basis of their level of development, with a distinction often being made between oil-exporting and -importing less developed countries. Many large banks have found that once-lucrative loans to less developed countries have turned into some of the largest problems in their loan portfolios. Thus asset size alone is no protection against loan losses.

Banks engage in both spot and future foreign currency transactions for their customers. Spot contracts settle within a few days and pose a limited risk to the bank. Future contracts are for the purchase or sale of foreign currency for delivery at some date up to six or more months in the future. The rate is established, however, at the time of sale. Generally, banks do not speculate but cover future contracts with hedges that protect the dollar conversion. While covering contracts are generally available, there may be occasions when they are not available for the exact amount or maturity, or when they cannot be arranged in a timely fashion. The result is a foreign exchange risk if currency prices change before a covering contract can be entered into. Unless the bank wishes to speculate, the net uncovered position in a foreign currency a trader can hold should be limited to that necessary for operating flexibility in servicing customer needs. Limits on the size of individual customer transactions also exist in some institutions, since a customer could default on a contract and leave the bank with a payment/exchange risk.

Loan policies vary among banks, depending on their size, expertise, markets, funding sources, extent, and sources of noninterest income, liquidity and interest rate policies, and management style. Profitability requires not only prudent loan policies but also loan pricing that is consistent with the costs of servicing an account, including the costs of funding and the "premium" associated with self-insuring the credit risk (loss of principal, nonpayment of interest, and loan work-out costs).

Trust Group

The trust group is strictly separated from the wholesale group. It is essential that confidential information acquired by the wholesale group while servicing a commercial loan be prevented from reaching officers in the trust group who may be making investment decisions involving the commercial customer's stocks or bonds. Since most trust investments are in major corporations, this is an area of particular concern to the larger regional and money center banks that lend to major corporations.

This group markets services to corporations and high net worth individuals, and possibly provides accounting and safekeeping servicing to other institutions and lawyers. If the bank offers private banking services where the target market is individuals with high net worth, this function may be housed in the trust group. The principal services to corporations are pension fund management and acting as stock transfer agent. The trust group may also act as corporate trustee for a corporation's bonds and represent the interests of the bond holders.

The trust group may be responsible for a customer's total account—making the investment decisions as well as providing servicing. In other instances, investment decisions are made elsewhere, and the group is responsible only for custody of the securities, accounting, tax preparation, and other services. The trust group may manage funds where monies from a number of individual accounts are commingled. These pooled investment funds provide the opportunity to service smaller accounts at lower costs as well as to permit those accounts to have a greater diversification of investments than would be possible if each account's money were invested individually.

The directors are concerned with the investment strategy being pursued by the group. They may be called on through a committee of the board to approve a list of specific stocks and bonds from which trust officers can select when making investment decisions. The approved list reflects the investment strategies being pursued for customers with various investment objectives. The board's participation in the process provides for outside input to the investment decision-making process and a review of the trust group's activities, particularly for the proper exercise of prudence and fiduciary responsibility. Investment performance is also important because it determines fee income for the area and affects the acquisition of new trust customers. To a lesser degree board participation may reflect the bank's investment position with regard to the social responsibility of some firms, independent of the outlook for dividends and appreciation in stock price over time. Directors are often expected to assist in marketing trust services.

Bank Investment Group

The bank investment group may be a specific organizational unit, but in smaller banks it is often an additional duty of the president or treasurer. This group is responsible for management of the bank's portfolio, which primarily consists of investments in government and municipal securities and sale of federal funds. Federal funds are the bank's temporarily not-needed funds lent unsecured to other banks, usually overnight. The bank investment group is usually also responsible—through the money desk—for the purchase of federal funds, issuance of repurchase agreements, and the generation of large certificates of deposit. In a repurchase agreement part of the bank's portfolio is sold to a customer with an agreement that the bank will repurchase the security at a specified time and price. Earnings are created because the original maturity of the security is longer than the time between issue and repurchase, and the customer receives credit only for an amount approximating the interest that would have accrued on a security of the short maturity. This arrangement works because interest rates are usually higher on longer maturity securities of equal risk.

As well as being a source of earnings in its own right, the bank's portfolio is a source of liquidity, since securities may be sold to provide funds to support additional lending activities or to offset deposit run-offs without reducing the loan portfolio. When interest rates are expected to peak, the maturity of the bond portfolio is lengthened; conversely, when interest rates are expected to rise to the extent possible, the maturity of the large denomination certificate-of-deposit portfolio is lengthened. Because of the difficulty in consistently predicting interest rates, extreme portfolio positions are avoided because they can have significant adverse impact on earnings as well as liquidity. Since banks are allowed to carry investments on their books at acquisition cost rather than market value, the sale of items with a fair market value below acquisition cost can result in an adverse impact on earnings in the period of sale. Consequently, banks will occasionally carry items that really should be sold for liquidity reasons because they cannot afford to recognize the loss on sale.

Directors are concerned with setting broad guidelines for the portfolio as well as setting leverage, interest sensitivity, and liquidity policies for the institution. Other prime concerns of a director are the capital adequacy of the bank and the establishment of dividend policy.

Staff and Services Group

In addition to the groups that have regular contact with customers, most banks have various support functions, among them the following:

- Auditing: is responsible for monitoring the activities of the other parts of the bank to assure compliance with banking regulations and internal policies and procedures. Auditing generally works closely with the regulatory agencies as well as with the audit committee of the board.
- Marketing: is usually responsible for corporate public relations, advertising, market research, and providing support to the marketing activities of the customer contact groups.
- The data processing or operations unit: provides back-office services to the other groups. Because the processing of data is such an integral part of a bank's activity, this unit tends to represent a much larger percentage of total noninterest expense in banking than in most other industries.
- Legal: works with outside counsel as well as handling more routine matters. Smaller institutions often rely entirely on outside counsel.
- Finance: maintains the general accounts of the bank, monitors performance against budget, and coordinates the budgeting and planning processes.
- General services: maintains the bank property, provides mail, messenger, and guard services. This is the housekeeping part of the bank.
- Personnel: advises on personnel policies and practices, performs recruiting, hiring, and payroll functions, administers the employee benefits program, and assures compliance with equal opportunity regulations and goals. Personnel may also run training programs of various kinds.

Directors are concerned with reviewing reports prepared by the auditing division and the applicable regulatory agencies. From time to time they may be called on to act on investments in data processing equipment or in the selection of a data processing service bureau. The board also approves the election of all officers and often determines employee benefits. It monitors hiring, promotion, and training practices not only for regulatory compliance but to assure personnel development for future management needs. The board is also concerned that management succession be an orderly process.

Holding Companies

Larger banking organizations may have subsidiary corporations engaged in consumer finance, commercial finance, discount brokerage or mortgage banking, as well as a variety of other businesses. A bank that is part of a holding company may be provided with staff or service functions by the holding company or by its flagship bank. At the same time, the provision of these services may limit the options available to the directors of an individual bank within the holding company. A balance must be maintained because the director represents the interest of the owner holding company but at the same time is accountable to the regulators for the health of the individual bank.

Summary

Within the confines of a regulated industry whose primary product is money—a commodity—bankers try to differentiate their institutions via specialization, quality of service, and delivery system locations (branches, ATMs, other electronic access). The geographical franchise, bank size, local market demographics, and organizational affiliation further define the options available to the bank. Within this framework the banker may choose a market focus—consumer, commercial, or a combination—and an institutional style—innovative, follower, or traditional. These choices may suggest greater emphasis on the elements of a market-oriented organization than on the more traditional functional organization. However, the limitation of bank size will in most cases prevent development of a strict market organization. The typical bank of the late 1980s will in all likelihood continue to have major customer contact units servicing consumers, commercial customers, and trust customers, although the products and methods of delivery will change.

The regulatory and environmental changes begun during the first half of the decade are likely to continue for some time. This includes further deregulation and equalization of allowed activities among various types of financial institutions and continued movement toward regional and national banking. It probably does not mean an end to regulation or to all references to particular institution types. In fact, recent failures of financial institutions suggest that in some areas there may be a return to greater regulation.

Increased competition—both regulated and nonregulated—the high cost of delivery systems, and the continued demand for more customer convenience and more sophisticated services with inter-relationships among products will tend to increase bank specialization, particularly in major markets with many providers of services of varying kinds. The 1980s are likely to see increased market or product specialization within institutions pursuing growth, while other banks position themselves for takeover or the arrival of national banking.

Chapter 3

ROLES AND RESPONSIBILITIES OF THE BOARD

by Robert K. Mueller

The Environmental Context

Conduct becoming a well-managed, properly governed bank is continually influenced by a host of shifting external and internal factors. These have been outlined broadly in Chapters 1 and 2. The role and responsibilities of the bank's board of directors are constantly shaped by a set of multiple criteria and multiple standards that evolve and change over time. The situation is compounded when an enterprising bank's objectives change and become multiple in nature and scope.

Certain criteria and standards for board conduct are established by statute and regulation. Others are shaped by public expectations and opinion, plus the all-important beliefs, values, attitudes, and ethics of individual directors. This is a complex set of abstractions. It impacts corporate conduct, the business philosophy, and the code of ethics (explicit or implicit) of a bank board. Board conduct and individual behavior patterns ultimately fall out of a composite of ethical orientation, beliefs, and value systems of the individuals on the board.

What we have is a complex frame of reference for a bank board's role and responsibilities. The board must be constantly concerned with clarifying what broadly constitutes human welfare and, more specifically, the kind of conduct of the bank's financial activities that is necessary to promote it. The normative behavior involved requires a process of deliberation and debate in the boardroom in response to new values and emerging technological and social developments in a shifting political, legal, and regulatory environment.

Human action falls into three domains. First is the domain of positive law and regulation. While constrained and complex, this domain is often a contradictory context for bank board functioning. The second domain is that of relatively free choice in banking affairs. It has opened up considerably with deregulation and the impact of innovative strategies of competing financial institutions. The third and most challenging domain of proper corporate conduct for a bank board implies "an obedience to the unenforceable"—directors do what they should do, although they are not obliged to do so by statute or regulation.

Banking Stewardship

The nature of the bank board is significantly different from that of a board of directors for most industrial and service corporations. In a general sense, a bank board becomes more involved in operations than an industrial board. Other differences have been set forth persuasively by William H. Bowen, president of Commercial National Bank in Little Rock, Arkansas.[1]

- Bank directors take an oath of office [12 U.S.C. (1973)]; business corporation directors do not.
- Bank directors have residence and citizenship requirements; their peers in business may, but often do not.
- Investment bankers may not serve as bank directors [12 U.S.C. (1978)]; no comparable barrier exists in business corporations.
- A bank director must make a financial commitment in the form of ownership [12 U.S.C. (1972)]; business corporate law typically exacts no such requirements of its directors.
- Statutory machinery exists for summary prohibition of unsound banking practices. The bank director may be

---

[1] Johnson, Richard B., *New Perspectives for Bank Directors* (Dallas, Texas: SMU Press, 1977), pp. 3, 4.

removed from office for unsound practices, with statutory liability for damages resulting from willful violation of the law [12 U.S.C. (1818)]; vague or less summary procedures, if any at all, appear in typical business corporation codes.
- With exceptions, national bank directors may not serve on more than one national bank board (15 U.S.C. 19); there is no comparable general prohibition in nonbanking corporations.
- Criminal laws abound which expressly prohibit certain acts by bankers, including embezzlement (18 U.S.C. 656), making false entries (18 U.S.C. 215), falsely certifying checks (18 U.S.C. 1004), making or granting a loan or gratuity to a bank examiner (18 U.S.C. 212), and borrowing funds entrusted to a bank under its trust powers. No such direct targeting or criminal law confronts the business corporate director.

Clearly, a higher level of performance and behavior is expected of the bank director than of the business corporate director.

In 1880, the New York State Court of Appeals captured the essence of a bank director's stewardship with this statement:

When one deposits money in a savings bank or takes stock in a corporation, thus divesting himself of the immediate control of his property, he expects, and has the right to expect, that trustees or directors who are chosen to take his place in the management or control of his property, will exercise ordinary care and prudence in the trust committed to them—the same degree of care and prudence that men prompted by self-interest generally exercise over their own affairs.

The Changing Nature of the Board

The role of the bank director continually expands and becomes more complex. Changes in the nature, the structure, the composition, and the process of bank directorship are leading the director toward a larger social consciousness and broader responsibilities. As presently pointed out by the American Bankers Association,[2]

Nowhere in corporate America is the disparity between myth and reality as great as it is on the boards of directors of commercial banks. Burdened with a maze of increasingly complex regulations

---

[2] American Bankers' Association, *Focus on the Bank Director: The Job* (Washington, D.C., 1977).

from various governmental agencies often proclaiming conflicting views, the bank director is expected to be a combination of Solomon and Medici. He or she must be well-informed and vigilant, legally responsible for the formulation of policy but not so attentive as to interfere with management. Although directors' own occupations may have very little to do with banking, they must be skilled in the knowledge of finance and economics. In spite of the limitations under which bank directors operate, as a group they are public-spirited citizens trying to fulfill their legal and business obligations in a responsible manner.

Without doubt, the powers, duties, and responsibilities of the board of directors are complicated by multiple sources of governance powers, many constraints, and varying degrees of freedom. A combination of common law, statutory law, articles of association, bylaws, and custom is involved.

Functions of the Board

The U.S. banking system, which encompasses some 15,000 banks, has a multiplicity of chartering, supervising, and examining agencies that makes it unique among the financial structures of the world. The function of the bank board is closely related to the nature of the system. This banking system imposes legal codes that involve both federal and state powers. To complicate matters further, there is diffusion of powers among different federal agencies.

Generalizing about the functions of a bank board is difficult. The board of a small community-oriented bank has little in common with the board of a large internationally oriented bank. Further, the structural differences in the banking industry may cause a particular bank board setting to be that of an independent unit bank, a branch banking system, a member of a chain group of banks, or a bank holding company. Regardless of the character of the bank, however, the board is the voice of the shareowners and the top echelon of authority and accountability. All corporate powers of a bank are exercised by or under the authority of its board. The directors manage its business and affairs except when such powers and authority are otherwise provided for in the relevant statutes and in the charter under which the bank functions. To serve in a responsible manner, directors clearly must be knowledgeable about the legal framework in which a bank operates. Such knowledge includes an awareness of the current federal and state statutes and regulations by the Comptroller of the Currency, the FDIC, and the Federal Reserve Board.

While national banks receive their charter from the Office of the Comptroller of the Currency, each of the states can also grant a charter to a bank that does not wish to be organized under federal law. Although the early U.S. banking system was predominantly one of unit banking, branch banking has developed in a context of uneven restrictions imposed by various state laws. Because of these restrictions, chain banking and group banking evolved. Chain banking refers to the use of interlocking directorates to link banks together; in group banking a holding company is formed to control the common stock of a number of banks.

A statutory web of regulations surrounds banking. It behooves the prospective director to appreciate fully the stewardship implications of bank directorship. The board has three very broad functions in directing the corporation: (1) to ensure that the bank complies with the law and regulations, (2) to assist the chief executive officer as necessary, and (3) to act as trustee for the bank's owners and depositors. These basic functions of any board of directors can become elaborate, depending on the size, location, maturity, ownership and type of bank. Specific functions normally performed by the bank board include the following:

1. To provide assurance that the banks' internal policies, procedures, and controls are designed in compliance with statutes, regulations, and good banking and business practice, and that procedures are carefully followed.
2. To assure formulation and adoption of major bank policies through formal statements of intentions, objectives, and specific goals. This function involves business philosophy, strategic parameters, organization, planning, measurement, and control. Specific bank policies are needed for matters of:
   (a) Lending: extent, nature, maturity, profiles, and risk assessment; loan risk parameters acceptable to the bank; geographical trading and transaction areas for the bank; authority and responsibility assignment for loan approval and lending limits; interest rates; credit worthiness of borrowers; and compliance with regulatory and statutory constraints.
   (b) Investment: including goals, reserves, money market

considerations, portfolio nature, quality size and balance; cash and tax management; risk analysis and risk management.

(c) Trust service management: including management philosophy, fiduciary responsibilities, legal and ethical considerations; investment philosophy and guidelines; and vehicles or fields of investment.

(d) Internal control and audit procedures.

(e) Employee relations policies.

(f) Security policies on programs and devices.

3. To provide general direction and governance of bank affairs, as distinct from operational management of the bank. The board must assure itself through knowledgeable and responsible inquiry that the bank's operating management has performed satisfactorily. The directors should direct and monitor the affairs of the bank without being entrapped in everyday managerial activities.

4. To conduct an evaluation of the bank's performance relative to corporate plan and industry and competitive norms. This evaluation includes assessment of the performance, integrity, and competence of the chief executive officer (CEO) and principal officers of the bank and a timely, adequate reporting and information system to keep directors knowledgeable at all times.

5. To anticipate the capital requirements of the bank in order to ensure appropriate growth and expansion of services and facilities. Profit performance must be sufficient to attract new capital as needed, and overall asset management is important to ensure adequate liquidity to meet extraordinary deposit levels or increase in loan demands.

6. To provide for executive succession. The board must ensure that personnel policies develop a pool of qualified candidates for the future.

7. To involve individual board members in various committee roles, thereby benefiting the bank by offering to management multiple perspectives, experience, and expertise.

8. To contribute to the business development of the bank, including suggestions for new business opportunities.

9. To furnish quality stewardship in the interest of shareowners, depositors, employees, and suppliers, and in the interest of the community where the bank operates.

Organization of the Board

The formal organization structure of a bank board is set forth in the statutes, in the corporate charter, and in the bylaws. There are two important features of any given board. One is the relationship and interface between certain company officers, particularly the chief executive officer and the treasurer. The other is the extent of each delegated power of the board. Corporate functional authority is normally described in the bylaws, and the accountability of each unit and its officers is defined. The degree of organization of bank boards is determined by the ratio of committee assignments to the number of directors willing to serve. Although many directors serve on committees of the board, others confine their directorship to a stewardship role in which there are no legal doubts about their responsibilities, liabilities, and privileges. A recent examination of U.S. bank boards revealed five committees as being the most common: (1) executive, (2) salary and bonus, (3) stock options, (4) audit, and (5) finance. Board officers usually number only a chairperson, perhaps a vice chairperson, a secretary, and a few committee chairpersons.

The corporate power conferred on the board under statute, charter, and bylaws can be divided into those the board delegates to the CEO and those the board retains for itself and its committees. Committees can deal with certain matters between board meetings. They often prepare recommendations to the full board; they may also be empowered to make commitments for the bank. For example, an investment committee of a bank board may decide to make a loan within a designated financial and risk range.

Some board committees are granted power to act on behalf of the board; the executive committee is an example. Other committees may be given responsibility for reviewing operations or subjects of interest to the bank and for making recommendations to the board (for example, the budget committee). A third type of committee is one that may be given decision-making authority combined with advisory responsibilities. An example is the audit committee, which has the authority to select auditors for board approval but may only recommend action on the audit itself.

Usually the articles of incorporation or the bylaws provide that the full board of directors may designate from among its members an executive committee and other committees. Each committee, to the extent provided in such a resolution or in the articles of incorporation, or the bylaws, shall have and may exercise all the authority of the board. No committee shall have the authority to do the following:

- Amend the bylaws or articles of incorporation.
- Designate candidates for director for purposes of proxy solicitation, or otherwise fill vacancies on the board or any of its committees.
- Approve actions or proposals which by statute must be approved by shareowners.
- Approve a plan of merger or consolidation not requiring shareowners' approval.
- Declare dividends or distributions.
- Authorize or approve reacquisition of shares unless so directed by the full board.
- Authorize or approve issuance or sale of a class of shares except when authorized by the full board.
- Reduce earned or capital surplus.
- Recommend to shareowners the sale/lease, exchange, mortgage, pledge, or other deposition of a substantial portion of the property and assets of the corporation.
- Recommend to the shareowners voluntary dissolution of the corporation or a revocation thereof.

So much for the general scheme of organization of the board of directors. Certain characteristics, responsibilities, and conditions of service are important to note as they pertain to directors as individual members of a bank board.

The Individual Director

To acquaint themselves with the background of specific board functions and responsibilities, the directors as individuals should be concerned about their own effectiveness, accountability, conduct, privileged position, liabilities, and relationships with each other and management. Federal and state statutes, regulations, customs, attitudes, and precedents shape certain policies and practices that are sensitive concerns for individual directors. These matters include the following specific areas of concern about individual directorship:

- Insider trading
- Legal responsibilities and exposures
- Fiduciary responsibilities
- Business and area development responsibilities
- Compensation and perquisites
- Retirement policy (of directors)
- Strategic planning oversight
- Indemnification
- Liability insurance
- Director nomination process and criteria
- Director performance appraisal

The effective bank director must also balance objective information against opinions about internal and external affairs of the bank. Thus, an open relationship between board and management is necessary if the board is to be fully informed. The board must make clear what it needs, and the CEO must respond. Certain categories of information are generally provided to the board in a timely fashion, among them (1) corporate objectives, including mission and strategic orientation; (2) objective review of historical results for perspective; (3) explicit statement of long-range business plans and alternatives; (4) statement of financial strategy and financial forecast; and (5) plans for management succession and development.

Information a director should expect, preferably in advance of each board meeting, includes the following:

- Minutes of the last board meeting and interim committee meetings
- Agenda of topics to be discussed or decisions to be reached
- CEO's report on operations
- Chief financial officer's report
- Project or appropriation proposals
- Resolutions bearing on policy, statutory commitments, legal actions, and other such matters
- Dividend proposals
- Significant public information releases by the bank

Given adequate advance information and a chance to come prepared to the formal meeting, certain conventional practices are to be expected in the boardroom.

Conduct of Board Meetings

Regular board meetings are usually private sessions attended only by official members of the board. On occasion, nondirector officers, counsel, auditors, or others may attend to discuss some specific matter.

A board meeting may include information exchange, close examination of performance, deliberation, debate, decision making, and executive personnel evaluation. A well-run meeting often calls forth manifestations of strength, weakness, tension, conflict, and resistance to change. A good chairperson will conduct meetings of a board in a progressive manner by applying accepted parliamentary rules of order and using leadership skills to foster cooperation and effective action. Bylaws and board policy set forth in varying detail procedures for the conduct of board meetings. The chief executive officer should give a full report to the board on bank affairs and should propose any considerations that require board action or merit board attention.

The agenda signals the significant items for board consideration. Since much activity occurs between meetings, the review and subsequent approval of the minutes of the previous meeting is important.

Directors should not be subjected to surprise. The conduct of the new business portion of the agenda is significant for a variety of reasons. The CEO can test the board's reaction to proposals or give early warning of trends affecting the bank. Discussion of matters affecting decisions to be made by the board or the CEO provides perspective and avoids surprise.

Length of the meetings is usually in inverse proportion to the amount of preparation of the board members on agenda items. Experience shows that only a few hours at one sitting are productive. Further deliberation can be carried on in committees or at a future meeting.

Board Composition and Conditions of Service

A bank board is usually made up of 15 to 19 persons. One 1981 survey of U.S. banks found the ratio of inside directors to outside directors averaged 3 to 16. (Manufacturing company boards generally ranged from 10 to 14 members.[3])

A smaller number of directors narrows the base of business perspective available for decision making. A larger number broadens the base and makes it easier to get a quorum. Bank boards tend to be larger in order to attract and hold important accounts. Balance of talent, skills, and representation is important for a bank board. Experience, skills, education, maturity, and reputation are conventional criteria. In addition, qualified directors are expected to have competence in some relevant areas, a reputation for ethical conduct, diplomatic talents, independence of thought, preparedness at meetings, demonstrated success in committee activity, regular attendance at meetings, an ability to serve as chairperson, and/or a capacity to provide special services.

Suggestions for director candidates may come from any source. If the bank board has a nominating committee, all prospective candidates need screening for propriety and qualifications for nomination prior to a deeper investigation. Ready availability, eligible age according to bylaws, lack of conflicts of interests, appropriate maturity, level of interest, reputation, business or professional qualifications, and other factors should be carefully considered before any overtures are made that lead to a formal, authorized, nomination proposal.

The nominating committee of the board is extremely important for improving the governance of a bank. The caliber of directorship depends on establishing and maintaining appropriate criteria and standards for nomination and renomination of prospective directors.

Ideally, shareholders should be advised that a nominating committee exists. They should be encouraged to submit recommendations, even though the practicality of shareholder input to the nomination process is questionable. Some proposals under discussion would provide shareowners a direct "right" of nomination. Such a procedure appears to be less desirable than the existing informal method of affording access to the nominating process.

According to a recent survey, most chief executives believe that

---

[3] Mruk, Edwin S., and James A. Giardina (of Arthur Young & Company), *Organization and Compensation of Board of Directors* (New York, 1981). Sponsored by Financial Executives Institute.

a director's compensation should approximate that received for an equivalent amount of time spent in the director's own profession or business. Others compare director compensation to consultant fees. There are three general classes of compensation: real income, psychic income, and perquisites. Real income varies with the scope and size of the bank. As stated in the Conference Boards' *Corporate Directors' Compensation, 1985 edition*, in 1984 the annual compensation for outside bank directors ranged from $2,000 to $41,000 for 73 U.S. bank holding companies. Annual compensation of outside directors of 32 commercial banks ranged from $1,200 to $28,000 in 1984. The median annual compensation for 189 financial services companies was $12,350.

Psychic income varies with the prestige of the institution, the stature of other directors, and public recognition and popularity of services the bank produces. Such income, of course, varies with the individual director's value system and peer relationships. Bank director perquisites are generally limited to annual or regular meeting dinners, indemnification policies, occasional social/business entertainment, and director pension plans.

The combination of an annual retainer plus a per meeting fee recognizes that the work associated with bank board membership consists of a constant and a variable. The constant portion of the role requires the director to stay informed and involved; the variable portion of the work requires attendance at meetings with the attendant preparatory homework and follow-up.

Stakeholder Relations

A modern stakeholder is one who holds that which is placed at hazard. In a corporate context this goes beyond holding ownership shares in the company or bank. It embraces those who hold money in custody for the institution or who hold contiguous land where the company or bank operates, those who hold jobs in the bank, and those who hold contracts to supply materials and services. It includes neighbors affected by unemployment or employment in the community. All who have a direct or indirect interest in bank activity are stakeholders. This constituency is thus greater than the conventional list of stockholders who—when things were less complex and interactive—represented the significant "holders of that which is placed at hazard."

The concept of stakeholders provides a relatively recent perspective on corporate governance with the board as part of a larger environmental and social system. Stakeholders are all those interested in, or affected directly or indirectly by, the corporation's existence and activity.

The stakeholder theory rejects the Victorian idea of profit for the owners as the sole or primary consideration. All who have a vested interest in the continued survival and prosperity of a corporation are considered participants. How to build bridges to relate to these interests is the issue. Public and stakeholder perception of, as well as actual linkages with these interests, are of importance to the board of directors of a bank.

The flow of power and information has shifted. Once it emanated mainly from the boardroom and executive suite into the organizations. Now, however, it must go outward among stakeholder groups, the public, and the government in order to obtain the consent and maintain the sanction necessary to govern a bank or other institution.

Enlightened directorates are examining this stakeholder concept as a more socially responsive perspective. The stakeholders, broadly stated, are essentially those whose collective behavior can directly affect the organization's future but who are not under the organization's direct control. Given this definition, the stakeholder concept has special aspects—for example, understanding how the free economic system provides goods and services. Some stakeholders enjoy a greater share of benefits than others. In the United States and Europe there is a rising tide of political and public opinion concerning responsible directorship. The public believes that directors have more freedom, access to corporate assets, and social concern as individuals than they actually do or are prepared to assume.

The main difference in dealing with stakeholders versus other dealings of a financial institution is that stakeholder relationships are rarely a one-time event or transaction-oriented. The relationships remain; a case in point is that of continued closely held ownership. Constructive linkages and mutual trust among interested parties, both inside and outside the owner circle of a closely held bank, for example, must be real and maintained. Ideally, the board of directors needs to monitor and guide this stakeholder network relationship in order that financial affairs are perceived to be, and are in fact, conducted in a socially responsive manner. As we know, this is not always the case when the owners are also the directors and managers. The reality, of course, is that common long-term welfare depends on a successful interdependent business and social community.

Directors could once content themselves with keeping stockholders happy, or at least pacified. Today, a large corporation or bank can be seen as having many stakeholders. This means having to function in an environment in which the classical distinction between public and private sector is often meaningless, because "private" decisions can have profound impact on the lives of many.

If boards of directors fail to deal with stakeholder interests, government regulators, lawmakers, and social activists will force more constraints on corporations. This appears to be the wrong way to improve social responsibility of banks. Directors as individuals and boards as groups must take the initiative in order to enhance corporate profitability and growth. This calls for paying directors well to govern properly, and replacing them if they fail to act in a responsible way in the stakeholders' interest as determined by the board.

As a board develops ability to conduct its affairs with responsible regard for all its stakeholders, no matter how diverse and scattered these interested or affected parties may be, the bank will present a more human face to the public. Such a posture involves an apparent willingness to consider trade-offs of certain private corporate interests in favor of public interests.

The "place of standing" of a board of directors in public judgment is becoming an increasingly important matter. Public concern mounts over accountability of directors, fear of power concentrated in corporations, secrecy of boardrooms, immoral bigness, and stakeholders' interest.

Because there are no generally accepted social standards of conduct or performance for an effective board other than economic-health and pattern-of-return to the investors in the corporation, the rating of a board is seldom attempted. Its role and *locus standi* in relation to other boards or societal norms are undefined but still a subject of concern. The concerns differ somewhat between closely held and widely held banks and financial institutions, between large and small banks, and with those further along in their corporate life cycle. A professional approach to stakeholder relationships requires the bank board to insist on and monitor the management's approach and system to ensure optimal stakeholder linkages.

Board Trends for the Future

A helpful step in assessing a bank's future corporate governance position is to contemplate likely trends in the industry. Such speculation should be in the context of a bank's operations and condition. A bank board of directors of the future will probably have different characteristics, requirements for future directorship, and expected board organization structure and policies.

Board Characteristics

The bank board of the future may be expected to display the following characteristics:

1. Be more assertive with respect to its evaluations, participation, resources, and roles. Even more rigor will be needed in the board's attention to statutory, regulatory, and fiduciary responsibilities to the bank's stockholders.
2. Have more nonconflicting linkages to important institutions or groups affecting or affected by the bank's activity, including schools, hospitals, churches, civic organizations, professional societies, consumers, environmental groups, foreign policy forums, and political groups. These are the bank's stakeholders.
3. Accept service, rather than competition, as the prime motivation for exemplary corporate governance.
4. Be alert to inroads into the conventional banker's domain by relatively new competitive business entrants. These entrants from nontraditional banking domains will include the brokers, real estate concerns, consumer services, and other enterprising sectors seeking diversification into banking. Banking regulations are being modified to permit greater degrees of freedom in meeting these competitive factors.

Future Directorships

Directorships in the future may be expected to require a greater commitment of time. Directors of U.S. financial institutions attended 4 to 18 meetings per year in 1984 (the median is 10). This number will increase in intensity, if not frequency, in the future. At least two additional trends are expected: First, all bank board members will undoubtedly have to be active professionally and intellectually or be otherwise gainfully employed; retired former directors may serve effectively in active advisory or emeritus roles when this is warranted. Second, continuing and formalized educational/orientation programs (within and outside the bank) will be valuable for all directors. Emphasis will be on evolving governance and management concepts as they are related to the changing nature of banking.

Future Board Organization

A trend toward separation of the chairperson and CEO roles will provide for the nonexecutive chairperson to be the agent of the board and a source of counsel and support for the CEO. In addition, there will be an expanded scope for banks' audit committees (or equivalent) beyond financial matters to embrace social responsibilities and corporate conduct, particularly in international banking practices. In general, committee activity will undoubtedly increase as directors become more active and board accountability becomes more evident.

As the determination of long-term strategy becomes more complicated and vital, the strategy review board committee (formal or ad hoc) will become a recognized organizational requirement.

Nominating committees composed of a majority of independent directors with formal criteria for board worthiness are generally accepted now. Shareholder participation in the director nomination process may become a more active issue, although such a movement may prove to be impractical.

Summary and Conclusion

Key words for bank boards to think about for the future are *legitimacy, relevance, integrity, interdependence, board worthiness,* and *independence*. These notions may be considered as follows:

- *Legitimacy* of the banking enterprise in terms of its purpose, powers, and identity.
- *Relevance* of the bank to society and the community.
- *Integrity* of the bank in terms of its viability and service.
- *Interdependence* of banking and other industries as vital in our complex, changing environment.

- *Board worthiness* as defined by director competence, ethics, integrity, ambassadorship, preparedness, and participation.
- *Independence* as manifested by confidence, courage, freedom from conflicts of interest, non-self-perpetuation in the bank's service, objectivity, and respected judgment.

Most elements of society, including banking, are being restructured. The most basic of prior understandings, assumptions, and institutions are being challenged and changed in the United States and abroad. The changes are political, economic, social, and cultural. Regulated sectors of society will also change, albeit slowly, to reflect the general shift from a mass industrial society to an information society.

With 55 percent of society working in the information sector (compared with 17 percent in 1950), the strategic resources of knowledge and data (both renewable and self-generating) must be considered in addition to monetary capital. The conduct of economic activity will shift with these contextual changes. In turn, banking functions and the role of those who regulate and govern financial intermediary activities will shift. Interactivity and interdependence of global economies are growing, and banking institutions will have to resolve who is going to do what in a world of instantaneously shared information and supersonic transport.

With this contextual transformation under way, certain issues are important to the governance of financial industry institutions. The public is increasingly concerned about standards of care and loyalty that are too low, increasing social costs, and too much power being concentrated in the hands of corporations and financial institutions. Further law and structural reforms can be expected in an attempt to improve the effectiveness and accountability of banks, other services, and industrial corporations. In banking the concerns will be about the accountability of management and directors, regulations imperiling the effectiveness of financial institutions, stockholder interests, and a growing realization that statutes and regulations are not necessarily the optimal vehicles for dealing with social problems.

These problems raise major issues for bank directors. Three of these issues are prominent: (1) Does the goal of long-term profit maximization continue to serve as an accurate description of bank objectives? (2) Should banks be further regulated? and (3) What is the proper balance of legislative reform at national and state levels for improving the effectiveness of bank governance with regard to standards of fiduciary responsibility, standards of care, and regulation of challenges to management from shareholders or bank outsiders?

The role and responsibilities of the bank board in the remaining years of this century will be interesting and challenging. Bank boards cannot afford to remain insular and unresponsive to the changing requirements of an interdependent and interactive world that affects every banking community and environment.

Chapter 4

ASSET/LIABILITY MANAGEMENT

by Charles J. Thayer and Maurice D. S. Johnson

Introduction

The balance sheet has for centuries been viewed as the primary indicator of a bank's financial position. Depositors, borrowers, investors, and even directors and regulators often glance only at total assets compared with the previous year to measure growth, review the loan-to-deposit ratio as the measure of risk, and consider the holdings of government and municipal securities as a vague message of liquidity.

This superficial review is, of course, inadequate. A successful bank, like all business enterprises, must be able to produce consistent earnings growth and achieve a return on capital that provides a base for future growth. Producing solid operating results against a background of a quality balance sheet can only be achieved by careful and dynamic balance sheet architecture.

The board of directors' challenge is to address the following question: How can the skillful management of the bank's balance sheet (generally called asset/liability management) become the backbone of consistent earnings growth? Each member of the board should be familiar with the subject of asset/liability management, since it has received a substantial amount of attention from the press, bank analysts, bank regulators, and bank managements.

Let us first recap the development of balance sheet management. The 1950s were the era of "asset management." The banking system's source of funds was primarily demand deposits supplemented by retail savings deposits. Loan-to-deposit ratios generally averaged less than 50 percent, and the test of bank management was the skillful investment of these funds—primarily in the securities market.

During the 1960s "liability management" was born. Loan growth at the money center banks exceeded the growth of their traditional sources of deposits, thereby creating the need for the development of the negotiable certificate of deposit, the federal funds market, repurchase agreements, commercial paper, and Eurodollar deposits as additional sources of funds. Each of these instruments is discussed in more detail later in the chapter.

The 1970s were described as the decade of "asset/liability management." Bank managements recognized the need for a coordinated strategy that would combine both the source and use of rate-sensitive funds. The risks of an unmatched asset/liability position were painfully illustrated by those banks that experienced significant earnings declines created by rate sensitivity mismatches during both 1973–1974 and 1979–1980. History should clearly illustrate the benefits of a hedged asset/liability strategy to bank management.

Perhaps the key word for the decade of the 1980s is "profitability." In the final analysis, the objective of any asset/liability strategy is to manage the profitability of the balance sheet—the net interest margin. Another specific measure of profitability that merits attention is the profitability of equity capital—that is, the return on equity. It should be remembered that the equity capital account can be built only through retained earnings or from the issuance of new stock. Dividend policy and the stability of earnings growth are the key ingredients of internal capital generation. It is very important to remember that the continued growth of bank capital is required to support future growth of earning assets.

Interest Rate Risk

The increasing volatility of interest rates and the changing structure of bank balance sheets require that bank management adopt increasingly sophisticated techniques to manage the bank's asset/liability position. The first decision that bank management must face is either to hedge the rate sensitivity of the balance sheet or to speculate on interest rate movements. The key assumption for this chapter is that management's objective is to hedge interest rate risk by establishing a balance sheet structure that will produce consistent growth of the net interest margin.

The temptation to speculate on interest rate movements to optimize earnings is always present. If management elects to "take a view on rates," a variety of methods are available. However, the structure of the balance sheet is seldom flexible enough to permit timely adjustments if management's interest rate forecast is wrong. If interest rate speculation to maximize earnings is your objective, it is suggested that the most appropriate approach is to take positions in the trading account that can be sold quickly to correct for errors in market judgment.

During the 1950s the cost of funds was relatively fixed, and net interest income was primarily a function of the changing level of interest rates and the resulting yield on rate-sensitive earning assets. The development of liability management during the 1960s created a source of funds that is also rate-sensitive. As a result, bank management now has the opportunity to match interest income and interest expense in a manner that will produce the same level of net interest income regardless of the level of interest rates. In other words, in theory, banking earnings no longer need to be at the mercy of changes in the short-term rate environment. Once rate-sensitive assets are matched with rate-sensitive liabilities, the net interest margin can theoretically be controlled. Unfortunately, the solution to asset/liability management's impact on the net interest margin is not this simple. The concept of rate sensitivity is explored in more detail later in this chapter.

Balance Sheet Growth and Asset/Liability Management

One of the functions of the board of directors is to ensure that the appropriate management systems are utilized to achieve that bank's financial goals. Any number of combinations of management personnel can serve to manage the balance sheet. Success can be achieved, however, only if certain authority and information are consistently available to and analyzed by management. Consistent financial performance requires management discipline.

Because of the volatility of the money markets and the constantly changing balance sheet of the bank, the asset/liability management group should meet frequently, generally on a weekly basis. Usually a well-organized hour will be sufficient.

The chairperson of the committee responsible for asset/liability strategy should be senior enough in the management group to provide appropriate perspective concerning strategy and tactics. The other members of the committee should represent the primary balance sheet portfolios for the bank. These may include the investment manager, the commercial loan manager, the construction loan manager, the retail banking manager, and the funding manager. The organization's chief financial officer should be present at these meetings to ensure that all financial data are accurate and represent the consolidated financial position of the total organization, not just the primary bank subsidiaries. Finally, the chief executive officer should attend to provide the management guidance required to achieve the financial objectives established by the board of directors. The financial information provided by each of these managers at the weekly asset/liability committee meeting should be brief and forward-looking. The primary objective of the committee is to plan the future structure of the balance sheet, not to discuss history.

The foundation for any asset/liability program should be a thoughtful and realistic strategic (three- to five-year) plan with a detailed one-year budget. These two documents, which obviously must be based on identical financial objectives, provide the strategic course for the company and the tactical operating plan for the coming year. The actions taken by the asset/liability committee should be directed toward keeping the bank on its planned course. A computer model may be utilized by bank management to assist the asset/liability committee in its task. However, we would suggest that the model be kept very basic and that the forecast be provided by the appropriate line managers rather than determined by staff personnel or sophisticated programming techniques. The model should be run monthly to illustrate management forecasts for the next several months to determine the impact of the most recent balance sheet projections on the budgeted net interest margin. This gives management the opportunity to restructure short-term strategies to maintain net interest margin growth.

Modeling techniques also permit bank management to analyze the impact of changing interest rate levels and money market spreads on balance sheet profitability. By continually analyzing the impact of restructuring the balance sheet in a changing economic environment, bank management can more effectively hedge the growth of the net interest margin during a rapidly changing economic and interest rate environment.

Asset Management: Strategic Elements

As the asset/liability management committee pursues its objectives, it should not change basic policy guidelines (such as trying to increase loan growth or yields by taking greater risks) without appropriate approval from the board of directors. Policy on credit risk should be established by executive management and the board of directors, not the asset/liability committee. Using that as a given, the committee looks at all acceptable alternatives to maintain the spread as planned, broadening the earning asset base as budgeted, and adjusting to the constant ebb and flow of the market. A more detailed discussion of loan policy and portfolio management was presented in Chapter 2. The following material addresses only the strategic elements of asset growth as they relate to liquidity and asset/liability management.

Money Market Assets

The primary source of short-term liquidity is the bank's money market asset portfolio consisting of federal funds sold to other banks, time deposits placed with other banks, and other short-term liquid assets. This portfolio represents the first source of funds to replace a decline in the bank's basic source—that is, deposits—and the source of funds that may be utilized to fund an increase in either the investment or loan portfolios.

Investment Portfolio

Executive management, using the best information from the asset/liability committee and other sources, normally targets the level of securities during the budgeting process. Usually, the level is a percentage of total assets and should be reviewed and adjusted during the year. Income tax considerations determine the amount and mix of tax-exempt loans and municipal securities. Historically, the traditional second source of liquidity—after money market assets—was the government portfolio, and a third source was the municipal and loan portfolios. However, as a practical matter, today the government securities are generally already sold on repurchase agreements. Therefore, asset liquidity is limited to the money market portfolio, followed by the quality and marketability of both the municipal bond and loan portfolios.

Commercial Loans

Professional bankers have long believed that they must always be prepared to make loans to their local businesses, even if in tight situations part or all of such loan growth must be shared with correspondent banks. Thus commercial loans have not provided a very flexible part of the asset portfolio for balancing against available funding. Occasionally, officers can prevail on good multibank customers to use or not use their line of credit, but too much of this practice does not represent good customer relations.

Consumer Loans

These loans have historically been considered to be funded by non-rate-sensitive consumer deposits. The modification of Regulation Q, which removed the ceilings on the rate of interest banks could pay on deposits, and the introduction of the T-Bill certificate in 1979 changed this historical relationship by making consumer deposits more rate-sensitive. Because all fixed-rate assets must be funded with fixed-rate sources of funds, the future of fixed-rate consumer lending will be directly related to a bank's ability to attract longer maturity—three- to five-year—fixed-rate consumer certificates. Of course, another alternative has been the introduction of floating rate consumer loans.

Real Estate Loans

Construction lending is not only more cyclical than most loan categories but also more easily financed directly. Usually tied to the prime rate and thus related to federal funds or money market CDs, properly managed construction lending may provide a good source of earning asset growth. Mortgages should be written as carefully as possible to conform to the private and public mortgage markets. Permanent mortgage loans have been resisted by most banks because of fixed rates and long maturities. The growth of the Government National Mortgage Association (GNMA) and other pass-through security instruments permits banks to participate more actively in the origination of loans for resale in these secondary markets.

Leasing

The typical lease usually matures in five to nine years with a rate that normally can be funded with an acceptable spread. Money market funding cannot be acquired easily for this maturity, and as that part of the portfolio grows, it lends itself to term fixed-rate borrowing, possibly using fixed-rate consumer deposits as a funding source.

In summary, the most important strategic elements of asset growth are pricing (fixed or floating rate) and liquidity (quality and marketability). The ability to fund asset growth is directly related to the ability to acquire funding that matches the pricing characteristics of the new asset.

Liability Management: Strategic Elements

Most discussions of liability management address the various funding instruments—that is, balance sheet categories used for financial reporting. Such a view of the sources of funds available through liability management, however, is very superficial. As in all businesses, the key to success is not the identification of the product but the identification of the customers who purchase the product. Table 4–1 illustrates the relationship between the various liability instruments and the basic customer groups that generally purchase these instruments.

Obviously, the availability of funds from these various instruments depends on the marketing skills exercised by management toward each customer group. Intelligent marketing programs are the key to continued growth of reliable funding sources. The primary sources of bank deposits, both demand and time, must be markets that are reliable providers of such funds during all periods of the economic cycle.

However, it must be acknowledged that any change in the

Table 4-1 Sources of Liability Funding

Instrument	Domestic Banks	Foreign Banks	Business	Individuals	Governments	Dealers
			Primary Customers			
Demand Deposits	Yes	Yes	Yes	Yes	Yes	No
Consumer Time	No	No	No	Yes	No	No
Money Market:						
Fed Funds	Yes	No	No	No	No	Yes
Large CDs	Yes	Yes	Yes	Yes	Yes	Yes
Repo Agreements	Yes	Yes	Yes	Yes	Yes	Yes
Eurodollars	Yes	Yes	Yes	No	No	Yes
Commercial Paper	No	No	Yes	Yes	Yes	Yes

bank's financial record might impair its ability to continue to utilize such money market sources of funds. It is obvious that a fortunate banker can nevertheless report satisfactory profits for short periods of time by stretching for high-risk, high-income loans or speculating in the securities portfolio. However, growing sophistication of both bank analysts and corporate treasurers will quickly penetrate those practices, and such bankers will find it difficult to obtain the required money market funds to fuel continued earning asset growth. The funding and liquidity problems experienced by banks during the early 1980s were created by asset quality deterioration—that is, excessive loan losses.

The price of various liability instruments should be considered from two viewpoints. The first is the interest cost associated with each instrument, and the second is the supporting or operating cost required to issue each instrument. The interest cost component of liability management also must be separated into two distinct categories. Those instruments whose costs do not fluctuate with changes in the level of money market interest rates, consumer savings, and demand deposits should be viewed as non-rate-sensitive funds. Those instruments whose interest costs do fluctuate with the changing level of money market rates are, of course, rate-sensitive liabilities and are the essential ingredient to understanding the rate sensitivity characteristics of the balance sheet.

One final type of cost associated with liability management that should also be considered is a regulatory cost such as reserve requirements of the Federal Reserve, an additional cost that is outside the control of bank management.

As previously mentioned, three primary categories of liabilities are available to bank managements: demand deposits, consumer time deposits, and money market sources. We will briefly discuss the key markets that provide funds within each category.

Demand Deposits

The checking account is the traditional source of deposit for the banking system and has historically represented a unique service provided by banks within our financial structure. The growth of demand deposits within the banking system is subject to Federal Reserve monetary policy, and represents the slowest growth source of funds to the banking system.

Corporate Customers. Private businesses provide the largest amount of demand deposits to the banking system, and this source of deposits is related to loan growth through the compensating balance requirements of the traditional lending agreement. The growing sophistication of corporate treasurers in the techniques of cash management will continue to put pressure on this source of demand deposits, and very careful customer profitability analysis systems must be put in place to monitor the relationship between services provided and the value of the demand deposit.

Retail Customers. The retail market has been a smaller but stable source of demand deposits for the banking system. However, various studies have shown that approximately 20 percent of the customers provide 80 percent of the deposits. As a result, the remaining 80 percent of customers may represent unprofitable accounts unless priced appropriately. This profitability paradox could be tolerated so long as the remaining 20 percent of the customer base was willing to keep significant balances in their demand deposit accounts. However, the nationwide introduction of NOW accounts and money market accounts into the banking system in the early 1980s provided the mechanism for these individuals with high balances to shift their funds into interest-bearing accounts. The remaining retail demand deposit base consists of the low balance, less profitable retail checking accounts. Bank managements are clearly faced with a challenge of repricing their checking services to the retail markets to provide adequate profit margins.

Correspondent Relationships. An important source of demand deposits for many regional and money center banks has been the correspondent banking relationships that they have historically served. Again, we see growing pressure from the Federal Reserve to provide many of these same services for a fee. The apparent desire of the Federal Reserve to enter into competition with the traditional correspondent banking relationships will provide growing pressure on both the availability of these deposits and the profitability of the correspondent banking relationship.

Government Deposits. Demand deposits maintained by cities, states, and the federal government also are under growing competitive pressure. Regulatory changes such as the conversion of the traditional Treasury tax and loan demand deposit account into an interest-bearing note arrangement with the Federal Reserve in 1979 illustrates the desire by government to obtain higher value for deposits in the banking system. As a result, bank management again must install accurate customer profitability analysis to ensure that pricing and services rendered are realistic.

Consumer Time Deposits

Consumers have provided a growing source of stable funding for the commercial banking system. The growth of consumer savings and certificates of deposit has been significantly above the growth of demand deposits. However, again we have seen increasing pressure put on these instruments, primarily as a result of regulatory and money market changes. The recurring upward changes in Regulation Q interest rate ceilings during the 1970s simply provided a stair-step increase in cost for the commercial banking system. The elimination of interest rate ceilings during the early 1980s converted non-rate-sensitive consumer time deposits into a more rate-sensitive deposit. The financial press, brokerage industry, and competition within the banking industry all have served to educate consumers as to the value of their funds.

Money Market Sources of Funds

These markets have expanded in terms of instruments and are utilized by the same customers: corporations, wealthy individuals, and other financial institutions.

Federal Funds. The federal funds market developed during the 1960s as a way for community banks with low loan demand to sell excess funds (usually on a one-day basis) to regional and money center banks to supplement their earning asset growth. A significant change may be underway in this market during the 1980s as the acceleration of local loan growth at these community banks diminishes their ability to sell federal funds. The liquidity provided to the banking system in prior years may now be utilized by these community banks to fund their own future loan growth. As a result, the federal funds market may not offer a growing source of funding for regional and money center banks in the future.

Repurchase Agreements. The ability to sell government securities and other assets on agreement to repurchase (repo) was recognized by all sophisticated bankers during the 1970s. As a result, the liquidity once provided by the government securities portfolio has been diminished because, as a practical matter, a large share of these securities already are sold on repurchase agreements. The availability of funds from the repo market is directly related to the collateral available to be sold. Therefore, repos represent a funding source only for those assets that are eligible for resale into this market. Historically, this has been a fairly dependable source of funding since the bank issuing the repo agreement has the underlying collateral as credit, and therefore very little credit risk is apparent to the purchaser. However, the failure of several government bond dealers during the early 1980s illustrates the need for careful credit evaluation for all money market activity, including repurchase agreements. The importance of payment against delivery of collateral should never be ignored.

Large Certificates of Deposit. The removal of Regulation Q from the large ($100,000 and larger) certificate of deposit permitted the development of this instrument as the primary source of funding growth within the banking system. The characteristics of the instrument are not nearly so important as the purchasers. The key to continued growth in this category of funding is careful development of the customer base served by the bank. The issuance of negotiable CDs through dealers appears to be an easy option to obtain additional funds; however, tight money market conditions limit the availability of funds from this market, and only limited amounts should be issued by banks that are unable to demonstrate superior financial performance.

Commercial Paper. This instrument was developed as a result of the conversion to bank holding companies and the impact of Regulation Q in the late 1960s. It does not currently represent a significant source of new funds for the banking system because of many restrictions on its use and the fact that commercial paper interest rates are very similar to those for certificates of deposit, normally a more marketable instrument.

Eurodollar Deposits. These deposits, with the exception of those in the large money center banks, generally represent deposits from other financial institutions. In many respects, this source of funds should simply be viewed as another technique for shifting funds between banks within the banking system. Such deposits may be booked between two domestic banks or purchased from a foreign bank for domestic use.

In summary, the increasing complexity of bank funding has created an environment that requires very careful coordination between the users and providers of funding within the bank. The most important strategic elements of liability management are the dependability of funding and the pricing—that is, fixed or floating rate.

Asset Liability Management and the Net Interest Margin

The traditional financial presentation of the bank balance sheet and income statement did not adequately illustrate the earnings equation for banking. One of the objectives of the restructured financial presentations required by the Securities and Exchange Commission in 1979 was to illustrate better the "earnings equation" for bank income. Table 4–2 illustrates the key components of the bank earnings equation required by this new reporting format.

The largest and generally most volatile component of the bank earnings equation is the net interest margin. As previously stated, the objective of asset/liability management should be to stabilize the growth of the net interest margin's contribution to operating income. This stabilized growth can be achieved through careful management of the bank's earning asset growth in relation to the rate sensitivity mismatch. The concept of rate sensitivity and its impact on bank profitability is illustrated in detail in the next section.

The primary external factors that influence the level of the net interest margin are earning asset growth (principally loan demand), interest rate levels, and money market spreads. The objective of asset/liability management is to structure the financial

Table 4-2 Bank Earnings Equation

Income Statement		Description
Interest Income	=	Earning Assets × Yields
Interest Expense	=	Source of Funds × Cost
Net Interest Margin	=	Interest Income less Interest Expense
Loan Loss Provision	=	Contribution to Reserve for Future Loan Losses
Net Financial Contribution	=	Net Interest Margin Adjusted for Loan Loss Provision
Noninterest Income	=	Service Charges and Fees
Noninterest Expense	=	Salary, Occupancy, Equipment, etc.
Pretax Income	=	Margin Adjusted for Noninterest Items
Income Tax	=	Tax Rate Affected by Amount of Tax-Exempt Income
Operating Income	=	Profit from Operations
Securities Transactions	=	Restructuring (Losses) Improves Future Year Earnings
Net Income	=	Profit Contribution to Capital and Dividends

position of the bank in such a manner that the level of interest rates and the money market spreads tend to offset one another. As a result, the principal component in determining earnings growth then becomes the level of earning asset growth, which is more easily controlled through such management actions as purchase or sale of securities and loan participations.

The Concept of Rate Sensitivity

The objective of rate sensitivity management is to offset the relative impact of changes in the level of interest rates and money market spreads on the net interest margin. To accomplish this objective, bank managements must analyze the relationship between money market spreads and the level of interest rates. Table 4–3 illustrates the relationship between the prime rate and the cost of money market funds.

Three significant items should be noted. First, interest rates have become increasingly more volatile. Second, the historical spread between the cost of funds and the prime rate has changed dramatically. Third, there has been more stability in the relative relationship between market spread and interest rate levels since the introduction of the prime rate formula by Citibank in 1974.

Table 4-3   Money Market Spreads

| Annual Average | Prime Rate | Federal Funds | 90-Day CDs | Prime Rate vs. | |
				Federal Funds	90-Day CDs
1960	4.82%	3.26%	NA	1.56%	NA
1961	4.50	1.53	NA	2.97	NA
1962	4.50	2.65	3.08%	1.85	1.42%
1963	4.50	3.21	3.40	1.29	1.10
1964	4.50	3.46	3.87	1.04	.63
1965	4.54	4.00	4.31	.54	.23
1966	5.62	4.94	5.43	.68	.19
1967	5.63	4.25	4.99	1.38	.64
1968	6.28	5.58	5.79	.70	.49
1969	7.95	7.71	7.66	.24	.29
1970	7.91	7.32	7.68	.59	.23
1971	5.70	4.65	5.07	1.05	.63
1972	5.25	4.40	4.61	.85	.64
1973	8.02	8.57	8.21	− .55	− .19
1974	10.80	10.53	10.28	.27	.52
1975	7.86	6.15	6.61	1.71	1.25
1976	6.84	5.15	5.31	1.69	1.53
1977	6.78	5.49	5.55	1.29	1.23
1978	9.06	7.88	8.05	1.18	1.01
1979	12.67	11.19	11.02	1.48	1.65
1980	15.29	13.48	12.97	1.81	2.32
1981	18.90	16.40	14.90	2.50	4.00
1982	15.02	12.48	12.41	2.54	2.61
1983	10.80	9.06	8.98	1.74	1.82
1984	12.06	10.15	10.40	1.91	1.66
1985	9.58	8.15	8.11	1.73	1.77

Source: Salomon Brothers.

The introduction of the Citibank pricing formula provided a money market benchmark for establishing bank loan pricing. However, spreads between the prime rate and the cost of funds have tended to widen during periods of extreme interest rate volatility and to stabilize during periods of interest rate stability.

Bank managements are certainly not immune to the desire to maximize earnings given a predicted interest rate environment. If, in fact, a bank management's forecast of interest rates proves correct, it is certainly possible for their performance to exceed that of the banking industry. On the other hand, given the instability and inaccuracy of interest rate forecasts, combined with the need to maintain a steady financial performance to maintain continued access to money market funding required to fuel asset growth, it would seem prudent for bank managements to adopt a strategy of stabilizing rather than maximizing net interest margin growth.

The following tables illustrate in detail the concepts of balance sheet management and rate sensitivity. The section is complex and represents material that may be of interest only to directors with a specific interest in this topic.

Table 4–4 illustrates a $1-billion asset bank that has successfully "matched" a $400-million prime rate loan portfolio with $400 million of money market liabilities—for example, federal funds, large CDs, and short-term consumer certificates. (Refer to Item A.) The interest rate on both the prime rate loan portfolio and money market liabilities changes under the two interest rate scenarios. The remainder of the assets and liabilities are not rate-sensitive, and the interest income or expense on these items is identical under both the 15 percent prime rate scenario and the 10 percent prime rate scenario.

Next, let's examine the impact of the two interest rate environments on the net interest margin of this "matched" bank. Total interest income (Item B) increases from $88 million to $108 million as a result of the increase in the prime rate from 10 percent to 15 percent. On the other hand, total interest expense (Item C) has increased more rapidly from $55 million to $77 million as a result of the increase in the cost of money market liabilities from 8.50 percent to 14 percent. Therefore, the net interest margin (Item D) decreased from $33 million to $31 million. Note that in this example we have restated interest income to a taxable equivalent (TE) basis, thereby stating all income in terms of taxable dollars to illustrate better its relative relationship to earnings.

The net financial contribution (Item E) is the net interest margin adjusted for the loan loss provision. In this example we have not changed the level of the loan loss provision. However, the impact of providing for increasing loan losses during periods of economic stress can also be illustrated by increasing the provision using this analytical procedure.

In our example, we have held noninterest income constant at $14 million and noninterest expense constant at $30 million. Therefore, the net noninterest expense (Item F) is $16 million. We will not make any adjustments to this noninterest category; however, even modest changes clearly illustrate the importance of noninterest income and the control of overhead expense on bank earnings.

The impact of increases in noninterest expense becomes appar-

Table 4-4   Rate Sensitivity Analysis: A "Matched" Bank Balance Sheet

		Interest Rates and Interest Margin			
		10% Prime Rate Environment		15% Prime Rate Environment	
ASSETS (MILLIONS)		Rate	Income	Rate	Income
Cash and Due	$ 100	0%	$ 0	0%	$ 0
Investments (TE)	200	9.00%	18	9.00%	18
Fixed Loans	250	12.00%	30	12.00%	30
*Prime Loans	400	10.00%	40	15.00%	60
Total Earning Assets	850		88		108
Other Assets	50	0%	0	0%	0
(A) Total Assets	$1,000		$88		$108 (B)
LIABILITIES AND CAPITAL		Rate	Expense	Rate	Expense
*Money Market	$ 400	8.50%	$34	14.00%	$ 56
Retail Time	300	7.00%	21	7.00%	21
Demand Deposits	250	0%	0	0%	0
Equity Capital	50	0%	0	0%	0
Total L & C	$1,000		$55		$ 77 (C)
Net Interest Margin			$33		$ 31 (D)
Loan Loss Provision			$ 3		$ 3
Net Financial Contribution			$30		$ 28 (E)
Noninterest Income			$14		$ 14
Noninterest Expense			30		30
Net Noninterest			$16		$ 16 (F)
Pretax Profit			$14		$ 12
Income Tax (TE)			7		6
Earnings			$ 7		$ 6 (G)

Table 4-5   Market Spread and Rate Sensitive Earnings

	Balance Sheet	Rate	Income Expense	Rate	Income Expense
*Prime Loans	$400	10.00%	$40	15.00	$60
*Money Market	$400	8.50%	34	14.00	56
Rate Sensitivity Mismatch	$ 0				
Market Spread		+ 1.50%	$ 6	+ 1.00	$ 4 (H)

* Interest Rate Sensitive

ent when this type of analysis is computed for a longer time period, such as five years. Appropriate pricing for bank services and the control of noninterest expenses are an essential part of managing bank profitability.

Obviously, the next step is the pretax profit generated by this "matched" bank under the two interest rate scenarios—the income tax adjustment and finally the net after-tax profit (Item G). In the final analysis the higher interest rate scenario generates $6 million of earnings, a decrease of $1 million from the $7 million generated under the lower rate scenario. Therefore, this "matched" bank would experience a decrease in earnings during an increasing interest rate environment—that is, the "matched" position has a negative impact on earnings. A bank with no money market liabilities would experience no increase in interest costs and as a result would experience an increase in both net interest margin and earnings during periods of increasing interest rates.

Now let us adopt a different viewpoint. Obviously, if this "matched" bank maintained a static balance sheet during a declining interest rate environment, it would experience an increase in earnings as a result of the increase in the net interest margin. The obvious conclusion is that the "matched" balance sheet has not stabilized the net interest margin's contribution to earnings. If we examine the interest rate environment in more detail, we will discover that the "market spread"—the spread between the prime rate and the money market sources of funds—causes the net interest margin's instability.

Table 4–5 highlights the impact of the market spread on the interest margin (Item H) within the two interest rate scenarios. Note that we have a positive 150 basis point (1.50 percent) market spread in the low rate environment and a positive 100 basis point (1.00 percent) market spread in the high rate environment. This change in market spread of 50 basis points changes the profitability of the interest-sensitive portion of the balance sheet from $6 million during the low rate environment to $4 million during the high rate environment. The question, of course, is, "Are these representative spreads?" In fact, we have experienced approximately a 100 basis point variation in annual average market spreads during the late 1970s and early 1980s.

Now that we have looked at the impact of the rate sensitivity position on earnings, let's examine two techniques for evaluating balance sheet profitability and the return-on-equity capital. Table

Table 4-6   Balance Sheet Profitability

Interest Yield (Interest Income/EA)	10.35%	12.71%	(I)
Interest Cost (Interest Cost/EA)	6.47%	9.06%	(J)
Net Interest Spread (Interest Margin/EA)	3.88%	3.65%	(K)

4–6 illustrates a technique for measuring the profitability of the balance sheet. The source of balance sheet profitability is the yield and the level of net earnings assets (EA). Therefore, this technique utilizes earning assets (EA) as the common denominator to determine both the yield on net earning assets (Item I) and the cost of funding earning assets (Item J). The difference is the net interest spread (Item K).

Table 4–7 illustrates a technique for evaluating the return-on-equity capital. First, we calculate the net after-tax profit margin (Item L) realized on total assets. Then we calculate the amount of equity capital leverage (Item M) employed to fund total assets. The return on equity (Item N) is simply a function of the return on assets times the leverage employed. This technique permits one to examine the components of a bank's return on equity.

Table 4-7   Return on Equity

Return on Assets (Earnings/Assets)	.70%	.60%	(L)
Leverage (Assets/Equity)	× 20	× 20	(M)
Return on Equity (Earnings/Equity)	14%	12%	(N)

Table 4–8 illustrates the relative impact of earnings and dividend policy on retained earnings and capital growth. If the management of this "matched" bank had established a dividend payout of $2 million (Item O) less than 30 percent of earnings during the low interest rate environment, then retained earnings (Item P) would have been $5 million, representing a 10 percent growth in equity capital. This would have permitted a 10 percent growth in assets

Table 4-8   Internal Capital Growth

Net Profit	$7	$6	
Less: Dividend	2	2	(O)
Retained Earnings	$5	$4	(P)

without creating additional capital leverage. However, during the high interest rate environment, this same $2 million payout would have represented 33 percent of earnings, limiting retained earnings to $4 million, representing an 8 percent growth in equity capital. This earnings instability has a direct impact on internal generation of capital and the ability to support future earning asset growth.

In conclusion, we have illustrated that "matching" rate-sensitive assets with rate-sensitive liabilities did not completely insulate this "matched" bank's earnings from the impact of a changing interest rate environment. In fact, it contributed to a decline in net profit, a decline in balance sheet profitability, and a decline in internal capital generation during a period of narrowing market spreads.

The point of this analysis is not to illustrate a right or wrong approach to rate sensitivity management; it is to illustrate the complexity of the issue. Appropriate rate sensitivity management is a dynamic exercise that requires constant management attention.

The money markets provide the first method of managing the rate sensitivity of the balance sheet. In other words, the bank can just match the growth of rate-sensitive sources of funds. However, the bank's customers may not always select pricing alternatives that provide matched growth; therefore, it may be necessary to utilize other hedging alternatives provided by the money markets.

The Management of Rate Sensitivity

The financial futures markets have become one of the fastest growing, most publicized markets in the financial community. Articles written by both professionals and nonprofessionals frequently suggest that these new markets provide the solution for nearly every investment problem faced by the financial community. The ever-growing selection of financial futures, forward contracts, standby agreements, debt options, and interest rate swaps have provided bank managements with new or expanded alternatives for minimizing or hedging interest rate risk. However, financial futures do not provide easy answers for complex asset/liability management problems.

The publicity concerning the development of the financial futures markets during this period of significant interest rate volatility has attracted the attention of bank managements eager to find solutions to the problems of hedging balance sheet rate sensitivity. Although the introduction of financial futures is a relatively new development, the use of futures contracts traces its history to the ancient days of Greece and Rome.

Futures contracts have historically been used to hedge the production of agricultural products. For example, the market price of grain to be produced by the farmer is subject to a variety of uncontrollable worldwide forces such as weather, disease, and politics. Over the centuries, grain producers, dealers, and buyers developed markets to price the future delivery of grain to protect their individual profit margins.

The growth of the financial futures market has its roots in these futures markets for agricultural products. As a result, to the amusement of many bankers, we find financial futures listed side by side with sugar, coffee, and hogs in the *Wall Street Journal*.

It is also important to understand that the concepts of futures and forward transactions are not strangers to the financial markets. The introduction of the first interest rate futures contract in the GNMA mortgage-backed certificate by the Chicago Board of Trade in 1975 was preceded by an active market in GNMA forward agreements. In addition, the use of forward agreements in foreign exchange transactions has been a part of international trade for centuries.

Although the concepts and techniques for futures and forwards have existed for centuries, it is the growing volatility of interest rates that is primarily responsible for the recent growth of the financial futures market.

The Futures Contract

Each contract represents a firm commitment to buy or sell a specific financial instrument during a specified time at a specific price. Transactions and prices are established through "open out-cry" in one of the regulated marketplaces. Buyers and sellers of financial futures contracts have no direct relationship, and once their trade is completed they are free to buy or sell their contract in the open market. For example, all trades on the Chicago Board of Trade are processed by the Clearing Corporation. As a "party to every trade," the Clearing Corporation guarantees the opposite side of all transactions made on the Chicago Board of Trade. Buyers and sellers do not have credit exposure to one another. However, bank managements must also understand that the Clearing Corporation does not guarantee customer accounts maintained by the broker.

The Forward Agreement

Each forward agreement also represents a firm commitment to buy or sell a specific financial instrument at a specific time at a specific price. Although certain financial instruments—for example, GNMA securities—have relatively liquid market quotations, the markets are not restricted to specific securities, and a wide variety of individual transactions may be negotiated. Transactions are obligations between the buyer and the seller, although they may be negotiated through a broker. Therefore, the buyer and seller of a financial forward agreement do have a direct relationship, and each has a credit exposure with the other for the duration of the agreement.

The forward agreement is normally negotiated between sophisticated credit-worthy investors who do not require margin from one another. However, each transaction is individually negotiated, and margin may be required by either the investors or the brokers participating in this market.

Standby Agreements

The standby agreement, normally used in the GNMA market, gives the seller the right to make delivery in the future. The seller of the agreement pays a fee to the buyer of the agreement. The delivery price is negotiated at the time of the commitment. As with forward agreements, these transactions represent obligations between the buyer and the seller, and the buyer and seller have credit exposure with one another for the duration of the agreement.

Debt Options

During 1982 a variety of new option instruments were introduced for financial instruments. Just as with stock options, the holder of a debt option pays a premium for the right to buy (a call) or to sell (a put) a specific financial instrument during a specific time period at a specific price.

As with financial futures, the buyers and sellers of debt options will have no direct relationship or credit exposure with one another. The debt option is not an obligation to buy or sell but a right to buy or sell a specific security. As a result, the owner does not risk having to provide additional margin; however, the owner of the option will lose the entire amount (premium) paid for the option if it is not exercised prior to the expiration date.

Interest Rate/Currency Swaps

An interest rate or currency swap allows the bank to synthetically change one or all of the following characteristics of its borrowing portfolio:

1. The mix between variable and fixed-rate debt (the interest rate sensitivity).
2. The index on which your debt is based.
3. The currency denomination of your debt.

The primary advantage of an interest rate or currency swap is that it allows the bank to hedge or arbitrage its borrowing portfolio without disrupting the underlying borrowing agreements.

An interest rate swap involves an exchange of interest payments. The bank normally enters into an agreement with another bank or securities dealer to make interest payments based on either a fixed- or variable-rate index in exchange for interest payments based on another fixed- or variable-rate index. These interest payments are calculated on the principal amount that you either want to protect or arbitrage.

A currency swap is the exchange of principal and interest payments denominated in one currency for principal and interest payments denominated in a second currency. A cross-currency interest rate swap combines aspects of both the interest rate swap and the currency swap. Not only are different currencies exchanged, but additionally, one party can agree to pay a fixed-rate, while the other pays a variable interest rate.

While an interest rate or a currency swap may be designed to match the bank's exact borrowing arrangements, this may not always be possible. If you are not matched exactly, you will have to consider the effects of basis risk (i.e., the risk that the index on which the swap is based does not correlate exactly with the index on which your borrowings are based).

Management Objectives

If a bank's management elects to enter this multidimensional world of financial futures, forwards, options, and interest rate swaps, it has three basic types of activity to consider: trading, microhedging, and macrohedging. These complex financial concepts represent the basic financial accounting framework for futures and forwards transactions.

Trading Activity. Open positions (long or short) may be taken by management to accommodate customer transactions or in anticipation of trading profits.

Microhedging Activity. Specific assets or liabilities may be identified for hedging to reduce interest rate risk or to ensure an interest rate spread. Microhedging or arbitrage activity may be defined as matched transactions utilized to hedge money market instruments, such as the following, generally with a maximum maturity of one year:

- Domestic time deposits
- Eurodollar time deposits
- Repurchase agreements
- Reverse repurchase agreements
- Term federal funds
- Commercial paper
- Futures and forwards
- Standby agreements

Macrohedging Activity. The objective of macrohedging activity is to reduce the interest rate risk associated with a consolidated balance sheet rate sensitivity mismatch, rather than hedge a specific asset. Such activity may utilize any balance sheet category to reduce a net rate sensitivity mismatch within a given maturity range.

Bank management today must attempt to monitor and control the interest exposure inherent in the bank as a whole rather than specific segments of bank assets and liabilities. The futures market can add considerable flexibility in the management of interest rate risk in this period of volatile interest rates and changing financial structure, as the use of financial futures becomes an increasingly important tool for banks in asset/liability management strategy. However, it is clear that because the accounting rules are complex, it is essential that any plans by bank management to engage in financial futures transactions must be reviewed by the bank's independent accountants prior to entering into any trades.

Conclusion

The sharp increase in the volatility of interest rates during the past two years, combined with the increasing rate of deregulation within the banking industry, has forced bank managements to explore all options available to them to hedge the asset/liability positions of the balance sheet. This section has outlined only the primary elements of a growing array of products designed to assist managements with this task. However, it is essential that bank managements develop a solid understanding of these complex markets prior to attempting to use them to hedge interest rate risk.

Balance Sheet Growth and Capital Leverage

Loan growth within the banking system has exceeded the internal generation of bank capital provided by retained earnings during the past 25 years. However, bank managements have only supplemented this internal generation of capital with new equity from the capital markets in a very modest way. As a result, bank balance sheets continue to experience a higher degree of capital leverage (average assets divided by equity capital).

The quality of bank earnings therefore has gained new importance as a result of the higher degree of capital leverage and the reliance on money market sources of funds to finance future asset growth. The credit standing of the bank determines its capability to access additional money market funds to finance future asset growth. As with any company, the quality of earnings provides a key ingredient for credit evaluation. In addition, it is the quality of bank earnings that provides access to the capital markets.

Both the marketability and price of a bank's debt and equity securities are significantly influenced by the financial performance of the bank. The ability to access capital funds has been further eroded by the relatively high levels of interest rates experienced during the past 15 years and the relatively poor performance of bank stock prices during most of this period. As a result, this constraint on the availability of external capital places an additional burden on bank managements both to achieve an adequate return on their existing capital base and to retain a significant portion of operating earnings to build equity capital internally. The need to build equity capital with retained earnings is of utmost importance during the 1980s.

Consistent profitability and a realistic dividend policy are the essential ingredients that must be considered by bank managements in building an equity capital base that will prove adequate to support future earning asset growth.

Future Considerations

As aggressive and well-balanced banks become more at ease with various money market funding sources and exercise prudence in maintaining a hedged position as they grow, they will become more self-confident and broaden their marketing efforts. They have more experience available to them than nonbank competitors and thus hold an edge in being able to broaden their services, increase their products, and eventually strengthen their share of the total market.

Regulatory changes may threaten banks by providing more and more bank privileges to others, but at the same time banks will also be given more range both territorially and in product mix. A well-structured asset/liability management strategy could ultimately give professional bankers more total growth opportunity than their competitors.

The development of asset/liability management has provided bank managements with a tool for achieving better control of financial performance. However, significant challenges remain in (1) the identification of the appropriate mix of rate-sensitive assets and liabilities, (2) tax policy and the growth of tax-exempt loans and securities, (3) asset liquidity and improved loan portfolio marketability, and (4) asset quality. A variety of techniques and models are available to aid bank managements, but in the final analysis the key to success is the exercise of good judgment.

Chapter 5

BANK CAPITAL ISSUES

by Donald H. Korn

Introduction

Bank capital issues relate closely to the conduct of business of commercial banks. Of greatest practical concern to the bank director is the concept of capital as the ultimate source of the bank's solvency; sufficient capital must be available as a cushion to absorb losses and to protect the depositors. Next, the director must be concerned about the ability of the bank to earn adequate return on the shareholders' capital invested in the bank. Regulations that define and establish minimum amounts of capital a bank must hold relative to its total assets have only recently been promulgated. There are also nominal statutory requirements on "start-up capital" that are imposed by federal or state regulatory agencies in connection with the approval of new bank charters. This chapter deals with capital in the context of ongoing operations.

We shall discuss the meaning and significance of bank capital to the director and the reason banks are faced with pressure to increase capital. We shall also present some commentary on bank holding company issues and examine the effects of inflation and deflation on bank capital.

The Meaning and Significance of Bank Capital

Bank capital may be defined and its significance understood in both an economic sense and in a regulatory sense.

Economic Definition of Bank Capital

A bank's capital, in the economic sense, may be thought of as the permanent risk capital contributed by the owners of the bank or banking organization. If the firm is a bank holding company, we should distinguish between the capital of the underlying bank or banks owned by the holding company and that of the parent corporation, which in turn is owned by "outside" shareholders. This capital is the equity capital represented by common stock, any preferred stock, and retained earnings of the entity in question.

This definition may differ from that used in the regulatory or "capital adequacy" sense; the latter includes capital notes (subordinated debt) and provisions for loan loss and other reserves carried on the balance sheet. The arguable presumption is that in the long run reserves will be offset by realized losses (and the related tax effects) and thus not be available to shareholders. In practice, a change in the external business environment may lead to adjustments in such reserves.

The economic definition excludes all debt, including debt incurred by a bank as "capital notes," which are really subordinated debentures. However, long-term (20 to 25 years) convertible debt, which has been issued by bank holding companies without restrictive covenants or sinking funds and with a small premium for conversion into common stock, could likely be considered permanent capital in an economic sense. To paraphrase one banker's statement, if a security issue is not available to absorb losses and does not share in the profits, it is debt, not capital.

Regulatory Definition of Bank Capital

The regulatory concept of bank capital also reflects the banker's notion of a cushion to absorb losses on bank loans and investments. Surprisingly, neither bankers nor regulators—for example, Office of the Comptroller of the Currency (OCC), the Federal Reserve Board (FRB), and the Federal Deposit Insurance Corporation (FDIC)—have been able to agree precisely on what is bank capital, let alone how much capital is adequate for a commercial bank. We are referring to the notion of a "cushion" comprised of equity plus any debt subordinate to depositors' claims. It is the safety and ready accessibility (real and perceived) of bank deposits that is of paramount concern to regulators and the public. (There is also concern to shareholders and management, in the sense that operating any business with too little equity—that is, too much financial leverage—can expose the enterprise to a very volatile earnings and cash flow pattern and a greater risk of default and/or bankruptcy.)

Note that the concern on the part of regulators and the public implies that a bank maintain a certain liquidity of its capital. That the FDIC now insures deposit accounts up to $100,000 and that banks must maintain reserves with a Federal Reserve Bank are features that engender public confidence and provide liquidity in the U.S. banking system. Commercial banks in the United States operate with equity capital of about 8 cents for each dollar of deposits or, equivalently, about 6 cents of equity per dollar of assets (loans, investments, cash, and property). Further examination and discussion of these figures will be presented in Tables 5–1 through 5–3.

In March 1985, the OCC and the FDIC promulgated *rules* raising capital requirements for banks. The rules for the first time set the same capital requirements for all national and FDIC-insured state nonmember banks regardless of size.[1] The agencies estimated, based on data from the third quarter of 1984, that the capital shortfall in the banking system was about $6.3 billion. Also, the Board of Governors of the Federal Reserve System finalized its *guidelines* requiring identical minimum capital ratios for state member banks and bank holding companies.

The rules raise total capital levels in the banking system to 6 percent and require that 5.5 percent be in primary capital. The OCC's total capital requirement for national banks, previously set in 1982–83, was 6 percent for community banks and 5.5 percent for multinational and regional banks. The OCC's primary capital requirement for national banks was 5 percent for multinational and regional banks and 6 percent for community banks. Under the FDIC's previous guidelines, all state nonmember banks were subject to a 5 percent minimum equity capital ratio.

The new rules also define capital. The OCC and FDIC include in primary capital (1) common and perpetual preferred stock, (2) capital surplus, (3) undivided profits, (4) capital reserves, (5) some mandatory convertible debt, (6) minority interests in consolidated subsidiaries, (7) net worth certificates, and (8) the allowance for

---

[1]Joint News Release, NR 85-20, from OCC and FDIC, March 11, 1985. See FDIC Rules and Regulations, Part 325—Capital Maintenance, April 30, 1985, pp. 2241–2245.

loan and lease losses. All intangible assets except purchased mortgage servicing rights are to be deducted from primary capital. The rules proposed in 1984 deducted all intangible assets from primary capital but added them back to secondary capital. The OCC/FDIC final rules now define secondary capital to include *only* subordinated notes and debentures and limited life preferred stock. The total of these instruments is limited to 50 percent of primary capital. The capital ratio is calculated by dividing defined capital by the sum of assets plus allowable loss reserves.

The rules provide that the two agencies will set higher capital requirements when a bank's circumstances warrant. The rules also outline steps for issuing directives to enforce a specific bank's required capital levels. If the rules or the terms of an agency directive are violated, *officers, directors, or employees of a bank can be subject to civil money penalties*. In addition, banks that do not comply with the provisions of the rules will be subject to agency enforcement action. The FDIC may bring an action to terminate the insurance of any insured bank operating with a primary capital ratio of less than 3 percent, unless the institution enters into a satisfactory agreement to correct its capital deficiency.

The agencies are concerned that some banks may attempt to comply with the regulation in ways that reduce liquidity or increase risk. They admonish banks to avoid decreasing liquid asset levels to achieve the minimum capital ratios. The agencies will impose higher capital requirements on banks with low liquidity or high levels of risk, including standby letters of credit and other off-balance-sheet risk.

The FDIC has adopted the same minimum capital requirements for mutual savings banks. However, due to the recent adverse conditions in the thrift industry, the FDIC also set guidelines that permit mutual savings banks more time to achieve these requirements. Qualifying mutual savings banks with primary capital ratios of 3 percent or more have up to five years to attain the minimum capital requirements.

A determination of capital adequacy is one of the major objectives of a bank examination and is one of the five components that form the basis of the Uniform Financial Institutions Rating System used by the OCC in determining the condition of individual banking institutions.

The new regulations will supplement, rather than replace,

supervisory evaluations of capital adequacy. The process of determining the adequacy of a bank's capital on an ongoing basis begins with a qualitative evaluation of the critical variables that directly bear on the institution's overall financial condition. These variables include (1) the quality, present value, type and diversification of assets; (2) historical and prospective earnings; (3) liquidity (with emphasis on asset/liability management); (4) the quality of management; and (5) the existence of other activities that may expose the bank to risks, including off-balance-sheet items, the degree of leverage, and risks undertaken by the parent company or other affiliates and institutions with which the bank has significant financial relationships, including chain banking organizations. Banks with significant weaknesses in one or more of these areas will be expected to maintain higher capital levels than the minimums set forth in the regulation. In addition, the capital requirements set forth are minimums, and all banks are encouraged to maintain higher levels of capital in order to provide protection against unforeseen adversities.

Constituencies of Concern to Directors

The director faces several different constituencies simultaneously—stockholders, management, employees, regulators, security analysts, the public, and the bank board.

Stockholders, Management, and Employees

Assuming that the bank holding company is a for-profit business, the director has a legal responsibility to shareholders and employees that is common to all directors. However, the bank is not always expected to be, and often not allowed to be, a profit maximizer. The bank is entrusted with responsibility as a financial intermediary and depository institution for properly safeguarding confidential customer and depositor information—inside information that directors are legally restricted from exploiting, either for themselves or for the benefit of stockholders.

The bank director has a very difficult fiduciary task in representing so many different de facto as well as de jure constituencies. The interrelationship between external events or events seen in the loan department (but not shared with the trust department) and a real or perceived threat to bank capital (and hence a bank's stock price) has been tested with increasing frequency of late. Recall the banking collapses of 1974 (e.g., the Franklin National), the potential default on loans to LDCs (less developed countries), New York City's financial crisis, the rescues of Chrysler Corporation and First Pennsylvania Bank, and, more recently, the FDIC rescue and takeover of Continental Illinois Corp.[2]

If there is a holding company relation, the director of the bank may be in conflict with the director of the holding company. The point is that unlike most other businesses, there is likely to be more conflict or potential conflict of interest between a bank director's duties to shareholders and to that director's other actual and perceived constituencies. Controversies over the bank's capital needs will heighten the pressures on the director from these different constituencies.

Regulators

Regulators include the OCC, the FDIC, the FRB, the federal interagency committee established by the Depository Institutions Deregulation and Monetary Control Act of 1980, and the Federal Home Loan Bank Board (for S&L operations and some mortgage financing activity). The bank has to be operated in conformance with many regulations and guidelines, some of which are vague. The director thus has a responsibility to comply with the spirit of the regulations: How much capital is really desirable? How much of a return on equity (ROE) is commensurate with the bank (or holding company) risk exposure? Will competition allow higher interest rates? Will Washington accept higher interest rates?

There is some agreement that capital should be great enough to engender confidence in the bank's stability and capacity but not so large as to prohibit stockholders from earning a fair return. As stated by Professor William Staats of Louisiana State University, "Too much capital can be just as deadly for banks in a competitive environment as too little capital."[3]

---

[2]It is important to note also a number of serious failures in the thrift industry, after which S&Ls have been taken over by commercial banks, and the recent efforts to rescue the Farm Credit Banks, which have been self-regulated.

[3]William Staats, *American Banker* (September 12, 1980), pp. 4, 9.

Security Analysts

Bank stock analysts, along with many bankers, eschew undue reliance on rigid capital adequacy specifications determined by regulatory formulas. (This sentiment has been shared by the Federal Reserve Board in the sense that the FRB prefers minimum capital guidelines and the flexibility to take a case-by-case approach.)

Bank analysts, as well as regulators, tend to place significant emphasis on several other factors. Analysts examine the earnings "cushion" represented by recurring earnings, the quality of the assets, the strength of management, and the ability of the bank to access the capital and credit markets. In respect to the latter, note that one of the items recently of great concern to banking regulators is the large and increased volume of off-balance-sheet or contingent liabilities, such as standby letters of credit, commitments, and repurchase agreements. FRB Chairman Paul Volcker has spoken often to congressional committees about his concern here, and the OCC and FDIC have recently established task forces to study the matter of allocating a capital reserve to cover such off-balance-sheet items. Also likely to result is heightened attention to related footnote disclosures in bank financial reports. These will be of great interest to bank analysts. The upshot of these developments will likely be additional pressures on bank directors to approve new financings and disclosures.

Many of the key measures of capital adequacy and profitability used by bank analysts are shown in Tables 5-3, 5-4, and 5-5. There has been a general increase in capital ratios over the period from 1980 to 1984. Nevertheless, the bankruptcy and subsequent federal takeover of Continental Illinois National Bank in 1984 rocked the financial markets and the investment community. This was followed in 1985 by the stunning losses reported by BankAmerica, First Chicago Corp., and highly rated Texas Commerce Bancshares. Such "surprises" raised questions in many analysts' minds not only about the management practices of large commercial banks, but also about bank auditing practices.

Table 5–1　Loans, Deposits, and Capital Accounts of Insured U.S. Commercial Banks, 1970–1983 (in $ Billions)

As of Year End	(1) Total Loans	(2) Total Deposits	(3) Total Bank Capital	(4) Long-Term Debt Capital	(5) Preferred Stock	(6) Common Stock	(7) Surplus	(8) Undivided Profits and Reserves	(9) Equity Reserves	(10) Equity Capital
1970	316	497	42.57	2.09	.11	11.14	18.07	10.15	1.01	40.4
1974	506	746	63.29	4.26	.04	14.79	25.31	17.97	.91	59.0
1975	502	781	68.72	4.41	.05	15.57	26.71	21.18	.80	64.3
1978	708	1,016	93.28	5.86	.11	18.16	33.20	35.94	—	87.4
1983	1,300	1,843	147.60	7.10	.66	25.72	47.90	132.51	—	140.5

Source: Annual Reports of the Federal Deposit Insurance Corporation. Data are for the United States plus territories. Data for 1983 include foreign office deposits.

Table 5–2　Selected Bank Ratios of All Insured Commercial Banks

	1970	1975	1978	1983
Equity Capital/Year-end U.S. Assets	7.02%	6.75%	6.87%	6.00%
Total Capital/Year-end U.S. Assets	7.39	7.21	7.33	6.30
Net Income/Average Total Assets	0.80*	0.78	0.77	0.68*
Dividend Payout Ratio	0.42	0.42	0.34	0.49

* Author's estimate.

Source: FDIC data. Data for 1983 include foreign office consolidation.

The Public

A bank director's responsibility to the public is, for the most part, a matter of law.[4] However, in addition, there is political pressure in the United States for banks to participate in loans for certain socially desirable projects or purposes and to refrain from others (e.g., loans to South Africa). This presents a conflict between shareholders' interest in maximizing bank earnings in the short run and what is deemed to be in the long-run public interest. The rationalization is that the bank shareholders' long-run interest is to serve the public interest. Indeed, while not regulated like a public utility, the bank is definitely "affected with a public interest."

The Bank Board

Recently, several examples have been publicized of abuses of the lending powers of banks—improper and/or unsound intercompany loans or loans to affiliates, or overdraft privileges—which had the actual or potential effect of impairing the capital of the banks in question. These disclosures have sensitized directors to take precautions, to be more aware of and involved in bank examination and audit procedures, and to organize and/or serve on one or more committees of the board. The board should monitor at least the same indicators of capital adequacy as do regulators and bank security analysts. These include absolute measures such as capital/total assets, equity capital/risk assets, as well as relative measures—that is, how the subject bank's ratios compare with those of its peers.

Tables 5–1 and 5–2 show aggregate data for all insured commercial banks; Table 5–3 shows selected ratios and comparisons among the largest banks and holding companies. The data in Table 5–1 provide a perspective on the magnitude and growth of bank capital in comparison with growth in U.S. deposits and loans since 1970. Note that while the data indicate roughly similar growth rates, they do not present a complete picture, since foreign loans and deposits are not included in the figures for the 1970s. Federal regulators have required the reporting of such data only since 1981. Table 5–2 data indicate the earning power and dividend

---

[4]Robert K. Mueller, "What a Bank Director Needs to Know," *The Bankers Magazine* (September-October, 1979).

Table 5-3   Selected Bank Median Figures, June 30, 1980

Ratios	120 Banks	Group 1 Banks 1–18	Group 2 Banks 19–50	Group 3 Banks 51–120
Capital Adequacy				
1. **Equity + Res./Risk Assets**	**8.5%**	**6.4%**	**8.1%**	**9.0%**
2. Equity + Res./Total Assets	5.8%	4.4%	5.7%	6.2%
3. Equity + Res./Liab. less Cash	8.0%	6.3%	7.8%	8.5%
4. Equity + Res. + Cap. Notes/ Dep. + Net STB	7.5%	5.5%	7.4%	8.1%
5. Equity + Res. + Cap. Notes/Loans	12.3%	8.8%	12.6%	12.8%
6. Capital Adequacy—N.Y. Formula*	75.5%	64.1%	75.5%	79.8%
Liquidity				
7. **Loans/Dep. + Net STB**	**64%**	**65%**	**64%**	**64%**
8. Cash U.S. Gov'ts and Agencies/ Total Assets	25.7%	29.2%	27.2%	24.4%
9. Savings + Time Dep./Total Dep.	66.2%	69.1%	68.1%	64.8%
10. Net Short-Term Borrowings/Loans	19%	16%	20%	18%
11. Interest Sensitive Funds/Total Assets	34%	51%	36%	29%
12. Market Value Sec./Statement Value	95.9%	96.0%	95.1%	96.0%
13. Securities Maturing in 1 Year	14%	13%	12%	17%
Loan Quality				
14. **Net Losses/Average Loans**	**0.34%**	**0.28%**	**0.26%**	**0.36%**
15. Loss Reserve/Loans	1.13%	0.98%	1.14%	1.15%
16. Non-Performing Loans/Loans	1.9%	1.8%	1.5%	2.0%
Operations				
17. **Net Income/Average Equity**	**14.2%**	**15.0%**	**13.5%**	**14.2%**
18. **Interest Coverage (Incl. Int. on Dep.)**	**1.14X**	**1.12X**	**1.13X**	**1.15X**
19. Net Oper. Inc./Total Oper. Income	6.9%	5.0%	6.9%	7.8%
20. Net Oper. Inc./Avg. Earning Assets	0.93%	0.75%	0.95%	1.02%
Capital Stock				
21. **Mkt. Value Stock/Book Value**	**69%**	**66%**	**83%**	**68%**
22. Mkt. Value Stock/Earnings per Share	5.1X	4.9X	5.5X	5.1X
23. 5 Yr. EPS Annual Compound Growth Rate	12.1%	12.5%	12.1%	11.9%
24. Dividend Payout	32%	33%	30%	33%
General				
25. Bank Assets/Holding Company Assets	93.3%	95.6%	93.3%	90.5%

Source: Banks: Composite (New York: A.G. Becker Incorporated, March 1981). Used with permission.
* Equity plus loss reserves plus capital notes to 12 percent of loans (net of unearned income) plus 5 percent of securities plus bank premises and equipment.

payout ratio of banks, which come into play in determining the magnitude and rate of growth in bank capital that must be planned for. Tables 5–3 and 5–4 illustrate types of financing comparisons across peer groups. Table 5–5 illustrates important profitability rankings within the peer group comprising the largest banks.

Indications are that the principal measure of capital adequacy, equity to total assets (including foreign branch and subsidiary assets), is approximately in the range of 4 to 7 percent for U.S. banks. For U.S. money center banks, the average capital ratio declined from 5.4 in 1970 to 3.9 in 1979 (with a brief interruption in 1975–1976, when banking system expansion diminished).

The Continental and BankAmerica situations referred to earlier resulted in other disturbing developments: termination of directors' liability insurance coverage at Bank of America, followed by a class action against Bank of America, its officers, and directors; a class action against Continental and its former officers and directors, alleging breach of fiduciary duty and seeking to recover insurance proceeds on behalf of shareholders. The outcome of this litigation may set important new precedents regarding a bank director's responsibility and the terms of liability coverage.

Focusing on the Issues

Perspective on Tests of a Bank's Soundness and Capital Requirements

The directors should be aware that up until the recent change in regulatory standards on bank capital there were normally significant differences in capital and liquidity ratios, depending on the size of the bank and other factors. Table 5–3 indicates the differences among the 120 widely followed banks. Note that in regard to two key measures, the largest (Group 1) banks operated (and will probably continue to operate for some period) with significantly less capital than the average, and that the smaller (but still large, compared to some 14,000 commercial banks) banks (Group 3) operated with significantly more capital than the average; however, a converse relationship has existed (at least until recently) with respect to a liquidity measure: interest-sensitive funds to total assets.

These comparisons illustrate the difficulty in measuring "capital

Table 5–4 Capital Adequacy and Earnings Performance: Illustrative Data, New York City Banks, Covering Peer Groups 1 through 7

Company Name	Year	Return on Average Total Assets	Return on Average Earning Assets	Return On Average Equity	Internal Capital Generation Rate	Primary Capital to Assets (EOP)	Equity to Asset Ratio	Equity to Loan Ratio	Double Leverage Ratio*
Amalgamated Bank of N.Y.	1984	0.71%	0.76%	14.86%	4.02%	5.06%	4.81%	24.02%	NA%
New York	1983	0.82	0.88	16.27	3.44	5.07	5.02	30.05	NA
Peer Group No. 4	1982	0.88	0.96	21.12	7.23	4.58	4.18	37.30	NA
	1981	0.74	0.80	17.62	3.00	4.21	4.21	58.83	NA
	1980	0.55	0.58	11.48	2.47	4.65	4.76	57.51	NA
Atlantic Bank of N.Y.	1984	0.56%	0.62%	7.22%	7.22%	7.23%	7.74%	21.16%	NA%
New York	1983	0.64	0.71	8.41	8.41	7.41	7.57	25.36	NA
Peer Group No. 6	1982	0.41	0.42	5.16	5.16	7.53	7.99	23.83	NA
	1981	0.88	1.06	11.82	11.82	7.31	7.43	24.63	NA
	1980	0.95	1.17	12.59	12.59	6.79	7.57	24.67	NA
Bankers Trust N.Y. Corp	1984	0.68%	0.80%	16.20%	10.96%	6.23%	4.54%	8.28%	106.64%
Bankers Trust Co	1983	0.63	0.76	15.88	10.47	5.60	4.38	8.08	104.62
New York	1982	0.64	0.76	18.42	12.55	4.51	3.69	7.44	107.21
Peer Group No. 1	1981	0.56	0.69	17.28	11.29	4.05	3.66	7.16	110.86
	1980	0.68	0.86	23.81	16.63	3.49	3.34	6.70	117.08
Bank of New York Company Inc.	1984	0.74%	0.86%	15.70%	9.56%	6.29%	5.44%	8.28%	114.26%
The Bank of New York	1983	0.66	0.79	15.56	9.38	5.79	4.93	7.88	112.40
New York	1982	0.60	0.72	15.30	10.42	4.45	3.91	6.61	113.15
Peer Group No. 2	1981	0.52	0.63	13.91	8.93	4.24	3.72	7.00	119.07
	1980	0.42	0.52	11.06	6.34	4.13	3.82	8.00	111.95
The Chase Manhattan Corp.	1984	0.38%	0.45%	10.23%	6.13%	6.37%	4.40%	6.29%	128.09%
Chase Manhattan Bank, NA	1983	0.48	0.57	13.11	8.92	5.44	4.30	6.35	112.97
New York	1982	0.34	0.39	9.77	5.49	4.73	4.05	6.00	106.50
Peer Group No. 1	1981	0.50	0.62	15.87	11.62	4.17	3.71	5.86	111.75
	1980	0.48	0.60	15.30	11.08	3.76	3.63	5.86	114.59

Bank	Year								
Chemical New York Corp / Chemical Bank / New York / Peer Group No. 1	1984	0.56%	0.66%	14.36%	7.93%	6.26%	4.44%	6.61%	130.84%
	1983	0.57	0.67	14.89	8.27	5.48	4.42	6.63	116.75
	1982	0.48	0.57	13.14	7.46	4.98	4.07	6.16	123.78
	1981	0.49	0.61	15.07	9.91	3.95	3.39	5.69	123.42
	1980	0.46	0.57	14.12	9.24	3.69	3.25	5.52	119.88
Citicorp / Citibank NA / New York / Peer Group No. 1	1984	0.58%	0.67%	15.01%	8.74%	5.86%	4.38%	6.59%	178.75%
	1983	0.64	0.75	16.47	11.16	4.86	4.17	6.20	177.27
	1982	0.59	0.69	15.82	10.94	4.25	3.81	5.72	190.41
	1981	0.45	0.53	13.08	8.20	4.05	3.55	5.57	188.36
	1980	0.46	0.54	13.24	8.50	3.90	3.57	5.67	181.20
European-American Bancorp / European American Bk & Tr / New York / Peer Group No. 2	1984	-1.59%	-1.88%	-39.74%	-39.74%	5.28%	4.00%	5.85%	154.76%
	1983	0.23	0.26	5.05	2.16	5.11	4.46	6.75	126.79
	1982	0.36	0.42	8.83	6.50	4.97	4.10	6.02	NA
	1981	0.40	0.48	10.37	6.94	4.70	3.84	6.50	NA
	1980	0.41	0.51	10.24	7.58	4.65	4.02	6.89	NA
Irving Bank Corp. / Irving Trust Co. / New York / Peer Group No. 2	1984	0.44%	0.53%	11.67%	6.82%	5.87%	4.25%	7.58%	116.69%
	1983	0.41	0.49	10.89	5.96	5.21	4.12	7.67	119.71
	1982	0.42	0.51	12.06	7.60	4.70	3.55	6.57	120.80
	1981	0.53	0.67	15.93	11.56	4.25	3.31	6.58	124.33
	1980	0.51	0.69	15.75	11.36	3.57	3.26	6.90	126.25
J. Henry Schroder B & T Co / New York / Peer Group No. 3	1984	0.50%	0.55%	7.45%	7.45%	7.32%	6.70%	12.76%	NA%
	1983	0.41	0.45	6.84	6.84	6.77	5.92	10.75	NA
	1982	0.28	0.31	6.62	5.57	6.10	4.22	9.00	NA
	1981	0.48	0.52	10.38	7.39	5.29	4.64	9.56	NA
	1980	0.40	0.46	7.99	5.26	5.40	5.01	10.59	NA
Manufacturers Hanover Corp / Manufacturers Hanover Trust / New York / Peer Group No. 1	1984	0.41%	0.48%	11.20%	5.02%	5.72%	4.43%	5.81%	152.94%
	1983	0.47	0.56	13.31	7.07	4.97	4.23	5.73	115.45
	1982	0.46	0.54	13.18	7.51	4.59	3.82	5.35	94.81
	1981	0.46	0.57	14.01	8.81	3.77	3.28	5.21	116.52
	1980	0.48	0.62	14.02	8.76	3.57	3.41	5.77	116.47

Table 5-4 (continued)

Company Name	Year	Return on Average Total Assets	Return on Average Earning Assets	Return On Average Equity	Internal Capital Generation Rate	Primary Capital to Assets (EOP)	Equity to Asset Ratio	Equity to Loan Ratio	Double Leverage Ratio*
J.P. Morgan & Co. Inc.	1984	0.84%	0.97%	15.86%	9.91%	7.02%	5.71%	9.98%	102.09%
Morgan Guaranty Tr Co of NY	1983	0.77	0.89	15.29	9.37	6.91	5.38	9.70	105.29
New York	1982	0.69	0.82	15.50	10.15	5.61	4.48	8.29	102.77
Peer Group No. 1	1981	0.68	0.86	15.47	10.19	5.05	4.39	8.63	105.13
	1980	0.71	0.92	16.55	11.16	4.63	4.31	8.69	105.91
National Westminster Bnk USA	1984	0.50%	0.58%	7.89%	7.89%	6.61%	6.37%	10.04%	NA%
	1983	0.36	0.41	6.54	6.54	0.00	5.57	9.25	NA
New York	1982	0.26	0.30	4.82	4.82	0.00	5.48	9.69	NA
Peer Group No. 2	1981	0.22	0.26	4.09	4.09	0.00	5.38	9.17	NA
	1980	0.23	0.27	4.17	4.17	0.00	5.52	9.05	NA
Republic New York Corp	1984	0.71%	0.83%	14.40%	7.61%	7.13%	6.63%	24.12%	153.38%
Republic Natl Bank of NY	1983	0.74	0.83	16.22	8.74	6.30	6.05	19.95	163.83
New York	1982	0.62	0.71	14.92	7.69	5.06	5.36	16.83	147.17
Peer Group No. 2	1981	0.83	0.97	21.78	12.58	4.62	4.80	12.50	140.51
	1980	0.92	1.09	25.81	14.94	4.75	4.56	11.44	145.90
Sterling Bancorp	1984	1.01%	1.15%	13.69%	5.01%	6.54%	7.37%	21.76%	138.89%
Sterling Natl Bk & Trust Co	1983	0.82	0.95	10.98	2.00	7.93	7.43	21.62	134.01
New York	1982	1.07	1.26	14.94	5.56	7.84	7.19	18.04	148.76
Peer Group No. 5	1981	1.10	1.31	16.94	6.91	7.41	6.49	16.19	125.77
	1980	0.94	1.13	15.19	5.16	6.94	6.16	14.79	125.65
U.S. Trust Corp.	1984	1.15%	1.38%	17.10%	11.77%	6.16%	6.74%	15.98%	119.30%
United States Trust Co of NY	1983	0.99	1.25	15.07	9.88	5.40	6.60	16.89	112.64
New York	1982	0.83	1.15	13.37	8.15	5.71	6.24	16.74	99.15
Peer Group No. 3	1981	0.80	1.07	13.43	8.01	5.36	5.99	16.14	100.00
	1980	0.59	0.74	10.08	4.41	5.24	5.85	14.88	100.00

Source: Keefe, Bruyette & Woods, Inc.

*Double Leverage is the ratio of holding company investment in subsidiary banks to the book value of total bank equity.

Table 5–5 Ranking of the Largest Banks ($20 billion and Over Peer Group)

Company Name	Return on Assets			Return on Equity			Internal Capital Generation Rate		
	1984	1983	1982	1984	1983	1982	1984	1983	1982
1. Texas Commerce Bancshares	1	1	1	1	1	1	1	1	1
2. J. P. Morgan & Co. Inc.	2	3	7	3	6	8	5	10	9
3. Bank of Boston Corp.	3	6	6	5	8	9	4	6	8
4. MCorp	4	2	2	8	3	2	8	3	2
5. Security Pacific Corporation	5	7	9	4	2	6	3	2	6
6. Bankers Trust N.Y. Corp.	6	10	10	2	5	4	2	5	4
7. Republic Bank Corp.	7	4	4	9	10	5	9	7	5
8. First Interstate Bancorp.	8	11	12	11	14	13	11	14	13
9. First Bank System, Inc.	9	8	5	12	13	14	13	12	12
10. Citicorp	10	9	11	6	4	7	7	4	7
11. Wells Fargo & Company	11	12	13	10	11	15	6	9	11
12. InterFirst Corporation	12	22	3	14	22	3	12	22	3
13. Chemical New York Corp.	13	14	15	7	7	12	10	13	15
14. Mellon Bank Corporation	14	5	8	15	9	10	15	8	10
15. Marine Midland Banks, Inc.	15	18	17	16	18	17	14	17	16
16. Manufacturers Hanover Corp.	16	17	16	13	12	11	17	15	14
17. The Chase Manhattan Corp.	17	15	21	17	15	19	16	11	19
18. Norwest Corporation	18	13	14	19	16	20	19	18	20
19. Bankamerica Corporation	19	20	19	18	19	16	18	20	18
20. First Chicago Corporation	20	16	18	20	17	18	20	16	17
21. Crocker National Corporation	21	21	20	21	21	21	21	21	21
22. Continental Illinois Corp.	22	19	22	22	20	22	22	19	22

Source: 1985 Bankbook, Keefe, Bruyette & Woods, Inc.

adequacy." One cannot merely look at one or two simple ratios; the business risk exposure of the bank's portfolio of loans and investments has to be taken into account, as well as the sensitivity of the bank to interest rate risk, including that arising from a mismatch in maturities between, say, loans on the one hand and the various deposit accounts on the other hand. (Chapter 4 contains a detailed treatment of asset and liability management.) Growth and inflation affect bank capital requirements, of course, and these factors will be discussed specifically later in this chapter.

The federal regulatory agencies have thus used a combination of quantitative and qualitative measures of a bank's capital adequacy and liquidity, in conjunction with "early warning" systems, which in turn provide a capability to identify and track the list of so-called "problem banks." The factors that the FDIC and FRB have used focus on bank capital adequacy, asset quality, management quality, earnings, and liquidity—the so-called CAMEL rating system. At this writing, the OCC and FDIC have been expressing concern about the number of problem banks. A director should, obviously, make every effort to keep informed as to whether the bank is approaching a condition that would likely result in its becoming classified as a problem and take or recommend actions to correct the situation.

Behavioral Aspects of Deposit Insurance and Bank Capital

Federal deposit insurance for banks is normally not taken explicitly into account by management, examiners, or bank analysts when looking at various ratios. Rather, many of the ratios observed are in large measure the consequence of bank regulation stemming from the statutory provisions for FDIC insurance and examinations by the federal banking authorities. Nevertheless, academicians concerned with the economics of banking point out that the insurance of bank deposits (in return for the relatively small FDIC insurance premium) affects the perceptions of bank capital adequacy. Without FDIC insurance, management might not be allowed to incur risk to the same extent that it does with insurance, for a given amount of capital.

Professor R. C. Merton, at MIT's Sloan School of Management, applied modern option pricing theory to determine the cost of deposit insurance (and loan guarantees). He showed that the guarantor (FDIC) has in effect issued a put option on the assets of the bank "which gives management the right to sell those assets for [the value of the insured deposits] dollars on the [effective] maturity date of the debt."[5] Now, several years later, the regulatory agencies are studying the possibility of adopting a system of *risk-adjusted insurance premiums, as well as risk-adjusted capital reserves*.

Governor Henry C. Wallich of the Federal Reserve System summed up the issues nicely during remarks he made at a conference entitled "The Roundtable of Credit Systems in the 1970s" held in the late summer of 1980:[6]

> *The downward trend in capital ratios has been a serious concern to U.S. bank regulators. They see bank capital principally as a means of protecting bank depositors and other creditors. . . . Some banks, to be sure, seem to believe that losses even of a size very unlikely to occur could and should be taken care of out of earnings. With pre-tax earnings of leading banks in the range of 20-30 percent of capital, there is indeed much scope for absorption of losses before capital would have to be invaded. Nevertheless, capital remains the ultimate source of solvency.*
>
> *A bank whose solvency is beyond question is unlikely to find itself strapped for liquid funds, because it can buy money. However, if its solvency comes into question, this source of funds will begin to dry up and create a liquidity problem. If the bank is then compelled to liquidate assets at depreciated prices, as may happen if interest rates have been rising, these efforts to provide liquidity may further endanger solvency.*

Deregulation vs. Reregulation

Commercial banks play a special role in the economy, and thrift institutions have been granted new powers, making them more like commercial banks. Both types of institutions have operated now for more than five years under a mode of deregulation. However, banks and thrift failures in 1984 and 1985 exceeded those in any year since the Great Depression (and 1986 may be worse). These years saw the uncovering of unsound banking, fraud, and other scandals involving banks, thrifts, and securities firms. The results were well-publicized runs on many institutions.

---

[5]Robert C. Merton, "An Analytic Derivation of the Cost of Deposit Insurance and Loan Guarantees," *Journal of Banking and Finance* 1 (1977), pp. 3–11.

[6]Henry C. Wallich, "American Banks During the 1970s and Beyond," remarks at the Roundtable of Credit Systems in the 1970s, sponsored by Ente pergli Studi Monetari Bancari e Finanziari "Luigi Einaudi," Perugia, Italy (September 5–7, 1980).

To many in government these events served to dramatize and bring second thoughts about the extent to which deregulation can and should occur. Indeed, for this author, the events of 1985 are clearly leading to forms of *reregulation* of depository institutions. One of the most eloquent and knowledgeable spokespersons from the private sector is Henry Kaufman of Salomon Bros., who presented a set of recommendations to Congress to deal with the increased strain on depository institutions and the danger that strain represents to a well-functioning market economy. In essence, the point is to recognize that market forces alone will not ensure smooth operation of the banking system and the safety of deposits; nor will 6 cents in capital per dollar of assets as of a particular statement date. To quote Kaufman,[7]

> *The underlying issue still involves the proper role of financial institutions in our society. . . . Financial institutions have an extraordinary public responsibility . . . For financial intermediation to work, however, the public's perception must always be that institutions are managed by people who merit public trust and who are dedicated to the preservation of the integrity of credit. How can this goal be achieved? . . . There are two directions. Underlying both is the question of which is the best way to discipline institutions— through market forces—or regulation. There is philosophical support for each . . .*
>
> *The driving force is credit growth . . . The heroes of credit markets without a guardian are the daring—Those who . . . revel in the present-day casino-like atmosphere of the markets.*
>
> *Because of their wide-ranging and extensive impact, financial institutions must be effectively guided through legislation and supervision to balance their entrepreneurial drive with their public responsibilities.*

Mr. Kaufman offered several recommendations for reforming the system of financial regulation, including disclosure of changes in official regulatory ratings of financial institutions to provide more market discipline, and reporting of loans and investments at the lower of liquidation value or cost so that true capital position would be known, instead of being a "regulatory accounting fiction" as in many instances today.

---

[7]Henry Kaufman, "Reshaping the Financial System: Market Discipline Is Not Enough," *New York Times*, Sunday, July 14, 1985, p. 2F. See also, "The Integrity of Credit," a statement before the Committee on Energy and Commerce, Subcommittee on Telecommunications, Consumer Protection and Finance, U.S. House of Representatives, Washington, D.C., June 5, 1985.

A few months after Kaufman's recommendation, FRB Chairman Paul Volcker testified before Congress and echoed in many respects Kaufman's concerns over new and growing sources of instability in the banking system due to aggressive banking practices. The FRB moved to limit use of so-called daylight overdrafts, citing their threat to bank capital. In September, Volcker went much further; he proposed raising bank capital requirements from 6 to 9 percent (including subordinated debt) and establishing guidelines for restricting dividend payouts under certain conditions. Subsequently, the FRB (and OCC) put out for comment formal risk-adjusted bank capital requirements.

The Bank's Capital Needs

The rate of growth in a bank's assets, and hence its capital requirements, is a function of the external demand for credit (and hence inflation effects), the capital adequacy requirements of the various bank regulatory agencies, the profitability of the bank's operations, and the bank board's dividend payout policy.

Growth

Historically, under moderate inflation bank enterprise expansion can occur without recourse to the capital markets. For a given ratio of capital to assets, a bank can expand its operations at a rate, g, financed entirely by retained earnings, as determined by the profitability of its operations and the payout of earnings as dividends.[8] Thus, with no external equity financing, the growth in assets that can be supported by the bank may be determined simply as follows:

Growth in Capital = Growth in Assets

$$g = \frac{\text{Average Assets}}{\text{Average Equity Capital}} \times \frac{\text{Net Income}}{\text{Average Assets}}$$

$$\times (1 - \text{Dividend Payout Ratio})$$

---

[8]This assumes normal liquidity conditions and the ongoing ability to attract and retain deposits.

To illustrate, if the ratio of assets to capital is 16 to 1, the return on assets 0.8 percent, and dividend payout is 40 percent of net income (see Table 5–2), then assets will grow at an annual rate:

$$16 \times 0.8 \times (1 - 0.4) = 7.7\%/\text{year}$$

Assets can grow at a greater rate if the bank increases its leverage (reduces the capital ratio) and/or obtains external financing. For a given set of earnings and dividend ratios, there is only one self-financing growth rate for bank assets consistent with a particular capital-to-asset ratio. Other things being equal, then, this example would support loan growth of nearly 8 percent per year. However, most large publicly owned banks would like to expand at a greater rate, and the Federal Reserve Board often allows (causes) the money supply to increase at a higher rate than this. Inflation may cause bank loan demand to grow more rapidly.

It may be observed that the product of the first two terms above is return on equity. The return on equity has averaged about 13 percent during recent years, with a little over 60 percent of this income retained (the third term above), so that internal capital growth has indeed been around 8 percent. The presumption is that over any long-term time frame, bank earning assets growth should be in line with nominal growth in GNP. Thus, on the assumption that real growth will be of the magnitude of 3 percent per annum, one has to be willing to theorize that inflation will be at a 4 percent annual rate or less to conclude that the banking industry will be able to totally meet its capital needs internally (even then, some individual, faster-growing and/or capital-deficient institutions would have to finance externally).

Financing Details

Table 5–6 illustrates the type and amount of debt and equity capital raised by banking organizations from 1980 to 1984. During the period 1971–1979, banks raised a total of about $18 billion (net) in external capital, which represented approximately one-third of the increase in total bank capital over the period. Figure 5–1 illustrates the trend in the type and amount of capital issued by banks. Even with the dramatic increase in recent years, it should be noted that retained earnings have continued to play the dominant role in providing increases in equity capital.

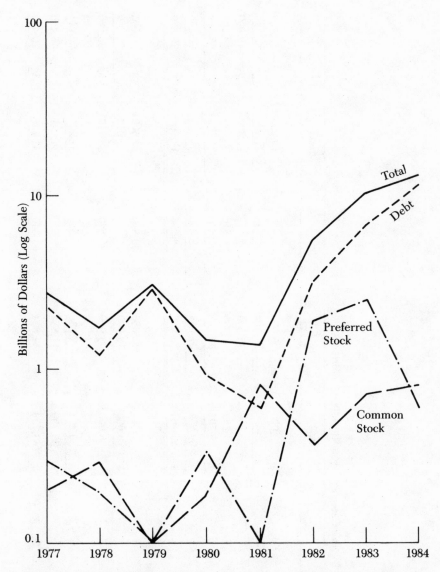

Figure 5–1   Capital Securities Issued by Commercial Banks and Bank Holding Companies

The year 1984 was a record year for capital financings by commercial banking organizations. According to the annual review by Irving Trust, $12.5 billion was raised through 133 issues. There were two major reasons for this record volume: First, overall conditions in the debt markets were favorable throughout the year. Debt accounted for about 94 percent of the total funding volume in

Table 5-6 Bank Financing by Size Category, 1980–1984 (000's omitted)

	1980	1981	1982	1983	1984
Assets under $500 million					
Public debt	$ 3,000	$ 9,000	—	$ 10,000	$ 19,000
Private debt	300	6,500	—	7,500	0
Total debt	$ 3,300	15,500	—	$ 17,500	$ 19,000
Preferred stock	14,162	300	10,816	—	4,661
Common stock	25,702	60,748	17,440	—	55,889
Total equity	39,864	61,048	28,256	—	60,550
Total financing	$ 43,164	$ 76,548	$ 28,256	$ 17,500	$ 79,550
Assets of $500 million—$1 billion					
Public debt	—	$ 15,000	$ 40,800	$ 30,500	$ 30,000
Private debt	$ 8,000	18,000	—	8,012	0
Total debt	8,000	33,000	40,800	38,512	30,000
Preferred stock	26,315	4,500	—	—	26,269
Common stock	9,424	7,334	22,540	54,221	20,211
Total equity	35,739	11,834	22,540	54,221	46,480
Total financing	$ 43,739	$ 44,834	$ 63,340	$ 92,733	$ 76,480

Assets of $1 billion–$5 billion					
Public debt	$ 145,000	$ 115,000	$ 268,400	$ 581,500	$ 210,000
Private debt	25,000	57,300	—	95,000	7,000
Total debt	170,000	172,300	268,400	676,500	$ 217,000
Preferred stock	69,083	32,000	237,843	428,110	38,805
Common stock	—	173,677	91,574	152,898	169,950
Total equity	69,083	205,677	329,417	581,008	208,755
Total financing	$ 239,083	$ 377,977	$ 597,817	$1,257,508	$ 425,755
Assets over $5 billion					
Public debt	$ 725,000	$ 375,000	$2,898,923	$5,990,000	$10,853,120
Private debt	60,000	—	—	—	50,000
Total debt	785,000	375,000	2,898,923	5,990,000	10,903,120
Preferred stock	234,384	—	1,661,313	2,076,813	526,828
Common stock	150,215	551,532	241,495	511,266	531,893
Total equity	384,599	551,532	1,902,808	2,588,079	1,058,721
Total financing	$1,169,599	$ 926,532	$4,801,731	$8,578,079	$11,961,841
Total Bank Financing	$1,495,585	$1,425,891	$5,491,144	$9,945,820	$12,543,626
Percentage due to Institutions with Assets Over $5 billion	78%	65%	87%	86%	95%

Source: Capital Securities Issued: Commercial Banking, 4th Quarter 1984, Report 116, Irving Trust Company, James W. Leong, Editor (New York: Irving Trust).

this period. Significantly, bank institutions in the over-$5 billion asset category have dominated the financing picture. These holding company institutions were also able to tap a receptive Euromarket. Bank offerings in the Euromarket totaled $4.5 billion in 1984 compared to $405 million and $1.1 billion reported in 1983 and 1982, respectively. These increased financings can be attributed to the overall attractiveness of U.S. dollar obligations due to the strong dollar in 1984.

The second reason for this record volume was that continuing industry problems intensified regulatory resolve on minimum capital standards. This was clearly evident from actions taken against several major bank organizations during the year. The resulting regulatory climate was undoubtedly a major factor in the record $5.7 billion of primary capital financings. However, analysts also point to favorable market conditions.

The data in Table 5–6 compiled by Irving Trust indicate that the five largest bank holding companies accounted for approximately *half* of all bank financing volume in 1983 and 1984. In general, the larger banks were most active in the debt markets. In contrast, bank organizations with less than $1 billion of assets were active in the equity markets, with these offerings representing over two-thirds of their total funding.

The most prominent trend has been the extensive use of debt instruments qualifying as primary capital (i.e. equity commitment or equity contract issues). These issues typically featured maturities of 12 years or less, yields at a premium over a floating rate index (usually the 3-month LIBOR—London Inter-bank Offered Rate), and either a mandatory conversion to capital securities or a commitment to sell such securities to retire the debt. With declining interest rates, these debt instruments represented a cost-effective method of raising primary capital compared with other equity alternatives. This was especially true for banks whose stocks were trading below book values.

Floating rate issues accounted for about two-thirds of the debt volume in 1984 and more than half of the debt volume in 1983. Greater interest rate uncertainty is one explanation for the popularity of this feature; moreover, increased floating rate loans have created the need for such matching liabilities.

Commercial banks were not a big factor in the equity markets in 1984, with only $1.4 billion in equity financings. This lower volume reflects a decline in preferred stock offerings, as adjustable rate preferred stocks (ARPs) lost their favored status as the major source of primary capital ($481 million of offerings in 1984 compared with a total of $2.1 billion in 1983).[9]

Both the FDIC and the FRB have been advocating risk-adjusted capital ratios—that is, capital reserves above the minimum for those bank investments and activities that are riskier than normal loans. Loans to less developed countries now require extra reserves. Moreover, the FDIC has proposed in effect a higher insurance premium for banks whose deposits it insures if such banks' financial ratios indicate they are in a high-risk class.

Total long-term debt and equity financing by commercial banks in 1983–84 exceeded that of the previous ten years combined. The new capital adequacy guidelines, together with the concerns over the quality of loans and off-balance-sheet liabilities, suggest a sustained high level of external financing for 1985–86. The extent to which common stock financing will be attractive to banks depends on the retained earnings growth, in conjunction with the price-to-book-value relationship, and relatedly the price-to-earnings ratio and return on equity. The higher these ratio values, the more attractive will be the sale of new common stock to improve the capital ratio and conversely (other things being equal).

Regulatory Concerns about Credit Expansion

Regulators have been uncomfortable with the observed long-term decline in capital ratios, especially among the largest banks (which hold most of the deposits). This decline is due to a profit squeeze and perhaps to bank managements succumbing to pressures for asset growth at any price. Directors should be concerned that the rate of return on equity be compensatory—that is, reward investors for the greater risk of more leverage, the risks associated with the loan and investment portfolios, and any erosion of shareholder wealth due to inflation. (We discuss this latter concern later in this chapter.)

Regulators agree that bank profitability is a key to an adequate capital position. (As noted earlier, other concerns are liquidity and capital availability.) However, while bankers should strive to earn

---

[9]The 1984 data and analysis are abstracted from Irving Trust's Report 116, *Capital Securities Issued: Commercial Banking*, Fourth Quarter 1984, James W. Leong, Editor (New York: Irving Trust).

enough net interest margin to achieve compensatory return, doing so means very high prime rates during periods of high inflation, and directors have been aware of much political pressure to keep rates low.

Managerial Concerns

The cost and availability of equity financing are always of importance. If market values are below book value for bank issues, equity financing would generally dilute shareholders' equity per share. The ratio of market to book value is in itself an important parameter for directors to monitor, because it presents valuable signals from the capital market. Another related concern is that the public capital markets are only available to the 300 to 400 largest banks. These have a large enough market capitalization to be followed by institutional investors, and the size of their financings would normally fall in the $20 million or more category for debt (capital note) issues and $5 million or more for common stock issues that permit underwritings by major investment banking firms for public offerings.

As pointed out in a 1980 study by F. Pape and J. Wooden[10] of Merrill Lynch White Weld Capital Markets Group, external financing by banks and bank holding companies has traditionally been almost exclusively for capital purposes, whether common stock or certain debt instruments. In recent years, however, long-term financing has been used for supplemental funding purposes, with the objective being to more closely match maturities, rate sensitivities and, in some cases, currencies. This trend is expected to continue, as the penalties for mismatching are becoming more visible, costly, and frequent.

Trends in bank financing, whether capital-related or for funding, should be viewed from the perspective and in the context of the changes occurring within the banking industry. There has been expansion in the concept of what commercial banking encompasses: holding company activities, international activities, real estate lending, credit card lending, mortgage banking, lease fi-

---

[10]F. Pape and J. Wooden, *Bank Financing Review* (March 1980); Merrill Lynch White Weld Capital Markets Group, "Bank Financing Review, March 1980," presented at the Financial Analysts Federation 10th Annual Banking Industry and Bank Stock Symposium (New York City, March 26–27, 1980).

nancing, factoring, and merchant banking. A critical factor is expanded loan demand without a corresponding increase in "core" deposits. The upshot has been to increase perceived capital needs of the banking industry. Directors should make sure that the bank management provides them with timely and convincing studies about when, how, and in what amounts to add to the bank's capital base.

Bank Holding Companies vs. Banks

Table 5–3 indicates that among the 50 largest banks, bank assets represent 93 percent or more of total holding company assets. Among the next 70 largest, bank assets average more than 90 percent of total holding company assets.

In its early 1981 study of 120 banks covering data through June 1980, A. G. Becker found that the five-year compound growth rate in earnings per share was 12.5 percent for the 18 largest banks and about 12 percent for the other banks. In a similar study in 1977, Becker found that for 102 large banks, the 1972–1977 earnings-per-share growth averaged 8.6 percent for the largest 18, 5 percent for the next 32 largest, and 2.9 percent for the next 52. This spotty record was below overall average loan growth (Table 5–1) and indicates the profit squeeze that put management under pressure to raise more capital to finance growth.

The market/book value for large holding companies in many cases has not been attractive for equity financing, and most external financing has been in the form of debt. Thus direct holding company debt issues have dominated the banking industry's external capital requirements.

In examining the financing picture, the Association of Bank Holding Companies (ABHC) has looked beyond the domestic banks per se to take into account the holding company status and influence on the nature of capital flow.[11] ABHC has also taken into account foreign branch subsidiary data for holding companies' affiliate banks when assessing the financing implications of asset growth, with the resultant asset picture representing at least 75

---

[11]See Association of Bank Holding Companies, "The Financing of Bank Holding Companies, Theory and Practice" (Washington, D.C.: 1977).

percent of the total consolidated assets for all commercial banks in the United States. (Not only has foreign asset growth been greater than on the domestic side, but leverage has effectively increased while return on assets decreased.)

Bank holding company bank affiliates are thus expected to require about 75 percent of the total additional bank capital needed by the industry in the next several years and 75 to 80 percent of the capital to be raised externally. There has been argument over whether it would be difficult to raise most of this capital through the parent holding company—for example, through "downstreaming" of holding company debt as equity for subsidiary banks, as was substantially the case through 1979.

Of more recent interest is the impact of the accelerating trend toward bank mergers and acquisitions, and recently authorized regional banking compacts, on the need for bank holding company capital. As this was written, it was too early to know what regulatory and legislative policy would be controlling.

A Closer Look at Inflation Effects

Accounting Framework

The essence of commercial banking is the holding of bank capital in the form of net monetary assets, attracting deposits, and making loans and investments at a positive "spread" or net interest margin. Monetary assets are money and claims to receive or pay a sum of money, the amount of which is fixed or determinable without reference to future prices of specific goods or services. During periods of inflation, the holding of cash and other monetary assets results in a loss of general purchasing power because a given amount of money will buy less at the end of the period than it would have bought at the beginning of the period. Conversely, continuing to owe monetary liabilities results in a gain of purchasing power because cheaper dollars will be used to repay the obligations.[12] Banks generally have a positive shareholders' equity, represented largely by net monetary assets. In a period of inflation, the purchasing power of that shareholders' equity may be

---

[12]Ernst and Whinney, "Inflation Accounting: Implementing FASB Statement No. 33 for Banks and Bank Holding Companies," December 1979.

eroded because the purchasing power of the underlying net monetary assets has declined. Large publicly owned companies, including banks, are now required to provide annual report information on the effects of inflation on the financial statements, in accordance with the constant dollar and current cost measurement concepts as set forth in Statement No. 33 of the Financial Accounting Standard Board (FASB-33). Publicly held banks and bank holding companies having either $1 billion of assets or $125 million of gross properties (before accumulated depreciation) at the beginning of the year are required to present the supplemental information. For purposes of the size test, the term *properties* would include bank premises and equipment and other real estate owned. The disclosures are effective for fiscal years ending after December 24, 1979. The principal disclosures required under the board's dual measurement approach are shown in Table 5–7.

In regard to 1(a) of Table 5–7, most banks will *not* have to present either the constant dollar information on income from continuing operations or any of the current cost disclosures because the related conversion adjustments will probably not be material. The FASB considered the purchasing power gain or loss on net monetary items (1[b] of Table 5–7) to be relevant to both constant dollar and current cost accounting. Therefore, separate disclosure is required under both measurement bases, although the concepts and amount presented are the same.[13] The FASB does not deal with the important changes in bank customer strategies in

Table 5–7 Principal Disclosures Required Under Dual Measurement Approach

	Constant Dollar	Current Cost
1. Current year data		
(a) Income from continuing operations	X	X
(b) Purchasing power gain or loss on net monetary items	X	X
(c) Increases or decreases in the current cost of properties, net of inflation		X
(d) Properties at year end		X
2. Five-year summary of selected data	X	X
3. Footnotes and narrative explanations	X	X

---

[13] Ernst and Whinney, *ibid*.

an inflationary environment, nor with the preferred strategy in asset/liability management to be adopted by banks. Such strategies will impact the sources and uses of bank funds. The important point is that bankers and bank directors should understand the effects of the inflationary environment on operations and devise an appropriate strategy to cope with these effects.

The most disturbing effect to be reckoned with is the shrinkage of stockholders' equity in real (constant dollar) terms. A higher return on equity is needed to offset this effect, but without resorting to higher capital leverage. This could be accomplished by:

- Higher/widening spreads.
- Lower reserve requirements.
- Lower income taxes.
- More fee income, which requires little equity.

However, competitive, regulatory, and/or tax conditions would have to be modified from those now extant to allow these benefits for banks and their owners. As important as these developments would be to the profitability of the banks, political considerations suggest they will be slow in coming.

Bank directors should recognize that bank customers can be a mixed blessing—to the extent inflation (including the still-soaring inflation in LDCs even though not in the United States) causes loan demand growth, in current dollars, but the credit environment yields an insufficient real, risk-adjusted rate of return to bank stockholders. Perhaps the lower price-earnings multiples that have been accorded bank stocks over the past several years reflect this picture.

Reported bank net cash flow, in current dollar terms, is still a basic measure of bank earnings to investors, and this figure will not be affected by accounting changes unless the IRS allows additional tax deductions for reserves for losses. The matter has received considerably more favorable attention in the United Kingdom and countries in the British Commonwealth.

The perception of the effects of inflation on bank equity capital could cause a propensity here in the United States to invest more bank funds in assets (land, buildings, equipment, art) that appreciate in value under inflation and inflation accounting, unlike net monetary assets. This may be counter to established regulatory policy, which favors "safety" and liquidity of bank investments and bank capital. The impact on dividend policy is less clear. One view is to favor full payment of earnings to stockholders. Obviously, a higher payout means less retained earnings, which means less capital for growth (or conversely, more external capital to be raised). Bankers could play the same game as their customers, retaliating against inflation, as it were, by borrowing more capital in the form of capital notes and debentures. The presumption is that the capital markets, in any case, exercise some "discipline" over bank capital-raising activities.

Recent developments, such as revision of the usury laws in many states and the move to variable rate loans, allow banks to better cover their costs of funds and protect the shareholders' equity.

Inflation vs. Disinflation

The period 1982–1985 was one of lower-than-expected inflation, with the latter years experiencing actual deflation in many basic commodity prices. Because banks hold net monetary assets, their real rate of return is enhanced by deflation as purchasing power increases. A 12 percent return on equity in 1985 is thus a much better result than a 15 percent ROE would have been in 1975.

At the same time, the shift toward variable rate financing tends to insulate bank operating earnings from inflation and deflation. But this is not to imply that deflation is favorable to banks. By definition, it means the physical assets that represent customer collateral for working capital loans and lease financing are worth less and less. Banks cannot look forward to growth in such an environment. Although paradoxically the banks' book net worth will have increased purchasing power, the value of common stocks, including bank stocks, in such an environment will probably be depressed.

Growth Impact

As Warren Marcus of Salomon Brothers observed in the 1977 ABHC study, as the rate of inflation increases, banking's need for external financing increases. "A 10 percent growth in nominal GNP—versus banking's internal equity generation capability— would translate into roughly $2.0 billion of required external financing annually. Higher rates of growth in nominal GNP would further enlarge this requirement." Growth at high rates of inflation can be accommodated in a number of ways—for example, increased leverage, external financing, increased bank earnings and profitability, and/or reduced dividend payouts.

All responses could, in theory, occur simultaneously. In the absence of regulatory constraints, if banks wanted to expand their loan portfolios as rapidly as possible (and could not sustain that growth rate by internal financing), there would be some limit to their leveraging possibilities, set by the risk aversion of the board and management; or, the stock market would "discipline" the bank (or holding company) by lowering the value of its equity. Whether or not the market actually disciplines a bank when it leverages itself too far is a question now being addressed by regulatory agencies.

Summary

- Investors' equity and reserves of a commercial bank represent permanent risk capital. From the standpoint of creditors and regulators, it is this capital that underlies the strength of the bank and provides the ultimate source of bank solvency.
- For the investment of this capital and the risk to which it is exposed, bank shareholders expect to earn a fair rate of return.
- Many difficult issues surface when dealing with the notion of bank capital as a cushion to absorb losses and protect the depositors. A central question is in defining and measuring capital adequacy for a commercial bank, given the scope of its operations, involvement in the money and capital markets, and its difficulties in matching maturities of assets and liabilities. Use of a risk-adjusted capital approach is now coming of age.
- Because of legal and fiduciary responsibilities of banks, the bank director represents not just the shareholders but many other constituencies and competing interests simultaneously.
- Because capital is vital to the growth of the bank, as well as to its soundness, the bank must maintain an adequate ratio of equity capital to assets. The minimum at this writing is 6 percent. Trade-offs must be made, especially in expansion periods such as those recently experienced, during which many bank stocks were selling below book value and equity financing would be dilutive.

- Banks could expand without recourse to external financing, given a high enough rate of return on equity and earnings retention and moderate GNP growth, as well as limited foreign opportunities. These conditions have not existed for the large U.S. banks, and because equity financing has not been attractive (aside from the significant increment flowing from retained earnings), banks have considered operating with more risk and augmenting their capital with the sale of notes and debentures.
- Holding company debt issues have dominated the banking industry's external capital-raising activity. Funds so raised have been "downstreamed" to the bank(s).
- The role of federal deposit insurance in facilitating the accommodation of U.S. commercial banks to increases in credit demands and response of bank management to increased opportunities for expansion abroad is under scrutiny. Recent work in extending modern option pricing theory to deposit insurance and loan guarantees suggests that the interaction between FDIC insurance and management behavior is rational and complex. Indications are that a new system of deposit insurance that penalized abnormal risk-taking will be attempted.
- Some data on bank stocks suggest that the capital market operates to provide some discipline in regard to the extent of risk-taking by a bank.
- No one single quantitative measure or ratio is satisfactory in assessing a bank's risk and, relatedly, its liquidity. Several are therefore used.
- The shift toward variable rate financing tends to insulate bank operating earnings from inflation and deflation. But deflation is not necessarily favorable to banks, because loan collateral may diminish in value, and because banks cannot look forward to growth in such an unstable environment. Although each dollar of a bank's book value will, by definition, have increased purchasing power, the value of common stocks, including bank stocks, in a deflationary environment will probably be depressed.
- Inflation has the effect of eroding bank capital that is held in the form of net monetary assets. To grow and maintain a fair rate of return in an inflationary environment, banks need to improve the return on capital—for example, through such

means as higher spreads, lower reserve requirements, and lower taxes—such that return on equity is fair and reasonable in light of the risk to the stockholders and the opportunity cost of capital.

Chapter 6

MEASURING MANAGEMENT AND BANK PERFORMANCE

by George B. Rockwell and S. Theodore Guild

Introduction

The popular *In Search of Excellence: Lessons from America's Best-Run Companies* by Peters and Waterman (1982) deliberately excluded all banking companies from its sample of 66 "excellent" companies. The authors thought banking companies were "too highly regulated and protected—to be of interest." While such an assumption had a sound basis in history, it is increasingly suspect in today's banking environment. Deregulation of the trucking and airline industries focused attention on the capability of management in companies in those industries. Certainly, the question of "excellence" among individual banking organizations has "interest" and significance for those who wish to be survivors in the growing movement toward regional banking consolidation. Moreover, we now know that banks, both large and small, can and do fail.

The primary responsibility of bank management is to maximize the wealth of the institution's stockholders, consistent with safe and sound banking practice. Increased wealth is represented by an increase in the value of the stockholders' investment. Every bank has a strategy, implicit or explicit, to accomplish that goal. In the past, implicit strategies within the industry were frequently based on the assumption that the experience of the past would continue relatively unchanged indefinitely. Deregulation abruptly ended forever the comfort of such a position. In meeting their stockholder responsibilities today, bankers are concerned with their ability to anticipate and manage change effectively. In this connection, we have found that identification of the critical factors for the success of an institution will provide a framework by which management and directors may assess their position, evaluate their strengths and weaknesses, and pursue appropriate change. In this chapter, we describe and discuss seven such critical success factors: marketing, innovation, asset/liability management, asset quality, expense control, planning and strategy, and performance comparisons.

Marketing

In an ordered, regulated world, aggressive marketing of one's services was not of high importance. Even the mild concept of "business development" was viewed by some as ill-suited to the professionalism of banking; a medical doctor did not go out and grub for patients—it was reputation that brought them in. Such attitudes generally disappeared from the industry in the 1950s, and the crumbling of protected franchises is revolutionizing financial service marketing. The key factor is that some are doing it better than others. The winners seem to be applying proven marketing techniques and methodologies taken from other industries.

Successful financial service marketing today must emphasize sophisticated retailing concepts such as market segmentation, product differentiation, product integration, and value added if traditional providers are to hold their own against new competitors who are aware of modern marketing concepts. Formalized competitive analysis and monitoring are also required.

The most effective marketing programs will emphasize (1) natural market segmentation, (2) tailoring of services and products for those segments, (3) development of a fully integrated marketing program, including the selection of appropriate media, and (4) use of the most sophisticated dimensions of sales training, sales management, and selling in both a retail and commercial context. Programs will be prioritized and launched, based on short- as well as long-term profit objectives. Product costing information will be available, and old products that are not profitable will be repriced or abandoned.

Marketing has sometimes been thought to be a separate function, more like public relations than anything else, relying heavily on the notion of community presence and stressing such catchwords as "awareness" and "image." In many institutions, market research, product design, product introduction, advertising, and promotion, along with appropriate sales programs, are not done or apparently well understood. Marketing management is a very complex skill, and many financial organizations—particularly small and medium-sized ones—have or will soon come to realize this if they are to survive.

In a commodity business—a business which demands efficiency and low-cost production as well as very little opportunity for market differentiation—customer or prospect needs have to be identified and then satisfied profitably. Over the next decade, technology and telecommunications will provide the opportunity to change the bank from a commodity business to a business in which technology can provide the bank with a unique and sophisticated competitive advantage. However, it is also important to monitor continually what competitors are doing. This means peer group comparisons as well as comparisons of specific institutions; thrifts as well as commercial banks must be evaluated.

Directors must keep well informed concerning the broad socioeconomic trends in the country and attempt to relate these trends to the responses that develop within the banking industry and to the environment in which a specific institution operates. Those whose marketing approach consists of blindly following after a few "leadership" banks will not be survivors under deregulation.

New products, such as specialized service departments for high net-worth individuals, personal financial planning for the income brackets from $25,000 to $100,000, or a new approach to service delivery, such as check truncation, may be highly successful for some. However, the fact that a "leadership" bank has a hot product does not imply that the product will be "hot" everywhere.

In the context of managerial responsibility, the role of the manager with respect to the marketing function is to:

- Have a thorough understanding of how the bank currently sells and markets its products.
- See that a basic marketing strategy and the related tactical programs are in place and congruent with current overall goals of the institution.

- Make sure that a relevant organizational form is in place and that the resources, both human and financial, are appropriate.
- See that program implementation responsibility has been assigned and accepted at all levels of the organization.
- Compare actual results over time with the achievement targets and understand the nature of the exceptions and any corrective action to be taken.
- Periodically recheck planning validity against evidence of real-world change.

A director may play an extremely valuable role in reviewing institutional competence in the marketing area. As an outsider to the industry, the director can bring a perspective that may well serve to correct the myopia from which many banks suffer. Banking industry experience is not a prerequisite for marketing success in a deregulated environment.

Innovation

Innovation was not always an important success factor for banking. Regulatory constraints on competition stifled innovation; experimentation was seldom rewarded. In contrast, the Peters and Waterman study equated "excellence" and innovation in other businesses. The first of the eight key attributes they found to "characterize most clearly the distinction of the excellent innovative companies" was a *bias for action:* "These companies may be analytical in their approach to decision making, [but] . . . the standard operating procedure is 'do it, fix it, try it.'" Regulation pervasively acts to transfer action decisions outside an organization. Thus, the management culture of banking has been less "do it" than "can we get it approved?" Conditional thinking of this nature is most difficult baggage to dump in a deregulated environment. Particularly traumatic may be the removal of the lawyer from the traditional place near the head of the table on policy issues. "Action" is a nonlegal quality.

Action is also a youthful quality. The automatic equation of grey hair with responsibility must be reexamined. Moreover, in the bureaucracies that now characterize large banking institutions, Darwinian selection frequently awards with promotion those with the most sensitive antenna for political consensus. Nonconformists have not been highly valued. "Action" does not wait for an internal political constituency to develop.

The proliferation of new financial products since the end of Regulation Q has been truly astounding. The money market mutual fund, a relatively new product, was developed and marketed to capitalize on an opportunity. Assets under management have grown substantially and continue to do so. The reasons are simple: fund marketing, good rates, and an innovative vehicle that meets customer needs. Related packaged products like the Fidelity U.S.A. Account and Merrill Lynch's Cash Management Account are further examples of timely innovation for consumers. The development of mortgage-backed securities and variable annuities demonstrate increasing product innovation in the investment banking and insurance fields. Further examples are insurance sales in bank branches, shared no-load mutual funds, and the Sears Financial Network. Technology-based innovations, such as automated teller machines (ATMs), cash management systems, banking at home, farm accounting, and the national credit card networks, have also flourished.

Innovation, limited to new product and new technology introduction (difficult and time-consuming as such undertakings may be), is not enough. Successful organizations must be sensitive to change in all areas of activity and have in place constructive methods to monitor change and make change happen.

Directors should be particularly sensitive to the leadership capabilities shown by key senior managers. It is no longer sufficient for a division head to display competence and expertise in a functional specialty. In a deregulated world, senior managers must possess leadership skills as well as professional skills.

Asset/Liability Management

With free competition on rates paid for deposits, banking now has much more freedom to make mistakes. For years, conventional wisdom held that bank failures were caused by bad loans or, occasionally, fraud or illiquidity from heavy deposit withdrawals. These traditional risks, however, pale in comparison with today's risk of making errors regarding the rates paid for deposits or the appropriate maturity of the deposit structure.

Many banks struggle to keep their reserve for loan losses at 1 percent of loans in the consumer area and even lower in the real estate area. At this level (unless the loans are particularly weak), the bank is thought to be prudently positioned with respect to credit risk. Ironically, however, in a matter of weeks, this same bank may lose 2 percent, 3 percent, or even more of its asset value due to changes in interest rates. The nature of this interest rate risk is beginning to be fully understood.

Examples of the extreme nature of interest rate risk can be constructed to show that a 20 percent change in the market interest rate—say from 10 to 12 percent—can dramatically reduce the value of fixed-rate loans. A decline in the market value of long-maturing assets in a rising rate environment is particularly harmful. A simple solution would appear to be matching maturities of assets and liabilities. This is easier said than done, however. Even if financial intermediaries simply match the maturity of their assets and liabilities, thereby avoiding the risk of interest rate gyrations, two other problems emerge. The first revolves around a primary function—that is, to "intermediate" the maturity preferences of depositors and borrowers. Thus, some mismatching of assets and liabilities is integral to the financial intermediary business. Most analysts agree that the degree of mismatching is the critical variable, not the avoidance of it.

Second, if financial intermediaries completely match maturities at all times, they may lose opportunities for significant profits. An example occurred briefly in 1980 when the difference between the cost of short-term funds and the rate available for lending long-term funds exceeded 6 percent. This extraordinary gap attracted the attention of even the most conservative managements. Unfortunately, the world of interest rate fluctuations often causes the initial profitability of such short funding to evaporate when short rates rise over the next interest rate cycle. What looks like an easy profit can quickly convert into huge losses. Thus, astute risk management and timing are essential, and they promise to be more so in the years ahead.

It would not be nearly so difficult to manage interest rate risk wisely if the temptation to mismanage it when short-term rates are low was not so great. Most banks, regardless of size, have found that they need an asset-liability committee (ALCO) to manage interest rate exposure safely yet profitably. Balance sheet management is not a function easily or wisely delegated. However, adequate commercial and some thrift bank experience, written material, and computer models are available today to create formal asset/liability management policies and procedures. Management of interest rate risk and the balance sheet clearly distinguish winners from losers. Winners will not be those who shrink entirely from this risk; they will simply be the ones who manage it well.

Balance Sheet Management

Balance sheet management is practiced both with a short- and long-term time horizon. In the short term, decisions tend to be focused on maximizing both near- and intermediate-term earnings while living within policy guidelines concerned with capital adequacy, liquidity, interest sensitivity, credit risk, and foreign exchange risk. Interest centers on the balance sheet changes that can be brought about relatively easily with only limited impact on noninterest expense or income of the institution. For the most part, these are balance sheet changes that only marginally affect core customers of the institution. Attention tends to be focused on changes that are more money market oriented such as interbank funds, investments, purchased funds, and so forth, rather than core customer deposits and commercial loans. Changes in interest rates naturally would tend to have a broader impact.

Long-term balance sheet management, on the other hand, tends to focus on strategic decisions and tends to be more customer market driven than short-term balance sheet management, which is more financial market driven. Uncertainty tends to be greater in the long term rather than in the short term, because so much more is variable; the long-term decisions tend to be directional, while short-term balance sheet management often focuses on marginal profit improvement. In the long term, one often seeks to achieve strategic flexibility through the selection of robust strategies which, to the greatest degree possible, can be successfully implemented, independent of exactly how the environment in the future develops.

A developing trend among major financial institutions is the securitization of the asset side of the balance sheet—that is, the sale of securities backed by loans originated by the bank, such as mortgages or auto loans. This generates fee income for servicing the portfolio but does not require additional capital since the balance sheet is not growing. Directors of major banks should understand the risk associated with securitization as well as the potential growth and earnings through fee income. Smaller banks or pension funds look to participate in the opportunities generated through securitization or syndications.

For these balance sheet management techniques to be successfully employed, they need a regular flow of accurate data. Short-term balance sheet management requires that the data, in order to be useful, be more frequent, more timely, and more accurate than for long-term strategic decision making. This has resulted in considerable effort being devoted to modifying the application accounting systems (loan, deposits, etc.) to provide these data as a by-product of the normal daily processing.

Measuring Interest Rate Risk Exposure

To measure the bank's exposure to interest rate risk, the asset-liability committee (ALCO) will see that the following reports are prepared:

1. GAP Report (monthly): This report will show the difference between rate-sensitive assets and rate-sensitive liabilities in various term categories.
2. The Funds Evaluation Matching Report: This report will estimate which liabilities fund which assets for the bank's balance sheet. After prorating liability costs to the assets funded, a net interest margin by asset category will be calculated.
3. Twelve-month projected Balance Sheet, Income Statement, and Cash Flow Statement, using high, moderate, and low interest rate scenarios, (quarterly): These statements will serve to analyze the impact on earnings and net worth of interest rate changes.
4. Market Value Balance (quarterly): This report will show estimated net asset values at various interest rate levels.

From the review of these reports, market conditions, and current asset/liability strategies, ALCO will develop the Interest Rate Risk Reduction Strategy and any subsequent revisions.

ALCO should *consider* a variety of interest rate risk-reducing strategies, including, but not limited to:

- Improved matching of maturities of liabilities with assets.
- Sale of fixed-rate mortgage loans with proceeds reinvested in

short-term or variable-rate assets or used to pay off short-term or variable-rate liabilities.
- Obtaining long-term fixed-rate sources of funds, with the proceeds used to pay off short-term or variable-rate liabilities.
- Interest rate swaps.
- Hedging via financial futures and options.
- Balance sheet growth via increased short-term borrowings with proceeds invested in short-term or variable-rate assets in an attempt to improve the ratio of rate-sensitive assets to rate-sensitive liabilities in the short-term categories.

Historically, long-term interest rates on average have been higher than short-term rates. Thus, long-term assets have higher average yields than short-term assets, assuming the same credit risk. Similarly, short-term liabilities are less expensive than long-term liabilities. Because of this, the board of directors and ALCO must realize that, in an attempt to shorten the term of assets and lengthen the term of liabilities, net interest margins may be narrowed significantly from what might have occurred if the borrow-short/invest-long policy were to continue, assuming a stable or falling rate environment. To compensate, the board and ALCO might find it necessary to consider investments with higher credit risks and correspondingly higher yields. The higher credit risks, properly assumed, would be undertaken in an attempt to reduce the bank's overall risk exposure without jeopardizing profitability.

Asset Quality

Maintenance of asset quality is not a responsibility that management can delegate to such bodies as the supervisory agencies, the external auditing firm, or a committee of the board. Such reviews may be helpful, but they have neither the frequency nor provide the depth of analysis necessary for adequate control.

The primary internal mechanism for asset quality control is an independent, comprehensive loan review system. Such a capability, however, is only the key component in the total administrative approach that is demanded. Four interrelated and properly functioning systems are called for: a supervisory system, an administrative system, an audit system, and a loan review system.

A *supervisory system* establishes periodic performance reviews of (at least) all officers who have been delegated authority to place the assets of the bank at credit or investment risk. Written current job descriptions containing a detailed statement of the tasks to be performed by an individual and the accountability and responsibility assumed in the position are a part of the system. A semiannual comparison of actual, individual performance against the institutional standard is normal. The written review and commentary of the immediate supervisor should become part of the individual's personnel file.

In their consideration of the supervision system and its impact, directors should be fully aware of the major impact that profit center accounting has made on the job of the loan officer. Historically, this officer performed a quality control function by accepting those asset risks believed to have met bank standards for quality. Today, as an individual profit center within the profit center, which is the lending division, the loan officer is responsible for producing a bottom-line result that meets budget. Thus, the loan officer is inevitably placed in the dual role of quality control officer and sales officer. Directors, therefore, should be satisfied that performance reviews focus not only on profit center performance, but also give adequate recognition to quality performance factors. The easiest way—on a short-term basis—for individual loan officers to exceed their profit center budgets is to process loans with less collateral, longer terms, and lower quality than their competitors or peers.

An *administrative system* is largely a management information system (MIS) that provides risk supervisors and administrators with appropriate, scheduled information with respect to individual assets and various asset categories within their portfolio. The reports should be current, accurate, and systematically distributed. Such reports serve to identify exceptions to risk policy statements and such specific matters as past-due notes, incomplete or inadequate collateral positions, financial statements due and not received, and so forth. This information serves as the basis for "follow-up" action by the responsible officer and for comment by the officer's supervisor. Directors should be concerned with the general level of "exceptions" reported in risk areas, and with the effectiveness with which the supervisory system acts to either clear up the "exceptions" or take other asset protection measures.

The *internal audit system* normally provides a form of independent review with respect to the condition of assets in all risk areas.

The following are key criteria for measuring the performance of this system:

1. The actual performance of audits in designated areas in accordance with a preestablished schedule.
2. The prompt distribution of audit findings to the areas and supervisory points concerned.
3. The integration of audit-discovered "exceptions" into the overall exception clearance system of the bank.

Obviously, audit schedules should also relate to depth and frequency of internal examinations and to the current risk exposure position within the portfolio. The proliferation of new asset products and risk acceptance points presents the auditor with a continuous challenge in this respect.

The *independent loan review system* provides for quality control performed outside the organizational units responsible for profits in the loan divisions. Prudent organizational practice calls for this system to report to an individual other than the chief lending officer, to have its reports considered by a committee of senior officers, and to have direct access to a committee of the board, when necessary. A strong capability in this system is demanded both by the changes and pressures on the traditional quality-control systems that have been discussed, and by the nature of the extremely sophisticated and specialized loan products that many banks now offer.

The independent loan review system, however, cannot and should not examine on an individual basis all portfolio risks. An appropriate minimum size should be established to (1) permit a greater focus on those situations that individually reflect a significant exposure relative to the size of the bank and (2) leave resources available for another most important review system task—that of monitoring portfolio trends with respect to exposure by type of loan, country, industry, location, and so on. Normally, some credit quality rating method will be utilized to facilitate quality and concentration analysis across the portfolio.

Finally, we should note the distinction between loan review and loan workout. The loan review system acts to scan the portfolio and identify deviations from standard expectations; loan workout assumes responsibility once a problem has been identified and its seriousness characterized.

Directors must reexamine their approach to monitoring asset

quality. Traditionally, executive committees have shouldered the responsibility of considering and approving or ratifying individual—albeit large—risks, without much time left over for attention to the condition of these systems within the bank. The lesson to be learned from the recent loan losses suffered by several large banks is that directors need to keep informed about quality control systems, as well as individual credits.

Today's lending environment has these characteristics:

- High volumes of activity, consisting of complex undertakings and subject to heavy competition and time pressures.
- Risk acceptance processing points that are geographically disbursed or organizationally separated.
- Staffs that are subject to rapid transfer and high turnover and with a lower experience level than was the case in the past.
- Supervision by managers whose careers depend primarily on profit center performance.

In this environment, the first questions for senior managers and directors to ask are, "Is the design of our asset quality control systems adequate for the risk on the books?" and "Are the systems in place actually functioning according to their design specifications?" After that, questions concerning individual risks are in order. Another lesson from recent experience is that quality control systems may, in fact, be overridden when a consensus develops within an organization that other strategic goals have higher importance.

Expense Control

A clear responsibility of any management is to control expenses and to establish prices for services and products in order to maximize profit for the shareholders. No business can be operated professionally without accounting records and a knowledge of costs.

One insidious effect of the protected and stable nature of profits prior to deregulation was a lack of attention to the intricacies of budgeting and cost control in almost all financial intermediaries. In comparison with the manufacturing sector, for example, the general level of management sophistication lagged by at least a full generation. Particularly in the thrift industry, the interest rate differential enjoyed largely obviated the need for a sophisticated cost accounting system for funds gathering, funds application, and customer service fees. Indeed, deposits were so profitable that this industry spent vast sums on branches and, in some instances, on gifts and premiums in order to attract deposits to these locations. When all these costs were considered together, even rough approximations showed that the resulting business was well worth the expense.

Moreover, those pricing and costing systems that did exist in banking usually measured profitability in the aggregate instead of analyzing specific accounts or products. Today, management in all financial intermediaries must know exact costs by products on both sides of the balance sheet, and also be positioned by reporting systems to measure actual aggregate income and expense experience against expectations.

Cost Accounting

The objective of a cost accounting system is to allocate all components of income and expense according to a logical plan so that the profit or loss for a product, department, division, or other profit center may be accurately determined. Within this objective is a need to maintain a level of system simplicity consistent with the need for adequate decision-making information.

The goal of simplicity in the design of bank cost accounting systems confronts the reality of the large number of individual products and services to be considered with respect to the analysis of direct costs, and a further requirement to rationally allocate major amounts of indirect cost. The system designer must not become overly fascinated with the design challenge but maintain a focus on the need for compatibility with the accounting system and the need for significant information.

Banks can no longer afford to introduce new services without knowing costs and their sensitivity to volume and interest rates. Cost accounting information in terms of acceptable approximations (coupled with detailed business plans) sufficient for new undertakings is relatively easy to develop. There is sufficient general cost information available from the Federal Reserve, U.S. League of Savings Institutions, Mortgage Bankers Association, public accounting firms, and the like so that the potential profitability of a proposed service or product can be identified and priced accordingly.

Budgets and Forecasts

The basic financial planning tool of many banks is an operating budget constructed for the year ahead. The budgeting process normally begins during the third quarter of the year and is often an extension of current trends into the future. The key elements to be considered in construction of the budget are anticipated (or desired) loan and deposit levels, interest income and expense, fee income, and the extent to which those items impact operations and personnel staff who must be geared to provide adequate support service.

The well-developed budget should be supported by specific programs designed to achieve the anticipated results. When it is accepted by management and the board, the budget becomes a tool for monitoring results and appraising the quality of management. Directors should be wary of accepting the recommendation of a budget that is simply an extension of the past and unsupported by programs to make this arithmetic statement of short-term plans actually occur.

Forecasting is separate from budgeting in the sense that it should reach out further in time and should be based on other than short-term internal expectations. The process of forecasting for longer-range plans should take place at a different time from the budgeting cycle. If the processes overlap, there is the possibility that forecasting will degrade into an effort simply to extend the arithmetic of the budget to a more distant terminal date. In giving effect to both internal and external factors, forecasting should encourage managers to ask, "what if" kinds of questions in other than arithmetic terms so that goals can be adjusted, set, or reinforced and then followed up by their financial implications. Forecasting for various elements of the bank may well be the basis for withdrawing from some activities while at the same time building up others. Forecasts by their very nature are subject to change, whereas a budget is less so, barring radical changes in the bank's environment.

Planning and Strategy

Successful financial businesses will conduct planning in a way not often seen within the industry in the past. All too often, sophisticated or detailed budgeting has been allowed to pass for planning. Budgeting is important; without it, no real planning can be implemented. But strategic planning will precede budgeting.

Planning is critical since few financial organizations can do everything well or profitably. Choices have to be made. Banks with $500 million in assets now have to make the hard decisions they avoided in the past by doing everything banks were allowed to do. With banks allowed to do more, and other institutions allowed to do what banks have been doing, letting the regulatory process guide the way won't be enough. Each institution will have to find its own way.

Successful planning is the CEO's job and cannot be delegated. Good planning may well mean survival itself; execution of a well thought-out plan will make the difference. Only the CEO can orchestrate effectively to bring the strategy through to successful implementation. Furthermore, the CEO and board must agree— "Here is where we are going, and this is how we are going to get there."

In our experience, the strategic planning process always contains three key steps or phases. While the planning focus, methodology, or task organization may well differ among institutions, the basic approach remains the same. The three phases are:

1. *Diagnostic*. Who are we; where are we? What are our strengths and weaknesses? What definition of the future do we want?
2. *Analytical*. What strategic options do we identify that will permit us to change from the condition we now own to the condition we aspire to own? How do we establish the cost/benefit implications of the identified options? How do we prioritize available options for decision making?
3. *Decision and Documentation*. How do we select those options that appear to be most suitable for us? How do we document these decisions in a form useful for implementation?

We have observed four almost universal weaknesses in the manner in which the planning process is actually managed. First, there is a general tendency for planners to slack off once the "mission statement" has been completed. We suggest that creating a fairly broad definition of the world you want is the easy part of the process; actually getting there is much more difficult. Second, there is a general tendency to believe that the "Planning Book" should equate with the Internal Revenue Code in size, detail, and complexity. It should be a reference tool—easy to use and understand.

A third weakness is that most plans and planners think in terms of five years. However, many strategic thrusts that improve shareholders' wealth in a significant fashion require thinking about the future and how to gain profitable competitive advantages as many as 20 years in advance. Examples of financial institutions that have looked far into the future in developing their strategic thrusts include State Street Bank, Bank of New England, Bankers Trust, and Morgan Guaranty of New York.

The fourth weakness we have identified is a general tendency to find fault in the plan when actual performance deviates from it. Certainly plans can be ill-conceived, but there is also a need within the industry to enforce standards of accountability rather than change the rules of the game.

We also urge most strongly that the strategic planning process include full attention to the "soft" issues that do not readily lend themselves to the quantitative methods so favored in this age of computer-based models. Soft issues include such factors as the following:

- *Human Resources*. We have a fit of numbers of people to our needs; do we also have appropriate experience and sophistication?
- *Capital*. We know the levels at which our capital needs are projected; can we also identify the potential suppliers?
- *Successors*. We know the run-off of our staff by retirement date; how realistic is our successor identification and training program?
- *Technology*. How do we propose to maintain an adequate understanding of the implications that technology may have on our plans?

It is a truism of management that any planning exercise is relatively easy compared with the task of implementing the plan. Directors should never equate their approval of a strategic plan with institutional accomplishment. The approval of a plan is merely the beginning of an exercise in which the goal is to realize change for predetermined reasons.

Plan implementation demands the following basic administrative skills, which are implied in the term "management-by-objective":

- Division of the total project into manageable, coherent tasks.
- Assignment and acceptance of individual task performance responsibility.
- Agreement on progress review dates and the level of accomplishment at each.
- Progress report meetings to monitor task performance.
- Consideration of adjustments based on valid, interim period information.
- Detailed comparison of final actual results against the original plan.

Directors should also be familiar with some of the more common strategies that exist, among them the following:

Asset Redeployment. Business segment managers within any organization suffer from tunnel vision; in banking they work mightily to maximize growth and return on that particular segment of the asset base for which they have responsibility. Understandably, they regard a decision to redeploy some of their assets into another area as a message of personal failure.

Successful institutions today do not automatically reinvest asset run-off in the same asset type. Instead, they seek to place available funds in those opportunities that are judged most attractive. Senior managers and directors must, however, have information about asset run-off by segment and redeployment opportunities ranked by attractiveness if they are to orchestrate a strategic program of asset management.

Expense Redeployment. Banking has such a large component of fixed expense that the industry has come reluctantly to the concept of expense redeployment. Successful institutions, however, will be committed to the strategy of spending in those activity areas that generate greater revenues in order to get back more value from the expenditure.

Space can be sublet; branches can be closed; equipment can be sold or leased; staff levels can be reduced by attrition or termination. At budget preparation time, these institutions do not automatically reinvest in the same activities each year (and then add discretionary efforts to this base, if conditions permit). Instead, they seek every opportunity to redirect expenses into those areas that return more.

BUSINESS SEGMENT NAME _____ DATE _____

RESPONSIBLE OFFICER/KEY MANAGERS _____

ACTIVITIES DESCRIPTION AND PURPOSE _____

KEY PRODUCTS OFFERED _____

LINKAGE TO MARKET SEGMENT STRATEGIES _____

EXPENDITURES AND PERSONNEL

	Actual	*Plan*

- **Head Count**
    - Front Office Delivery
    - Back Office Delivery

    Subtotal
    - Marketing
    - Finance & Administration
    - Communications
    - Computer

    TOTAL

- **Capital Invested**

FINANCIAL DATA

Interest Income
Fees and Service Charges
Revenue

Net Income
Net Cash Flow

Spread
ROA
ROE

DESCRIPTION OF RISKS AND THEIR IMPACT ON FINANCIALS

- **Strategies Current/Future**

- **Milestones/Measurement**

Type	*Objective Date*	*Significance If Not Met*

- **Effect on Other Profit Centers**

- **Effect on Bank Performance**

Figure 6–1 Business Segment Risks and Trend Analysis

Strength Redeployment. Every institution has one or more activities in which it has differentiated performance strength. With respect to certain products or capabilities, it supplies "added value" in the delivery of its services. Customer recognition of such "added value" can place the institution in a favorable pricing position. Recognition of such strengths offers the bank an opportunity to refocus its strategic thrusts in order to realize maximum value for its strengths.

Directors may also wish to have a system for tracking on a regular basis the circumstances of business units with important strategic responsibilities. Figure 6–1 illustrates a simple form suitable for such purposes.

Performance Comparisons

A successful financial institution has a large appetite for information about the results of its direct competitors and general peers. It is interested in measuring its own current performance against these standards, as well as its own past. It will seek out the causes behind identified differences, examine them in an organized objective manner, and consider such strategic adjustment as may be indicated.

Among the informational sources readily available for such comparisons are annual releases such as:

- The BAI Index of Bank Performance
- The Comptroller's Peer Group data series
- The Functional Cost Studies of the Federal Reserve
- Bank call report ratios in the FDIC "bank statistics" publication

Also available are more focused series, including:

- The Retail Credit report of the ABA
- The Loan Loss Experience Report of the Robert Morris Associates
- The Mortgage Bankers Association Annual Reports

Additionally, a number of suppliers stand ready at a relatively small cost to deliver precisely focused data on such subjects as market shares by products for the inquirer versus selected competitors.

Directors should become familiar with the standard performance valuation ratios that the industry uses for self-analysis. Among these are some that are unique to the banking industry and may not have been previously encountered:

- Demand deposits and time deposits, as a percentage of average assets: monitors the composition of the available funding base.
- Ratio of primary capital to average assets: the key institutional risk ratio in the eyes of the regulators.
- Ratio of earnings (after tax) to average assets—that is, return on average assets (ROA): the primary industry ratio for measuring the ability of management to translate assets into earnings and capital.
- Ratio of net interest margin to average assets: the "spread" ratio showing the return available from risk acceptance.
- Ratio of noninterest expense to average assets: the indicator of operational efficiency.

Directors should also understand the construction of the basic equation that determines profits. The simple logic of this equation may be summarized as follows:

	Interest Earnings
Less:	Interest Expense
Equals:	Net Interest Margin
Plus:	Other Earnings (fees)
Less:	Noninterest Operating Expense
Less:	Loan Losses
Equals:	Operating Earnings

When the four key elements of margin, operating expense, losses, and other earnings are thus highlighted, obvious opportunities for modeling operating earnings are created. An overlooked aspect of performance comparison is that of capital costs. Every institution must consider its ability to obtain capital on a basis comparable to that of its peers and competitors.

Managers become too preoccupied with the immediate bottom line and neglect to turn on themselves the spotlight of investment community perceptions of their results. Here, we move to the world of dividends and P/E ratios, and total return concepts with which directors are more generally familiar from their activities as personal investors. However, many bank directors do not have business experience with public companies and the issues of establishing marketplace value. Most banks do not have an "investor relations" function; nor do most banks consider formal programs to market themselves to the investment community as necessary.

The reality is that bank stocks are no longer directly owned by "widows and orphans." In fact, individual investors are of secondary importance in the capital markets. Institutional trading now accounts for more than 70 percent of public trading on the New York Stock Exchange and is assured of continued growth in all markets. Banking must recognize the special characteristics of those who will determine its access to capital in the future.

Information is the lifeblood of the network of broker-analysts, institutional analysts, and portfolio managers who influence and determine the investment actions of institutions. The information this network gathers is used to gain the differentiated investment performance results on which these information seekers' own professional careers depend. Successful banks will develop investor relations programs that will produce credibility, visibility, and a following in institutions relevant to their own position and long-term expectations in the capital markets.

Conclusion

It is broadly recognized that deregulation has changed the banking industry. Less discussed is an inevitable by-product of this change—that is, deregulation has also changed the job of a bank director. No longer is the position a form of community service, vested with a responsibility for custodial concern over the cycling of community financial assets in a wise and prudent manner. Nor is it just a position with visibility, honorary connotations, and business development overtones for the institution. These aspects all remain in place, of course, but with deregulation a new responsibility surfaces to ensure the long-term corporate survival of the business: to maintain competitive viability. A banking franchise is no longer granted for perpetuity.

To the traditional terminal threats of loan losses and fraud have been added the more usual business risks in marketing, operational efficiency in service delivery, technological obsolescence, and maintenance of adequate capital. The special industry risk of interest rate misalignment has become critical.

This is a period when pools of money can be quickly moved into a distressed, weak, or underperforming bank perceived as a capital appreciation opportunity from such seemingly remote places as Jeddah and Tokyo, regional centers such as Atlanta or Houston, or a next-state competitor. Directors must now exercise their community-related responsibilities by seeing that the management in place is adequate for the demands of this new world.

In this respect, the selection of a successor to the office of CEO is the single most important responsibility the directors face. While this is normally an infrequent task, it can be a most difficult one for a homogeneous group centered in a community. Banking institutions usually move into position as heir-apparent one who has been successful in meeting the challenges presented over time. The process is gradual and on a somewhat automatic basis. Competition is not broad and expectations grow.

Deregulation, however, presents the likelihood that new criteria should be established for the selection process. Personal success in a regulated environment may not be a valid indicator of success potential in a deregulated environment. Appropriate selection criteria may come from a different base. Quite simply, directors must ask: "Is this officer capable of leading this organization to our defined vision for the future of this institution? Do we have the best candidate for the assignment?" Successful banking leadership in the future will not be achieved by those who are clones of the leadership of the past.

Chapter 7

LEGAL CONCERNS
OF THE BOARD

by Blair C. Shick

Introduction: Banking, Regulation, and Change

On assuming the responsibility as a bank director, the experienced business person is apt to be struck by the profound dependence of the institution on law and regulation. All of us have perhaps learned to accept the fact that governmental controls constrain most forms of modern economic enterprise to one degree or another. There is, however, no industry quite like banking where law and regulations so pervasively dictate what can and can't be done, and how. A unique characteristic is that individual banking institutions are regulated along with their branch distribution system and many of the financial products and services they make available to the public.

At the heart of this regulatory complexity is the rarely defined notion that banking is quasi-governmental in function. In a capital-istic system, those institutions that play the primary role in allocating capital among competing interests bear a heavy public responsibility. Thus, banking is viewed as a profession, not just another business, and a great deal of the regulations that shape banking have the objective of assuring that banking services are rendered with the degree of professionalism commensurate with public expectations.

Bank Chartering

The notion that banking is clothed in the public interest is symbolized and perpetuated in the governmental chartering mechanism. It is easy to form a corporate organization to conduct most businesses; obtaining a corporate charter is a perfunctory exercise. This is not true in banking, where obtaining the business charter can be a rigorous exercise. Certain threshold legal requirements must be met. The key owners and officers involved will be closely examined. In many states, a demonstration must be made that a new financial intermediary is supported by the "public convenience."

Although the requirements vary among the states, and between the states and the federal government, bank chartering standards share a common central purpose. Regulators want to assure the public that the organization coming into existence—the new bank—is owned and controlled by people who know and understand the business and its public responsibilities, and is sufficiently capitalized to execute its business responsibilities. As a result, chartering authorities examine the background of the people involved and frequently require that directors have a stock ownership position as a way of assuring "at risk" involvement. It is also common that directors meet citizenship and residency requirements.

Examination and Supervision

The examination/supervisory function of bank regulatory bodies is an exercise in furtherance of the initial chartering objectives. After the institution has been legally born, the concern is that it stay on the publicly "right" track. Over the years, the notion of what is publicly "right" has been continually adjusted and refined based on experience. Large numbers of bank failures in the late 1920s and early 1930s gave rise to the Federal Deposit Insurance Corporation (FDIC) as an examination/supervisory body for state-chartered banks. The FDIC functions in addition to state authorities. That same period also saw strict federal prohibitions emerge against commercial bank involvement in investment banking, and in insurance and in other risk underwriting financial activities.

The major thrust of these regulations was to separate banking from other financial business activities, and from commerce generally, to minimize the risk of failure. This goes back to the basic concern that banking be maintained in furtherance of the public interest. Bank failures, it has been reasoned, do more than undermine the public faith in banking institutions; bank failures can send ripples of weakness that spread rapidly throughout the economy, indirectly causing or aggravating more general economic problems. Thus, banking stability has always been equated with economic and social stability. As a consequence, the bank director enjoys, and is beset with, stewardship responsibilities for constituencies that include depositors, borrowers, and the local community, along with management and stockholders.

Today's Dual Banking System

Historically, state governments had the primary, and sometimes exclusive, responsibility for chartering banking institutions. Recall, for example, the colorful events associated with early attempts to establish a national bank, culminating in the veto by President Andrew Jackson of a congressional renewal of an existing charter. The current federal chartering system was established during the Civil War, in part as a means to help finance rapidly escalating federal expenditures. To this day, the regulatory body for national banks—the Office of the Comptroller of the Currency—is part of the U.S. Treasury Department.

The federal chartering system was subsequently strengthened by the creation of the Federal Reserve System early in this century. The creation of the FDIC in 1934, together with other depression-era legislation, established the framework for the beginning of a growing federal regulatory edge over the dual banking arrangement. The growth in the nation's economic might since then has helped to catapult the nationally chartered banks into a position of dominance in the industry.

The last 20 years have been occasioned by a host of new federal statutes that reach out directly, and in many instances indirectly, to strengthen federal regulatory schemes that govern the affairs of both state-chartered and nationally chartered banks. Some of these statutes have a narrow focus—for example, consumer protection provisions such as Truth in Lending that are concerned with personal credit only. Others, such as the 1978 federal Change in

Bank Control Act, go to the heart of bank ownership and require administrative examination of the background of persons seeking to acquire control of an existing bank.

In all cases, the effect of this new federal legislation has been to add to the complexity of bank regulations. Moreover, since much of this legislation has evolved in recent years—notably the comprehensive Financial Institutions Regulatory and Interest Rate Control Act of 1978, the 1980 Depository Institutions Deregulation and Monetary Control Act, and the Garn-St. Germain Depository Institutions Act of 1982—one is apt to inquire about the possibility of additional federal regulation in the near future.

The answer seems to be yes; there probably will be more federal legislation affecting banking before long. For example, questions concerning the nature and extent of interstate banking activities that should be permitted, although hotly contested, are begging for near-term resolution. The rapid emergence and maturation of the so-called holding company "nonbank bank" loophole in 1983–84 and the enactment by a growing number of states of legislation authorizing regional interstate banking suggest the need for comprehensive revisions of the existing federal structure. In addition, there are continuing issues concerning bank holding company involvement in a large array of nonbank-related financial services.

As a result, it seems clear that we are bound to continue to experience increasing centralization of regulation of the American banking system, with "the Fed" (the Board of Governors of the Federal Reserve System) emerging as the primary regulator for both state- and nationally chartered institutions. This tends to spell the possible demise, over time, of the role of state regulatory bodies. A very recent example makes the point quite clear. Early 1985 publicity over the stability of a state-sanctioned insurance program for Ohio-chartered thrifts has led to the rapid movement of thrifts in yet four other states with nonfederal insurance programs to the federal insurance schemes.

The Need to Keep Informed

The already heavily regulatory content of the business of banking seems bound to become increasingly complex, subject to change, and more centralized. This places a burden on the bank director that differs substantially from that of other business boards. As the regulatory environment continues to change, directors nationwide will play a key role in determining the restructuring of the financial services industry that will eventually result.

Bank directors bear the same general corporate responsibilities for their bank as those of the directors of the more general corporate entity. Considerations of profitability and long-run stability are essential. At the same time, bank directors have additional legal responsibilities that are unique to banking. Nothing can be more important than the basic need to be kept fully informed of the changes that are taking place to be sure management is in full compliance with new requirements. Further, since new requirements present business opportunities as well as constraints, there is the additional need to assure that the institution is being steered in a direction that maximizes future potential.

Importance of Legal Counsel

The above introductory material is intended to apprise the bank director, particularly the new director, of the importance and value of the role of legal counsel to the proper exercise of board responsibilities. Counsel should be present at *all* board meetings and at many board committee meetings. In addition, any director should be able to consult freely with counsel at any time concerning the affairs of the bank.

Very often successful practicing lawyers sit as bank directors. However, bank regulation is so specialized that highly accomplished lawyers may still lack the necessary regulatory knowledge and insight needed by the board. There is, therefore, a need to differentiate between bank counsel and lawyers generally.

There are considerable differences in opinion in banking circles concerning the advisability of a bank's legal counsel occupying a directorship. If the bank is large enough to maintain a full-time legal staff, the officer designated general counsel may in practice be the board's primary source of legal advice. Many bankers believe that general counsel should not serve on the board directly in order to preserve the objectivity of his or her advice. Others feel that legal input is so important to banking that it is relevant both in advice and decision making—thus justifying board membership.

The same arguments and counterarguments are made with respect to outside lawyers who serve as general counsel. There is no hard and fast rule to govern decisions of this kind. More often than not the maturity and sophistication of the individual will be the deciding factor. In addition, many small institutions find it extremely convenient to involve counsel on the board.

Legal Responsibility of Bank Directors

An initial concern of the director might be his or her own exposure to personal liability for activities of the bank. Given the litigiousness of modern society and the extent to which minority shareholders, individual borrowers, depositors, and various community groups vociferously contest bank decisions, this is no small matter today. The importance that modern media journalists place on the behavior of financial institutions serves to exacerbate the problem.

The historical answer to questions concerning the basic legal responsibility of bank directors is easy to formulate. Initially, it is not that different from the responsibility of other corporate directors: *Directors are obligated to behave as prudent and reasonable persons*. This means that responsible supervision is expected over the institution's basic affairs. Due care should be exercised in the choice of management (principally the chief executive officer and the CEO's key officer nominations) and in the supervision of subsequent activities. Serious attention should also be paid to the reports and suggestions of regulatory examiners and independent auditors, and to the broader issues of the institution's overall legal compliance.

Personal Oaths

As a general rule, banking requirements dictate that directors take an oath that they will diligently direct the bank's affairs in accordance with applicable laws and regulations. Frequently, directors are also required to swear that they will not knowingly permit violations of state and federal laws.

Mandatory oaths of this kind are sometimes perceived as anachronistic, relevant only as a symbolic gesture to the public importance of banking. This perception is inaccurate. Directors have been held personally liable to shareholders and other persons—for example, customers or creditors of customers—in instances involving violations of statutory requirements.

Personal Liability

A basic characteristic of our legal system is that personal liability arises from the violation of a duty owed to another. The liability is for damages caused by the violation but only exists if the person damaged was one intended to be protected by the duty in question. In the context of banking, these duties are found in the various state and federal statutes directly concerned with banking. But, they may also be found in the more general case law and in securities, antitrust, and other legislative provisions, both state and federal. Again, this is the complexity of the regulation that is uniquely associated with banking. It evolves from various legal starting points and moves in many different directions. The result is a considerable number of legal standards with which directors are expected to comply. Further, the law generally presumes that directors know of these rules; ignorance of the legal obligations of the institution is not a defense. It should be noted, however, that personal liability is neither absolute nor arbitrary. Since a degree of willfulness or intentional violation is generally required before liability may be imposed, the alert and conscientious director has little to fear. As a practical matter, personal liability of bank directors is rarely encountered. Senior management inevitably knows the legal standards under which it is required to operate, and the techniques of the regulatory examination teams are calculated to disclose infractions and to bring them to the attention of the board directly. However, the potential for personal liability should underscore the needs of directors to be kept informed of the various laws and regulations and to take seriously the responsibility that the institution be operated in full compliance thereof.

General Requirements

In the search for guidance concerning legal responsibilities, the bank director should begin with the notion that the obligations are the same as those of any corporate director. Banking requirements impose additional responsibilities and do not detract from the more general corporate obligations of the director. The latter are inevitably phrased in broad legal terms, but nevertheless they provide an appropriate starting point for appreciating the expectations of the position.

As stated earlier, the basic obligation of a bank director is to behave as a prudent and reasonable person. The standard of conduct expected is one of ordinary care. Directors are not expected to be legally responsible for the day-to-day business of the bank. Nor are they expected to be responsible for *all* conduct of the executive officers. Losses can and will occur under the best of circumstances, and the exercise of even bad judgment is not a legal violation if, in fact, ordinary care has been exercised.

This standard of ordinary care is impossible to define precisely. It is usually phrased in terms of the same degree of care that prudent and diligent persons would have exercised under similar circumstances. Thus, the specific circumstances will always loom large in any court review of director conduct. This means that the facts that were known at the time will be highly determinative. Failing or refusing to act when confronted with knowledge that others would perceive as demanding action is perhaps a more frequently encountered infraction of duty than taking a wrong course of action.

Although directors are not expected to supervise everyday business activities, they should know the basics of the banking business. The outside director, in particular, should become familiar with capital requirements, lending limits, other loan controls, and the collateral basis of the more significant loans. In addition, the outside director should be able to evaluate and stay on top of the bank's financial status. Bank regulators and independent auditors routinely perform examinations that are calculated to alert board members to existing or potential problems. But this does not relieve directors of the responsibility to be alert to the need to conduct their own examinations and retain their own auditors, legal counsel, and so forth. In short, the onus is on the directors to secure the necessary protections for themselves and their institution.

Importance of Good Faith Loyalty

Loyalty to the institution is an important element of the director's basic legal obligation. Modern legal literature usually casts loyalty in the broader context of good faith. As a result, the maintenance of sound business and personal ethics lies at the heart of the director's obligation.

This means that the director should not be involved in interests that are competitive with or antithetical to those of the bank, should disclose all potential conflicts of interest, and, like Caesar's wife, should take care to avoid any personal or business dealings that lend the appearance of self-interest. Given the current public concern with financial institution governance, a good rule of thumb might be to avoid any involvement that would prove embarrassing to the bank if it appeared on the front page of the local newspaper.

Recent legislative proscriptions concerning loans and other business dealings with the bank are discussed next. However, it is important to note here that compliance with these new standards is often less than full compliance with the good faith loyalty requirement. Although it is difficult to articulate precisely, the good faith standard requires considerably more in personal ethical behavior than the bare statutory minimums. In a nutshell, while it is expected that the director be in a position to bring business to the bank, it is not acceptable that the bank be manipulated to bring business advantages to the director.

Some Specific Banking Requirements

Although the legal requirements for a bank are legion, it is perhaps worthwhile to point out a few of the more salient features of regulation that have given rise to director liability in the past. Loan limitations are a critical area. Federal law requires that the total obligations (loans and extensions of credit) of a single borrower may not exceed 10 percent of the amount of the bank's unimpaired capital surplus if the obligations are fully secured by collateral having an equivalent market value. The permitted amount rises to 15 percent if not fully secured. Losses sustained by loans exceeding these limits can end up as the personal responsibility of the directors. This requires close attention both to the regulatory definitions of capital and surplus. It also dictates that both board and management pay close attention to the need for a balanced portfolio, especially in times of low loan demand.

The collateral of loans is also important. As a general rule, loans cannot be secured by the shares of the bank. In addition, loans secured by other corporate shares on margin for the purchase of still other stock are subject to certain value prescriptions of the Federal Reserve. Further, real estate loans frequently must meet loan/value ratios, primacy of lien requirements, and other terms and conditions. Finally, there are a variety of limits on loans to bank officers, including those of other banks.

Federal law prohibits improper payment of dividends. They can be paid only from net profits, but not more than 10 percent of net profits can be paid out as dividends until the equivalent of the value of capital stock is equaled. The purpose of this and comparable state requirements is to alleviate shareholder pressure to pay dividends that would undermine the economic stability of the bank. Federal legislation formerly prohibited the payment of interest on all demand deposits for ostensibly this same purpose. This law was partially repealed with the authorization in 1980 of NOW accounts nationwide and the automatic transfer of savings deposits to checking. Until a scheduled phase-out in 1986, most depository institutions remain limited on the amounts they can legally pay on NOW accounts and regular savings.

An interesting prohibition in the federal law limits the amount of investment a bank may make in real estate used for its own business purposes. Any related indebtedness may not exceed the bank's capital stock outstanding. This may seem an anachronistic requirement in the context of the modern emphasis on productivity and profitability. It is in part intended to suppress any "edifice complex" of bank officers and directors, but, in fact, was violated on more than one occasion in the expansionist era of the late sixties and early seventies. The broader concern is to prevent banks from venturing too far into the field of real estate speculation.

The limits on loans, interest, dividends, and investments are described here to give the bank director a flavor of the kind of requirements commonly encountered in bank regulation. There are many more—for example, limits on the use of the name and certain words like "national" or "trust," on the maintenance of security devices and procedures, on premiums advertised or given for new deposits, and on disclosures to shareholders. The important point is that the legal limitations are many and varied. Some are obvious and easy to grasp, but many are obscure. It is the responsibility of both the board and management to keep abreast of these legal limitations and any new requirements and to keep the bank in full compliance.

Loan and Investment Policies

In the business policy direction of a bank, two major supervisory areas stand out as requiring special attention of the board. The first lies in the area of loans and investments; the second is in the maintenance of sound audit procedures.

Investment policy, in terms of the board's responsibility to the institution and its owners and other constituencies, means considerably more than steering a course intended to avoid running afoul of the strict legal prohibitions in investments. In this respect, the bank director's responsibility is not dissimilar from that of any corporate director. Being barely legal—in the narrow sense of statutory compliance only—can, in fact and in law, amount to being illegal in the broader sense of the fundamental responsibility to maintain the institution in an orderly course of stability and profitability.

This concept is not as tricky as it sounds. Since loans and other investments are the basic revenue generators of most banks, loan/investment policy is tantamount to sound business policy. As a result, while the board is not necessarily legally responsible for any particular loan or investment that eventually proves sour, it is clearly accountable for a policy that pursues kinds of loans that could threaten the solvency or the stability of the institution. This situation may be manifested in a disproportionate amount of the bank's portfolio being in a single industry, known to be negatively affected by business cycles, or having an undue tie to a group of related borrowers. To deal with this responsibility, most bank boards maintain a loan or investment committee that checks for statutory compliance with respect to specific loans. More important, the committee serves as a check on management's approach to loans and investments in general and as a vehicle for affirmative policy direction concerning portfolio management overall.

Audit and Other Special Supervisory Procedures

Audit procedures can and should be viewed as being closely related to loan/investment supervision. In both instances, the board is attempting to employ specialized analytical procedures to gain a critical view of internal aspects of the bank's operation. Although they move in different directions, each is vitally important to the overall economic health of the institution.

Most banks employ a person who is assigned the title of auditor. And many banks, particularly the large institutions, regularly employ the services of independent auditors. In both cases, the board's responsibility is to assure that sound auditing procedures are being routinely maintained and that auditors' reports are being taken seriously and acted on constructively.

In larger banks, audit committees are an important component of the board. In fact, an independent auditing firm may be retained by and directly report to the committee. This may not be realistic for smaller institutions. But, it does suggest the need for initiative and affirmative action on the part of the board to project itself as a positive force for review and guidance of internal operating rules and procedures.

Protection from Liability: Insurance and Indemnification

The best protection from legal liability, of course, is the director's own conscientiousness in the exercise of his or her responsibilities. However, this is not optimal protection, since there will always be marginal and spurious claims that will be expensive to defend against. Indeed, considering the rarity of final judgments against bank directors, the most important need is for coverage of the costs of defending and settling such claims.

Adequate protection for the director is available through insurance coverage procured and paid for by the bank. Due to the peculiarities of bank regulation, there are two types of insurance coverage available. Today's directors need and should insist on both.

The first kind of insurance is known as company reimbursement liability insurance. It covers the losses for which banks or holding companies are allowed by statute to indemnify their directors. In general, indemnification is allowed where the director has acted in good faith and in the interest of the bank. In some states, it may not be allowed if the director is found to have acted negligently or in violation of an administrative action.

The second kind of insurance is the more commonly encountered directors and officers (D&O) liability insurance. This is the broader of the two and covers losses ordinarily not covered by indemnification (company reimbursement liability). D&O liability insurance includes liability for breach of the duty of good faith and for negligence.

The two types of coverage are complementary and typically written by the same insurance carrier. Usually a "deductible" approach is taken, with the bank bearing the same percent of the loss. Due to some rather large liability situations in recent years, the approach of the insurance industry to coverages of this kind is rapidly changing. Larger institutions are finding it necessary to engage two or more carriers, the premium is rapidly growing, and deductibles are becoming the subject of intense negotiation.

Directors' liability is a very delicate area of the law that is in a state of considerable flux. The bank director should make this a priority area for obtaining very specific legal advice. Policy coverage should be carefully reviewed on an annual basis since the tendency of the insurance industry is to move to single-year coverages.

Personal Relationships with the Bank and Other Financial Institutions

The relationship of "insiders" to the bank has come under increasing regulatory attention in the last few years. This is a concept borrowed from securities regulation but made infamous for banks not too long ago with the notoriety associated with alleged noninterest-bearing overdraft loans of a key federal official. The public perception was that bank officials were receiving special personal advantages—usually of a financial nature—from their position with a publicly chartered institution, potentially endangering the stability of that institution. The resulting outcry gave rise to legal prohibitions that are not surprising. In fact, banking and legal attitudes against such abuses have existed for a long time. What is new is the detail of the prohibitions, many of which were enacted in the 1978 federal Financial Institutions Regulatory and Interest Rate Control Act.

Loans

Directors are prohibited from receiving preferential loans. While this prohibition obviously applies to lower-than-market rates, it also prevents other preferential terms. The test is that the bank not be subjected to a lower risk of repayment than for any other loan. The notion here is that directors should deal, if at all, with the bank on the same basis as any other borrower.

It matters little if the director is also a substantial stockholder. In fact, a workable rule-of-thumb might be that the greater the involvement of a director—in terms of stock ownership, being an officer of the bank, etc.—the more likely it is that any business relationship with the bank will be closely examined by the regulators. The same is true of outside corporate arrangements in which the director also plays a major role. For example, a bank director who is an officer, director, and shareholder of a nonbanking company can expect the closest of scrutiny of the company's business relationships with the bank.

The new federal law requires that all loans in excess of $25,000 to directors individually, to their controlled companies, or to political campaign committees must be approved in advance by a majority of the entire board. Included are advance lines of credit, provided the draws against the line are made within 14 months of the approval. Finally, the 1978 law limits any loans made to shareholder directors who own, control, or have the power to vote more than 10 percent of any class of voting securities to less than 10 percent of the institution's capital and surplus. This prohibition does not apply to a director who is neither a 10 percent shareholder nor an executive officer.

Overdrafts

Overdraft privileges on demand accounts are generally prohibited for directors and executive officers since this is an obvious form of preferential loan that is easily subject to abuse. The prohibition excludes overdraft situations handled pursuant to prearranged automatic transfers from other deposit balances or from interest-bearing extensions of credit. In addition, the federal agencies have issued regulations exempting inadvertent overdrafts in the amounts of $1,000 or less if they are paid within five business days and a fee is charged that is the same for other customers.

Disclosure of Insider Loans

Under the 1978 federal law, a bank must submit annual reports naming all executive officers and stockholders who own, control, or vote more than 10 percent of any class of voting securities. The report must also show any outstanding loans to each such person and any company or political or campaign committee individually controlled. Directors who are not executive officers or 10 percent stockholders are not included. The reports give the regulatory agencies the basic information to ensure legal compliance with the preferential loan/overdraft prohibitions and limitations. This regulation is significant, since the penalty for violation can go as high as

$1,000 per day and can be assessed personally against directors, officers, and others who participated in the violation. Finally, it should be noted that the reports made by the bank are not protected from the Freedom of Information Act and should be assumed to be available to a requesting member of the public.

Interlocking Directorates

Another major thrust of the 1978 federal Financial Institutions Regulatory and Interest Rate Control Act is to place substantial restrictions on interlocking management among potentially competing depository institutions. The legal restrictions on "management officials" specifically include directors—even nominal honorary or advisory directors. Thus, it is a matter of concern for directors personally as well as in their broader responsibility of policing the behavior of officers and management.

The law includes a general restriction, a special rule for large institutions, and a narrow exception for smaller ones. In general, a management official of a depository institution (or holding company) is prohibited from serving as a management official of any unaffiliated depository institution if both institutions (or their affiliates) have offices within the same standard metropolitan statistical area or within the same contiguous or adjacent city, town, or village. In the case of a depository institution (or holding company) with assets exceeding $1 billion, a management official is prohibited from serving as a management official of any other unaffiliated depository institution with assets in excess of $500 million. There are no geographic limitations to this prohibition. Finally, in the case of depository institutions with less than $20 million in assets, the prohibition only applies if the two institutions each have a branch or office in the same, contiguous or adjacent city, town, or village. The effect of this concession to smaller institutions is to allow minor degrees of management interlock within standard metropolitan statistical areas.

Depository institutions are defined by the 1978 act to include savings banks, trust companies, savings and loan associations (including building and loan and homestead associations), cooperative banks, industrial banks, and even credit unions, along with commercial banks. Thus the act, recognizing the market reality that the historical distinctions between different kinds of depository institutions are rapidly breaking down, created these rather strict prohibitions against management interlocks in the interest of maximizing opportunities for competition.

There are several very limited exceptions to these basic prohibitions against interlocks. For example, interlocks are permitted among subsidiaries of the same holding company and between the company and its subsidiaries. In addition, the prohibitions do not apply in chain banking situations in which the same individual or group of individuals hold 50 percent or more of the stock of each of the institutions, since an automatic interlock is already in place by virtue of the common stockholder control. Further, narrow exceptions exist when one of the institutions is a special-purpose, limited-operation-type of bank or trust company. Finally, there are grandfather provisions for interlocks in effect in 1978, which may continue up to ten years, and for changes in ownership patterns through mergers and other voluntary arrangements wherein the regulatory agency may allow a transition period for as long as 15 months.

Relationships with Correspondent Banks

Still another part of the 1978 federal law that applies to bank directors is a prohibition of preferential loans to an executive officer, director, or 10 percent shareholder of another (usually smaller) bank that maintains a correspondent relationship with the first bank. This restriction is intended to deal with situations in which larger banks made loans to key persons in a position to influence another bank's decision to keep funds on deposit or purchase other services from the lending bank. The law does not prohibit the making of loans in circumstances such as these. But, it requires that any such loan be made on terms that are substantially similar to those prevailing for comparable transactions with other persons. Only the preferential loan is prohibited.

This prohibition extends to both the bank making the loan and to the individual persons—directors or officers—participating in the loan transaction. And, it carries a $1,000-a-day penalty that can be assessed and collected by the appropriate regulatory agency. To aid enforcement, directors and others affected by this prohibition must make written reports to their board of extensions of credit from any bank that maintains a correspondent account with their own bank. The bank, in turn, must file this information with its appropriate federal regulatory body.

Relationships with Bank Regulatory Bodies

The existence of periodic in-depth examinations lies at the heart of the unique regulatory environment that characterizes banking and distinguishes it from other industries. Bank examinations are frequently perceived with mixed biases. To some they represent unbridled governmental intervention, emblematic of a willingness to override private business judgment for the sake of the exercise of public power. To others they represent a relatively inexpensive source of independent auditing and consulting expertise. As is true in most such polarized extremes, the truth lies somewhere in between and will vary, in specific applications, usually in a matter of degree only.

As a general rule, the members of bank regulatory examination teams, both state and federal, are well trained. It can and should be assumed that they know the law, the regulations, and their responsibilities. Thus, they can be expected to identify basic problems, and their reports should be received in this light, as a resource to the board that can be constructively utilized for the benefit of the institution. But, examiners are neither auditors nor specialized consultants in matters of business judgment, and the fact of their existence is hardly a substitute for the exercise of the board's own initiative and judgment.

Procedural Issues and the Range of Enforcement Powers

Formal regulatory examinations are periodically performed on every bank. In addition, follow-up or problem-specific examinations may be scheduled to assure that alleged or identified problems are being worked on or have been resolved. Knowing in advance when examinations are to take place or preventing or delaying them until the bank has put its own house in order as preparation is not a clear right. The assumption is that a bank should always be in a state of preparedness for independent scrutiny and that any problems identified should be a priority for immediate resolution. This is just another example of the special public obligations of banking institutions.

Under the various state and federal banking statutes, examination teams (and the regulatory bodies they represent) have differing degrees of legal powers to correct any deficiencies they find and/or to require that recommended actions be taken. As a general rule, informal techniques are relied upon. Written "letters of agreement" may be sought representing an acknowledgment of actions to be taken to stop questionable or illegal practices. More formally, regulatory bodies usually have the power to issue enforceable "cease-and-desist" orders, which may be enforced by monetary civil penalties for subsequent violation. In an extreme case of egregious violations, the FDIC can deny insurance, or officers or directors of the bank can be removed or suspended by the appropriate agency.

In all instances—that is, at each level of enforcement action—the bank or the officers and directors involved have adequate legal protection from governmental abuse. The different statutes create rights during agency proceedings, including hearings, and final administrative disposition is usually the subject of independent judicial review. Further, most such actions are rarely the subject of public information releases. However, formal cease-and-desist orders and appropriate corrective actions must be disclosed under Securities and Exchange Commission (SEC) rulings applicable to banks whose securities are registered. And, recent federal Freedom of Information Act decisions have required that edited versions of administrative enforcement orders—eliminating personal and specific factual references—must be made available to the public on request.

In the last analysis, bank regulatory agencies are empowered to refer to public prosecutors evidence that examinations may have revealed on criminal behavior. But, the specific enforcement powers available to examiners and their regulatory bodies are not quite as important as the fact that a rather extensive range of powers does exist and that ample legal protections also exist to prevent any such powers from being exercised arbitrarily. With this in mind, the director should approach and deal with the examiners, their reports, and any regulatory agency actions with respect—but neither reverence nor fear.

Trends in Public Enforcement

Traditionally, most issues turned up by examiners were quietly brought to the attention of management. Informal negotiations served to define areas in need of attention, and the matter stopped there. Unless management was resistant, the board never learned of it. To this day, examiners are not given to extending accolades. Thus, superlative reports of the kind that management might bring to the board for recognition have been and continue to be nonexistent. Such is the province of independent auditors.

In recent years, however (especially at the federal level), the regulatory agencies have taken a more aggressive role. This is partially due to the rapid escalation of the number of new statutes and regulations enacted, imposing new obligations on the banking community for which equivalent managerial compliance techniques have not yet been perfected. In this respect, a "new wave" attitude has emerged among bank regulatory bodies generally, which shows a greater willingness to go directly to the board in order to achieve quicker results. This more aggressive attitude is also being expressed in a greater willingness to resort to more formalized enforcement proceedings such as cease-and-desist orders.

It may be true that this change in attitudes concerning enforcement procedures is due to a certain impatience with the slowness with which banking institutions have responded to new regulatory obligations. The new style is unquestionably more hard hitting on the inertia that is inevitably built up in labor-intensive institutions that society expects to be cautious and conservative. But, this is not necessarily undesirable for the directorate, which is charged with the ultimate responsibility of stewarding the bank in the new direction that society has carved out. It seems threatening only for the board that is reluctant to pursue its own role. The responsible director should be anxious to meet the examiners head on. In fact, the attitude should be one of constructive but competitive partnership; the board should invite the examiners' attention and response, be willing to challenge their findings and recommendations, and anxious to do them one better in resourceful compliance.

Social Responsibilities and Relationships with Other Governmental Bodies and the Community

Bank directors are usually important figures in the community the bank serves. Since the overwhelming number of banks in our country are relatively small, with a home office and two or three branches at best, the community served is also relatively small, even if located within an urban area. For this reason, directors have been able to treat comfortably the community as another major part of their banking constituency, along with management, shareholders, and depositors. The personal background and experience of individual directors serve to keep the bank on a steady course between the demands of private enterprise and community needs.

The liberalization of branching in recent years, together with the gradual extension of banking across state lines through mergers, has contributed to an expansion of the breadth of banking markets. This trend makes it difficult for the director of the modern bank to identify with the community being served. And, since all existing trends point in the direction of more expansion through the reduction of regulatory barriers, it seems as if this difficulty is bound to spread increasingly to even smaller institutions.

The expansion of banking markets is significant because the element of community is rapidly becoming an important factor in bank regulation. We are currently witnessing a trade-off in a clear shift in regulatory attitudes toward community services. When banks were restricted to single offices or limited geographic areas, the community to be served was obvious; the directors were in a far better position to regulate the direction of that service than any remote legislative or administrative body. As geographic and other barriers have gradually broken down, however, many directors understandably find themselves remote from the community, and bank regulatory and other governmental bodies have begun to substitute their own judgment on the criteria to be followed in assuring community service.

One result is that the modern bank director finds that the historic responsibilities still exist, albeit with little regulatory pressure or risk of legal liability. Thus, it is still expected that the director will become involved in civic affairs, charitable drives, neighborhood revitalization, and other high-visibility matters that generate good feeling and attention for the bank. But, at the same time, a newer and different result is emerging. The director increasingly is expected to get involved with management in the way employees are trained, treated, and promoted, in the way consumers are being served, in how the bank is responding to regulatory demands, and in decisions concerning satisfaction of the deposit and credit needs of the community.

Under the present state of the law, these new community-related obligations are legal responsibilities of the bank; they are not particularly identified as individual standards for which directors will be held personally accountable. But, they have become so important to the continuing legal viability of banking institutions that they cannot be relegated to management as just another element of compliance with a complex regulatory system. As the law and politics have changed in this area, bank directors have found that they have had to establish new committees or strengthen and expand audit and/or other supervisory functions to assure that the institution is in proper compliance with emerging requirements.

Relationships with Other Government Bodies

Perhaps the most subtle change in attitudes in the last five years can be found in the relationship of the bank to other, nonbank governmental bodies. These include local city and town legislative and executive groups, along with their state equivalents. This point was dramatically illustrated by the publicity in the late winter and early spring of 1985 over the noncompliance of several major banks with the currency reporting laws. The responses of the bank regulatory bodies were in many respects of secondary importance. Many legislative and other political bodies—at the local, state, and federal levels—demonstrated strong concerns. In at least one instance, executive bodies of both the state and its major city threatened to remove all governmental deposits from the banks involved.

Circumstances such as these should be viewed in the larger context of the change that characterizes today's financial services industry. The financial media and the general press report stories of change on an almost daily basis. But it is the bad news that seems to get the lion's share of attention. Thus, the public and its representative bodies tend to remember the stories about the branches that are getting closed in marginal neighborhoods or the thrifts that were forced to close recently in Ohio and in Maryland.

It is probably true that the banking industry is one of the more convenient whipping posts for a sensationalist press. But it is equally true that banking leaders cannot ignore this fact. More than good public relations is at stake. Today's bank director should maintain effective linkages with the surrounding political bodies that govern the various aspects of the community being served.

This will help to protect the institutions against unnecessary adverse publicity in the event of problems that attract public attention.

Community Reinvestment

Perhaps the most far reaching of the socially oriented measures enacted in recent years is the federal Community Reinvestment Act of 1977. This act was passed to further a congressional intent that banks meet the credit needs of their local community or communities. The act requires something in the nature of an affirmative action plan for community investment. Whereas the employee or consumer protection measures discussed later focus on discrimination against an individual or a class of individuals, the Community Reinvestment Act focuses on perceived discrimination against entire neighborhoods or communities, especially low- and moderate-income areas. Although the act grew out of concern for alleged "redlining" against residential mortgage credit, it applies to agricultural, business, and other commercial credit as well.

The details on compliance with this act are primarily set forth in Regulation BB of the Federal Reserve Board. Enforcement sanctions exist in two forms. First, examiners are required to take into account the performance of the bank in helping to meet the credit needs of the entire community, including low- and moderate-income areas. In addition, the federal regulatory bodies are required to take this same record into account in considering applications (1) for new branches or relocation of an existing branch, (2) for merger and consolidations, (3) for the creation of a bank holding company, (4) for a holding company to acquire another bank or to merge or consolidate with another holding company, or (5) generally for other activities that require regulatory approval. The effect is an enforcement sanction that can result in a denial of business expansion plans for a bank or holding company that is considered to have inadequately served the credit needs of the existing communities.

The federal regulations for the Community Reinvestment Act require each bank to prepare, and annually review, a delineation (using maps) of the local community or communities that comprise the entire community. Low- and moderate-income neighborhoods cannot be excluded. The regulations leave it to the bank to prepare its own delineation. Of course, this action will be reviewed by the appropriate regulatory bodies. The regulations require that a local community consist of the "contiguous areas surrounding each office or groups of offices" and recognize that lending areas and other reasonably related criteria need to be used along with geographic or political boundaries.

Once local communities have been delineated, the board of directors is required to adopt a Community Reinvestment Act (CRA) statement for each such community. This statement must indicate the specific types of credit that the bank intends to extend in that community. The regulations do not require but encourage the inclusion of a description of the bank's current efforts, any special programs, records of results, and any research activities relevant to identifying community credit needs. The statement is required to be available to the public for inspection and for copying at the bank's head office and each office in the various local communities delineated. The bank is also required to maintain publicly available files containing written comments received from members of the public. Further, the board must review each CRA statement annually and act on any material changes.

In an examination, examiners will be verifying the accuracy of the communities delineated, the thoroughness of the formal CRA statement, and the record of the bank relative to meeting community credit needs. Significantly, examiners are required to review and assess the extent of participation by the board in formulating the bank's policies and reviewing its performance. Given the role that this act's enforcement sanctions may play in the long-term expansion programs of the bank, it seems vital that directors give it priority attention.

Experience with this act shows that examiners have been working hard with bank management to upgrade the quality of the formal statements and to assist in methods for identifying community credit needs. The federal regulatory bodies have taken their obligations under the law seriously, and there are numerous instances of denials of applications for branch expansion, acquisitions, and the like for failure of depository institutions to demonstrate they were meeting adequately the credit needs of existing communities.

The law does not require a bank to pursue types of credit that do not fall within its business objectives. For example, a bank that does not seek investments in residential property generally is not expected to change this policy with respect to a low-income neighborhood within a local community served by one of its branches. Nor is it particularly expected that a bank participate in subsidized government revitalization programs. But, it is expected that the bank pursue credit opportunities within the sphere of its loan expertise and objectives if similar community needs are going unmet. This seems to be the type of challenge that directors are uniquely qualified to help meet. Certainly, the regulatory bodies have gone out of their way to be sure that the objectives of the act are regularly placed before the board.

Equal Employment Opportunity

Although this subject is well covered in Chapter 9 on personnel management, it needs brief mention here because of the increasing emphasis that enforcement authorities, including private litigants, are placing on affirmative employment action in depository institutions, especially commercial banks. When the federal employment discrimination laws were first enacted, administrative enforcement was assigned to the Treasury Department. Later, due to accusations of lack of attention, enforcement was shifted to the Department of Labor. The shift has been accompanied by a dramatic rise in investigations directed at banks. A recent estimate indicated that about one-tenth of all investigatory enforcement actions of the Department of Labor today focus on depository institutions.

Banking by its very nature employs large numbers of clerical personnel. Thus, it seems only natural that a given institution's employment profile will mirror the socioeconomic makeup of society at large. The executive/managerial ranks tend to be Caucasian and male, while the clerical staff tends to be female, and, in some urban areas, increasingly black. Since equal employment actions are statistically oriented, financial institutions are highly vulnerable to accusations of noncompliance. Settlements of private litigation have proved particularly expensive for many of the larger money center banks.

The point is that directors should pay special attention to the bank's affirmative action program. Every bank should have one. Criteria should exist not only for entry-level positions, but for training and promotion opportunities as well. An affirmative action plan should be a subject of the highest priority with the board since an enforcement action may well prove to be a source of adverse publicity. Directors should bring to bear experience in their own business activities to shape constructively the bank's own program ahead of the demands of enforcement authorities and private litigants.

Consumer Protection

The subject of consumer protection could be a book unto itself. The dramatic rise in consumerism during the 1960s and 1970s was accompanied by an equally dramatic increase in the number of technical legal requirements intended for the protection of consumers of banking products, particularly in the area of credit. Starting with the 1968 Truth in Lending Act, the federal Congress legislated a new protective scheme for consumers on the average of every two years, well into the late 1970s. These schemes, many of which are highly complex, cover discrimination in credit granting, credit billing, credit reporting, debt collection, bankruptcy protection, home mortgage disclosure, real estate settlement practices, electronic funds transfer, and privacy of financial records. During this same period, many states enacted similar measures or imposed requirements that are in addition to the federal standards.

Most of these federal legislative schemes are enforceable by both private and administrative action. Private litigation, frequently cast in the setting of class actions representing large numbers of persons, have proved particularly costly to banks, in moneys paid for legal defense and final resolution as well as in bad publicity. In an attempt to minimize these actions, the federal regulatory bodies—frequently in consort with their state equivalents—have recently strengthened their examination techniques and requirements in this area. The result is that any examination today of a bank with a retail component will include a review of forms, procedures, and customer files by a team of consumer protection specialists.

This is one instance in which the examination can be viewed as a resource to the bank rather than as a nuisance or an adversary force. The various consumer protection measures are highly technical and have developed so rapidly that retail managers and legal counsel have had difficulty staying in compliance and keeping abreast of new developments. If the bank has an important retail focus, the board is well advised to stay active in this area with management until internal training programs are on top of this rapidly expanding area of the law.

Life-Line Accounts and Other Emerging Concerns

It was possible by the early 1980s to see the beginning of a cessation in governmental attitudes toward increased regulation of banking and other industries. For example, the Garn-St. Germain Depository Institutions Act of 1982 included provisions for the simplifications of the 1968 Truth-in-Lending rules, including the relaxation of entitlements to class actions. From the point of view of consumer or community issues, the trends here represent something different from those commonly expressed as "deregulation." New legislation is not appearing as frequently as in the past, but the underlying concerns continue to exist.

This is readily apparent in the attention that is currently (mid-1980s) focused on the need for "life-line" accounts. As a result of interest rate deregulation, banks and other depository institutions are returning higher yields to consumers and, to compensate, have recently raised their fees for many retail services. While understandable, raising fees has had the effect of changing the economic relationship of moderate-income consumers with banks. Basic low-balance savings and transaction accounts are no longer free, along with MasterCard and VISA credit lines. This has led to a certain amount of hue and cry over the economic disenfranchisement of the young, the elderly, and the poor. Some states, like Massachusetts, have enacted 18/65 laws requiring the availability of basic accounts at low or no fees for the young and elderly.

Many members of Congress have sponsored federal legislation that moves in the same direction. It is unknown whether proposals of this kind have a serious chance for enactment. Many banks have responded to the "life-line" movement by developing pricing options appropriate for low-balance accounts. What is important here is the extent to which the members of public bodies are motivated to influence banks to adhere to a perceived obligation to serve the public interest. Even in an era of deregulation, the pressure continues to be strong to perpetuate a regulatory framework for the industry that is more akin to that of a public utility than a private sector participant. The fact of the matter seems to be that there is in place today a longstanding set of attitudes and precedents in the regulatory approach to banking that is not likely to change drastically over the next few years, or even decades.

Banking occupies a unique position in the economy, and it is extremely difficult to assume that this is likely to change over time. Today's director should assume that continuing perceptions of economic problems might encourage experimentation with more governmental powers to direct banking or credit services into troubled areas of the economy.

The business and financial press of today routinely carries stories of the pressing needs for capital for small business, for agriculture, and for urban rejuvenation. Not too long ago, it was for alternative energy sources. The traditional approach of government to perceived problems such as these has been to create positive incentives—for example, direct loans from government agencies (or banks initially capitalized with appropriated funds), guarantees of private loans, tax preferences, and other forms of subsidies. This approach continues to be our dominant approach to allocate credit and other forms of capital.

The Community Reinvestment Act and various affirmative action programs are perhaps symptomatic of a change in the direction of the use of negative incentives. It is predicated, possibly, on the belief that positive incentives haven't worked very well for the problems of declining neighborhoods. It may be that this approach will be limited to this area and never be extended to any other. It may be that it may prove to be unworkable even in its present narrow context.

But, a precedent has been set, and it seems that bank directors should be alert to any trend that may be emerging along these lines. What is clear is that banks no longer have the unfettered freedom to set their policies on the basis of profitability and strategic considerations alone. This is perhaps an even greater challenge for the board than for senior management. The message seems to be that creativity, resourcefulness, and strategic thinking will loom large in the policy formation of financial intermediaries for the 1980s and 1990s. One objective will be to stay one jump ahead of governmental bodies.

Chapter 8

STRATEGY DEVELOPMENT

by George B. Rockwell

Introduction

The banking business can no longer be viewed solely in terms of traditional banking activities. Today, banks deliver a variety of financial services to individuals, corporations, other banks, and governments. Many of these services compete intensely with those provided by nonbank firms. This competition demands that bank executives possess both a sensitivity to change and a breadth of understanding never before demanded; commercial banks must be proactive rather than reactive to current and future marketplace needs and to new competitive entrants.

In recent years, competition has been intensified with the emergence of nonbank competitors—"quasi-bankers"—who are involved in the asset or liability side of financial intermediation. Examples of "quasi-banking" include:

- Money market funds.
- Asset-based management consulting firms.
- Thrifts converting to commercial banks.
- Finance companies expanding beyond personal credit.
- Mortgage bankers.
- Investment broker firms.
- Real estate and insurance firms combining to provide financial products.
- Captive commercial finance companies entering banking.
- Credit unions.

193

- Intercompany lending via commercial paper.
- Securitization of almost every conceivable asset.
- Corporations tapping individual savers for capital.
- The insurance industry broadening its lending base into commercial bank "turf."
- Most importantly, government banking activities.

This list is not only not an inclusive one, but over the next decade there will be even more new entrants offering repackaged or unique new services to the saver or the borrower.

Why are nonbankers entering banking? First, they can make a favorable return on their investment; second, they can circumvent regulations by being selective; third, market share may be gained through a better understanding of the needs of the financial service marketplace; and, fourth, it may make it easier to sell core business products.

Directors of banks need to understand this changing environment to guarantee their own survival and growth. Excellence and consistency in the delivery of financial services may be assured only by establishing effective planning and implementation systems. Directors must encourage a planning system that will require management to (1) establish goals and objectives, (2) reflect on marketplace needs, (3) allocate resources against the needs, and (4) provide a timetable for the orderly execution of the plan in the most beneficial way to assure shareholder returns. Today, most high-performance banks have in place a planning process to help them manage the future. The important question is, Can the plans be changed quickly enough to meet the changing environment and still achieve profitable and prudent growth?

Fiduciary Responsibility

Chapter 3 in this book is devoted to governance; strategy is an integral part of governance. Critical analysis and evaluation of the future are essential if financial failures are to be avoided. The fundamental problem is that the strategy, or even the tactics, may be speculative and not financially sound. Until a strategic plan is in place, directors have no way of distinguishing speculation from valuable financial services. The long-term viability of the institution is the responsibility of both management and directors. The planning process is the major means to redirect the institution in an orderly fashion for the long-term benefit of the shareholders. Therefore, it is the directors' duty to understand the plan and serve as a check and balance on management. The financial service business, now that deregulation has occurred, is not a long-term or short-term crap game. Prudence, conservation, and good judgment are what go into making a better-than-average bank or bank holding company.

The formal long-range planning process in banks is both simple and complex. Conceptually, the planning process is quite simple in that it progressively narrows strategic choices. Operationally, the process is much more complex. Good strategic planning can take place only when qualified personnel engage in creative and rigorous thinking and then reduce the emerging thoughts into a plan of action. Planning is important, but execution of the plans is more important and infinitely more complex.

By now there is little doubt that formalizing the planning process is worthwhile; it ensures that officers and staff at all levels of the organization will devote some time to strategic thinking, and it guarantees each of them an audience for presenting ideas. While formal strategic planning cannot guarantee profits for the services being offered in the marketplace, it can enhance profit potential and ensure that only those services that offer payoffs commensurate with the associated risks will be so offered. The benefits of planning and subsequent execution and monitoring of the plans are manifold. Planning provides a vehicle for (1) communicating—explaining where we are and where we are going; (2) analyzing competitive strengths and weaknesses; (3) defining more clearly and with a degree of newsworthiness our problems and opportunities; (4) allocating limited resources; and (5) measuring short- as well as long-range progress, along with providing a means for making appropriate mid-course corrections.

The CEO

Bank planning will not be successful unless the chief executive officer (CEO) believes in planning, works at it, and assumes a leadership role with the wholehearted support and understanding of the board of directors. At best, the management of change is not a problem that the CEO, board, or managers can solve; rather, it is a problem they all must live with and manage.

As a bank grows (and most grow at least at the rate of the GNP), it becomes more complex. In an earlier, simpler, less complex development stage, the chief executive officer typically knows all the details of the business and spends a great deal of time (1) carrying out major functions, (2) servicing key accounts, (3) raising capital, (4) managing the net interest margin, (5) introducing new services, (6) hiring and training people, (7) dealing with the regulatory environment, and (8) understanding the basis of competition. The "plan" may be in the CEO's head or on the back of an envelope. However, as the bank grows and becomes more complex, the number of decisions and activities outstrips the time available, and the CEO must rely on other executives to perform major functions. At this juncture, back-of-the-envelope planning ceases to be effective. Major shifts in emphasis begin to occur. Now the CEO must (1) spend more time selecting, motivating, allocating, and evaluating key officer talent; (2) devote a larger share of time to strategic planning to ensure that the assets and liabilities are effectively hedged and managed; (3) evaluate markets and allocate resources to assure rather than assume successful introduction of new services; and (4) become knowledgeable about the basis of competition both in the bank's market as well as in other markets by means of sophisticated and timely market research and through participating in trade association activities, serving on corporate boards, and dealing with regulatory officials.

All too frequently, unfortunately, the chief executive officer finds it impossible to change. The CEO's subordinates also fail to change, and then the bank may stagnate or get into serious earnings problems and be unable to meet the financial needs of its customers. As a consequence, the board steps in and removes the CEO or forces the CEO to adopt a different management style. The CEO who avoids those pitfalls may do so through formal training, counseling with experienced outsiders, or sheer determination. A successful CEO will develop a management team that can anticipate and solve customers' problems more effectively than the competition; with the formation of such a team, the bank can assume a leadership position—if not today, certainly tomorrow.

Strategic Management

Banking is a business that has changed dramatically in the past five years. Managing the marketplace used to be rather simple. The regulators told you what services to offer, and protected territories were established either by regulation or by antitrust boundaries. In a deregulated environment, hard-nosed strategic management is the only way to assure profitable growth. Figure 8–1 shows the change over the last 25 years, and demonstrates that a financial institution requires not only products but also solutions to specific market needs. Today this creates a new dimension of complexity for management.

Over the past few decades, the methodology for the development of management systems has been fine-tuned. In the 1970s strategic planning evolved as a replacement for a traditional profit center approach to planning. Current work is expanding the strategic planning concepts to a complete strategy management system. Strategy management requires not only the selection of a strategy to pursue from the alternatives available but also the process of establishing reporting and control systems. This involves determining management styles, performance measures, performance standards, and methods of reporting results. The emphasis is on monitoring the quality of strategy execution and the continuing appropriateness of the current strategy as the environment changes.

The approach described here has been proved worthwhile and not only helps management develop a strategic plan appropriate to a particular time but also develops in management an understanding of the principles underlying the process. As the process evolves, execution of tactics improves, and the changing needs of customers are anticipated and served.

The Principles of Planning

There are four underlying principles in strategic planning:

1. Planning is a process based on data.
2. Strategic business units serving specific markets can be identified within a bank or bank holding company.
3. Strategy is more condition-driven than ambition-driven.
4. There is a finite set of available strategies from which a business must choose.

Figure 8–2 demonstrates the flows of inputs, the development and process, and the outputs and consequences to be expected from a well-conceived system for strategy development.

Dimensions of Change	Low	Moderate	Substantial	High	Higher
A. SERVICES Number and Diversity of Services	Single Line	Several Related 1960	Several Related Some Unrelated	Diverse and Complex	Diverse
Compexlexity of Individual Services	Simple Design	Multiple Components, 1960	Highly Intricate, Technically Sensitive	Technical and Systematic	Integrating Services
Degree and Intensity of Interest Rate Cycle	None or Little, 1960	Some	Extensive	Volatile, Unpredictable	Volatile
Rate of Service Innovation	Slow, 1960	Slow to Moderate	Moderate to Rapid	Rapid	Rapid
B. MARKETS Geographic Scope	Local	Regional 1960	National	International	National Re-emphasized and International Growth De-emphasized
Distribution Channels	Single	Few, 1960	Several	Multiple Complex	By Market Needs and Sophistication
Customer Groups	Single, Well Defined, 1960	Few	Several Distinct	Multiple Diverse	Segmentation Becomes Commonplace
C. ENVIRONMENT Competitive Intensity	Low, 1960	Low to Moderate	Moderate to Intense	Very Intense	Regulation No Longer Factor
Number of Competitors	Well Defined, 1960	Few	Blurring of Intermediaries	Financial and Non-Financial	Everybody Who Needs Financial Services to Sell Products
External Forces (economic, government, social, labor)	Stable	Stable to Moderate, 1960	Moderate to Intense	Highly Volatile, Very Intricate	Limited-Level Playing Field Near

Figure 8–1   The Growth of Service Market Complexity in Banking, 1960–1985

CORPORATE STRATEGY DEVELOPMENT PROCESS

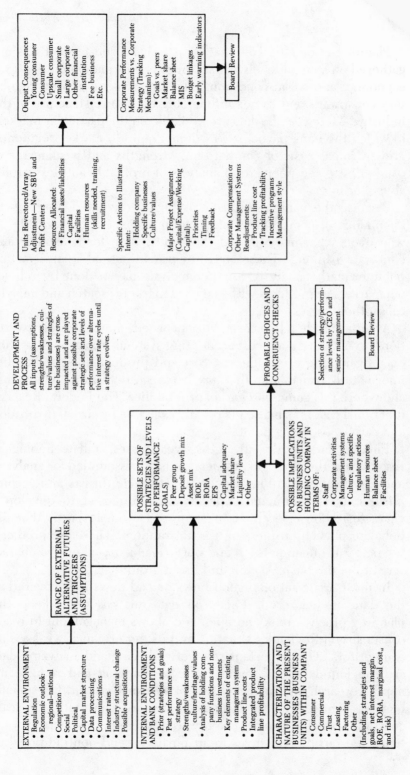

Figure 8–2 The Planning Process

ιg is data-based—that is, it is based on facts. Facts are
on several levels. First, there is information on political,
ιc, and social conditions affecting banking and on regula-
 nstraints and trends influencing the future structure of the
ι.. ιy. More specific data are available on the particular markets
in which the bank participates—demographics, market segments,
growth rates, basis of competition, strengths and weaknesses of
competitors, and peer group analysis of profitable and less profitable offerings.

Because the banking industry is highly regulated, there is an
abundance of competitive information and statistics available on
who owns what markets and the trends both for consumer and
corporate banking. These statistics provide an adequate starting
point for market analysis. Further analysis may be done by individual markets or products with standard market research and analytical methodologies.

As far as product line costs are concerned, most financial institutions do not have good cost accounting systems in place. However,
once again, there is sufficient cost and product line profitability
information available so that any bank can determine where it is
and where it is going in terms of profitability. The Federal Reserve
functional cost information is readily available by size of institution
and can be a starting point.

Finally, data on the strengths, weaknesses, and technological
resources of the strategic business units are assembled for analysis,
and a critical evaluation of previous strategic thrusts and accomplishments is conducted. Specific facts are used to develop a
characterization of each business unit. The idea here is that the
behavior of each business unit is not random. There are predictable patterns of competition and performance based on the characteristics of the business unit and its environment.

In most organizations, good news or bad news is uncovered as
the data are gathered. Focus on data analysis helps keep the
planning process frank and open and allows management to reach
consensus on the bank's situation and its performance, vis-à-vis its
competitors. The important steps of gathering and analyzing data
are the foundation of sound strategic planning and require in-
depth research and analysis. Out of the analysis will fall specific
business units. Typical business units are consumer, up-scale
consumer, small corporate, large corporate, other financial institutions, fee businesses, investment portfolio, and nontraditional or

new services. Each business unit has any number of profit centers and discrete products or services. Some will be integrated with others, and some will stand alone.

Business Unit Identification

For an individual institution the process of defining specific business units constitutes the next step in strategic planning. A business unit is a business activity possessing an identifiable marketplace. Working backward from the marketplace, one can determine objectives and relevant penetration strategies for the activity or "line" of business. Business units, however, are not necessarily traditional profit centers but are demand- or marketplace-defined. For instance, up-scale consumer as opposed to secured borrowing consumer and their appropriate market segments illustrate this orientation.

A business or service acquires identifiable attributes over time and can be classified as having a certain defined market or strategic condition that influences the strategic options open to management. However, a multilevel analysis should be performed to allow consideration of the organization as well as its business units and services. To ignore one's strategic condition is to court disaster. Too often in the past, banks have engaged instinctively in follow-the-leader tactics without regard for regional or individual institutional differences and frequently ignored other (nonbank) competitors. Thus, the bank's strategic condition should be determined before the alternatives are set forth.

The financial interaction of services or business units that are fund users with those that are fund providers demands an escalation of inquiry beyond product analysis. Because of this, the analysis of strategic conditions must be brought to the corporate and holding company levels. The strategic condition of the organization as a whole will, in part, determine whether services or businesses can follow the natural strategies selected for them.

Thus, an organization analysis sets the stage for evaluating the condition of, and developing strategies for, services offered by business units. More specifically, at the organization level, we are concerned with:

- Institution size, both absolute and relative to competitors.
- Condition of the balance sheet.

- Earnings performance.
- Regulatory and political environment.
- Organizational and management philosophy.
- Strength of the board, management, and staff.
- Past ability to manage the marketplace for both existing and new offerings.
- The ability to use technology to achieve competitive advantage.
- The ability to be a lean, low-cost operation.

Key Factors of Strategy Development

We believe there are nine key factors in determining strategic condition:

1. Alternative futures. (Although the future cannot be predicted, there are many possible futures. Once these futures are understood, a bank can determine their probabilities of happening and establish early warning indicators, coupled with sound, re-vectored strategies.)
2. Product or service maturity (particularly as related to new or emerging services).
3. Competitive position.
4. Strategic management of technology.
5. The net interest margin for lending products over differing economic cycles and related hedging possibilities.
6. The management of the balance sheet, including capital retention strategies.
7. Tax planning.
8. The breakdown of barriers to geographic or functional expansion.
9. Management's past performance.

Maturity

If a bank is to be successful, it must manage the market. This process begins with an understanding of the strategic position of each unit or service in its relevant market. We have found maturity positioning to be a powerful assist in gaining this understanding when it is linked to product profitability and market management and technological or operational capacity. In determining maturity, we look at the level and rate of change of a number of criteria, including:

- Growth characteristics
- Income generated
- Volumes outstanding
- Breadth of service line
- Number of competitors
- Market shares
- Customer base
- Technology
- Communications
- Product integration

Most of these factors receive extended discussion elsewhere in the book. Several, however, merit some comment here.

It should be noted that maturity is determined within a market; consequently, similar products or business units can be classified differently by two organizations. Services can be grouped into four convenient stages of maturity. First, an *embryonic service* is normally characterized by rapid growth, changes in technology, great pursuit of new customers, and fragmented and changing shares of market. Second, a *growth service* is one that is still growing rapidly, but its customers, market shares, and technology are better defined and entry is more difficult. Third, a *mature service* is characterized by stability in known customers, in technology, and in shares of market, although competitive markets are not precluded. Finally, *aging service* is best described by falling demand, a narrowing field of competitors, and, in some cases, a narrowing of service lines. The life cycle and duration of phases in the life cycle can be short or long. The essential point for a bank is to know where each of its services is positioned vis-à-vis competitors and then to develop appropriate strategies to dominate, further penetrate, or deemphasize the market.

Despite tremendous efforts, no one has been able to forecast interest rates. However, interest rates are cyclical, and if each service, along with its appropriate revenues and costs, is analyzed over different interest rate cycles, it becomes clear when to emphasize or deemphasize the service, or hedge your position. Recognition of turning points in the cycle, together with the formulation of strategies appropriate in each phase, assures a better return on assets with lowered risk.

Balance Sheet Management

An effective strategy cannot be executed without a well-rational-ized plan for managing the balance sheet—that is, assets, liabili-ties, and capital. Normally, an ALCO (asset/liability committee) establishes policy on funding an investment. This committee of senior management meets weekly in large institutions, less fre-quently in smaller ones. It focuses on (1) interest rates, (2) loan and deposit relationships and mix, (3) investment strategies, (4) tax planning, (5) budgeting, (6) alternative futures, (7) a heavy empha-sis on spread management and hedging, and (8) the maturity position of each service and profitability. Each service or business must be woven into the fabric of the plan individually. Each must be analyzed against the backdrop of changing cyclical expectations.

Competitive Position

Competitive position is one of the most complex elements of business analysis and one of the least researched. In the face of complexity, there is a temptation to fall back on a single criterion, such as market share. A competitive position embraces many factors, such as technological or market strength, breadth of ser-vice line, market share, cost structure, management skills, and special market relationships. The overriding objective is to move services toward profitable market dominance, regardless of the service positioning vis-à-vis competition. It is usually easier to do this in an embryonic or growth environment. Some strategies and tactics will make this easier to achieve than others. An ongoing process of competitive monitoring will assist in the identification of those market segments where competition is most vulnerable or the business unit may be becoming vulnerable. A formal market research program to identify both your and your competitor's strengths and weaknesses is essential if you are to achieve consis-tent market share penetration of these most profitable services.

Strategic Management of Technology

The objective of strategic management of technology is to bridge the gap between technical and business management, to improve the quality of technological choices and the effectiveness of resource allocation, and to achieve a broader stable of profitable new services which provide a competitive advantage or efficiency improvement, or both.

Selecting Strategies

Once an understanding of the strategic condition of the institution and its business units has been reached and the competitive position and maturity of each service ascertained, management is ready to consider appropriate profit-raising strategies. Figure 8–3 demonstrates how a bank's services are positioned in relation to several competitors and the strategic change that is desired over the next five years.

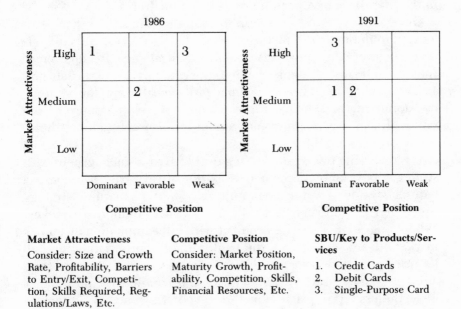

Market Attractiveness	Competitive Position	SBU/Key to Products/Services
Consider: Size and Growth Rate, Profitability, Barriers to Entry/Exit, Competition, Skills Required, Regulations/Laws, Etc.	Consider: Market Position, Maturity Growth, Profitability, Competition, Skills, Financial Resources, Etc.	1. Credit Cards 2. Debit Cards 3. Single-Purpose Card

Figure 8–3 Strategic Business Unit and Product Line: Market Attractiveness and Competitive Position

Strategies can be grouped by their focus. Some strategies are more appropriate to execute than others, based on competitive position and maturity. The following are typical strategies:

- Start-up
- Fast Grow
- Develop Niche
- Turnaround
- Retrench
- Grow with Industry
- Hang In
- Defend Position

Strategies tend to fall into periods of execution that relate to the stages of the interest rate cycle, market position, and risk. Therefore, a service can move from one stage to another and back again, depending on the business cycle, competition, the ability to stimulate the marketplace, and what is happening to interest rates. Some strategies are usually most appropriate to one or two phases in the maturity curve, as Figure 8–4 demonstrates.

Once each service or single-purpose business unit has been located in the matrix of maturity, market alternatives, and competitive position, the appropriate "natural" strategies are identified. In general terms, strategies fall into the categories seen in Table 8–1. By having a common language or vocabulary for strategy development, most officers and planners develop a sense of the range of available options and communicate freely among themselves on positioning.

It is desirable to execute strategies that are not incongruent with strategic positioning, but a unit is not always free to choose a natural strategy. A business unit may find its natural strategy precluded by internal trade-offs or external competitive moves. When long-term objectives conflict with full exploitation of a unit's market advantage or when the bank cannot appropriately fund all its prime opportunities, a unit may be assigned a strategy that, although "unnatural" for its maturity and competitive position, is nevertheless appropriate for the corporate good. An example would be the emphasis on fixed-rate lending because of competitive opportunities available to lock in more than one service.

Determining Strategic Risk

The likelihood of a selected strategy being successful is a function of the strategic competitive position of the service or business unit, as well as a function of the corporate environment. Certain strategies are more predictable and therefore less risky than other strategies, and past performance and the level of expected future performance give strong clues as to risk. The inherent strategic risk of a business unit or service is usually related to its place in the

Stages of Industry Maturity

Competitive Position	Embryonic	Growth	Mature	Aging
Dominant	Start-Up Fast Grow	Fast Grow Attain Cost Leadership Defend Position	Grow with Industry Attain Cost Leadership Renew Defend Position	Grow with Industry Focus Renew Defend Position
Strong	Start-Up Fast Grow Differentiate	Fast Grow Attain Cost Leadership Differentiate Renew Defend Position	Grow with Industry Attain Cost Leadership Differentiate Focus, Renew Defend Position	Grow with Industry Harvest Develop Niche Hang-In
Favorable	Start-Up Fast Grow Differentiate Focus	Grow with Industry Fast Grow Attain Cost Leadership Differentiate, Focus Renew, Develop Niche	Grow with Industry Attain Cost Leadership Differentiate, Focus Renew, Defend Position Harvest, Develop Niche Hang-In, Turnaround	Turnaround Retrench
Tenable	Start-Up Grow with Industry Fast Grow Differentiate Focus Catch-Up	Grow with Industry Focus Develop Niche Catch-Up Hang-In Turnaround	Harvest Develop Niche Turnaround Retrench	Retrench
Weak	Catch-Up Turnaround Withdraw	Turnaround Retrench Withdraw	Turnaround Retrench Withdraw	Withdraw

Figure 8-4   Guide to Strategic Thrust Options

Table 8–1 Categories of Profit-Raising Strategies

Strategy	Objective	Requirements	Expected Results	Risks
Start-Up	To develop a totally new industry to create and satisfy a new demand where none existed before.	Risk-taking attitude of management; capital expenditures; expense.	Negative cash flow; low-to-negative returns; a leadership position.	High to very high; demand, technology, channels of distribution, sourcing, basis of competition are all unknown.
Fast Grow	To grow volume and share faster than competition and faster than general industry growth rate.	Available resources for investment and follow-up; risk-taking management attitude; an appropriate investment strategy.	Higher market share; short-term, perhaps lower returns; above-average returns in longer term; competitive retaliation.	High; threat exists that someone else may play the game smarter, harder, or sooner.
Develop Niche	To retain a small, defensible portion of the available market by defining the opportunity so narrowly that large competitors with broad lines do not find it attractive enough to dislodge you.	"Think Small" management style; alternative uses for excess capacity; reliable sources for credit; superior quality and/or service with selected sector.	Stable volume and share; high to medium returns if special needs are served. More flexibility in pricing.	Medium; danger exists that segment was not well defined; danger from potentially powerful customer and/or supplier blocks; danger that niche will not produce volume sufficient for economical distribution or operations.

Turnaround	To halt further decline in share and/or volume; to bring about improved position; to protect the line from competitive and substitute products. (Make or break mode.)	Fast action to prevent disaster; redirection; change in morale.	Potential short-term losses followed by substantial improvements in competitive position.	High; a strategic thrust imposed by poor conditions, not selected; stronger competitors may have sealed off all reasonable routes to success; time may run out before improvement is possible.
Retrench	To stop unacceptable losses or risks; to prepare the business for withdrawal; to strip away loss operations in hopes of exposing a "little jewel," by cutting back investment, divesting a portion of the business, or contracting the scope of operations.	Highly disciplined management system; good communication with employees to prevent wholesale departures; clear strategic objective and timetable.	Reduced losses or modestly improved performance.	Low to medium; performance is predictable, but not acceptable.
Grow with Industry	To free resources to correct market, product, management or operating weaknesses, thereby maintaining market share.	Management restraint; market intelligence; some capital and expense investments; time-limited strategy.	Stable market share; profit, cash flow and ROA not significantly worse than recent history, and fluctuating only with industry averages.	Medium to high in strenuously competitive industries; essentially a defensive posture.

Table 8–1 Continued

Strategy	Objective	Requirements	Expected Results	Risks
Hang In	To continue funding a tenable (or better) unit only long enough to take advantage of unusual opportunity known to be at hand.	Clear view of expected environmental shift; a management willing and able to sustain poor performance; opportunity and resources to capitalize on new environment; a time limit.	Poorer-than-average performance, perhaps losses; later, substantial growth and high returns.	High; the future never comes as fast or is as favorable as a weak unit expects; stronger competitors probably will benefit most anyway.
Defend Position	To ensure that relative competitive position is stable or improved by creating barriers that make it difficult, costly, and risky for competitors, customer blocks, or new entries to erode the firm's market share, profitability, and growth.	Establishment of one or more of the following: proprietary technology, strong brand, protected sourcing, favorable locations, economies of scale, government protection, exclusive distribution, or customer loyalty.	Stable or increasing market share.	Low; by definition, you should have the resources to control your destiny.

matrix of maturity, market attractiveness, and competitive position. In general, the unpredictability of performance (hence the risk) is greatest for units with weak competitive positions in an embryonic business and least for those with a dominant position in an aging business.

By now, it must be clear that management information systems are needed in order to be supportive of a given strategy, but it still can be very difficult to implement such systems because of the constraints of established bank systems. In the volatile competitive environment of today, this is unsatisfactory. Knowledge is critical for success. Also, management activities or functions such as management styles, organization structure, communications, policy and procedures, and competitive monitoring systems may have to be adjusted. The effective management of change requires versatile management systems and style.

Corporate Strategies

After tentative strategies are selected for each business unit, a consolidated bank or bank holding company strategy session is required. Senior management considers the interaction of business unit strategies and pays particular attention to balance sheet structure, net interest margin, earnings per share, liquidity, and return on equity. Strategies appropriate to the corporation as a whole must be considered as well. The universe of corporate strategies seems to compromise five groups:

1. Corporate entity strategies pursued to defend or manage the identity of the corporate units.
2. Growth and renewal strategies for managing the present and future corporate array of businesses and services.
3. Managerial systems strategies that include resource allocation, reporting and control systems, and development of corporate style.
4. Financial strategies designed to develop and manage the corporate balance sheet.
5. External relations strategies designed to position the corporation with its various publics and clients.

Laying Out Strategy and Tactics

Once data are gathered, it is customary for senior management and line management for the particular business units to spend two or three intensive days together developing appropriate strategic options and necessary support programs for their own units. This is followed by a 30-day evaluation period that culminates in their consolidation into a corporate strategy and resource allocation

---

GOAL OR OBJECTIVE
- Should be very specific. Use quantitative terms. Address several items (i.e., ROE, RORA, improved competitive position, etc.).

STRATEGY
- The generic strategy selected.
- The specific interpretation of those words to this market/business.
- Results expected.

RATIONALE
- A terse explanation of why or how the strategy is expected to achieve the results.

PROGRAMS (TACTICS)

What to Do	What Is Required	What Results	Tracking Progress
Check action plans by function, customer product, or marketplace	Dollars	Translate into financial and strategic terms	How to measure (types of things that can be tracked)
	Staff		
	Agreements		Specific benchmarks
	Information		
			Who is responsible?
			Date of next review

Figure 8–5 Laying Out a Strategy

plan. Figure 8–5 details the planning and tactical process. Appropriate project management systems are used for monitoring new service development or repackaging existing services. Good tactical systems have a way of tracking development as well as operations and providing the tools to take corrective action.

Summary

The strategic planning process focuses first on making an objective appraisal of the position of each service, business unit, associated personnel, and the bank considered in its functional entirety. Once this objective determination has been made, strategy alternatives flow naturally from it. However, the choice of strategies for a business unit may have to be adjusted to take into consideration conditions at the corporate level that may suggest pursuing strategies that are not natural for individual business units.

Superior performance results from managing the balance sheet, the organization, personnel, and the firm's position in the marketplace. Planning facilitates objective thinking about the organization's current condition and the logical steps for growth and improved performance. Competitor and peer group analysis and comparisons help in establishing markets as well as financial initiatives. Analysis of nonbank competitors is also critical to strategic success. In any event, it is not enough to prepare a strategic plan. Reporting and control systems to monitor progress against that plan must also be established. This involves determining performance measures and setting performance standards for individual units based on the particular condition of that business unit singly and in concert with other units within the corporation.

The follow-up emphasis must be on monitoring the quality of the strategy execution and determining whether that strategy continues to be appropriate as the organization and the external environment change. By taking a disciplined approach to managing change and keeping score of planning successes and failures, a CEO and board can assure rather than assume excellence.

Chapter 9

HUMAN RESOURCES MANAGEMENT

by Lewis M. Rambo and Homer J. Hagedorn

Strategy and People

As the CEO and the board of today's financial institutions address the new and different strategies made necessary by the realities of competition in their now less regulated environment, "people" considerations cannot escape their attention. Human resource systems, practices, and procedures—which at one time might have gone unnoticed by the CEO and the board—now become an integral consideration in pursuing any selected strategy. The full array of human resource systems deserves review to assure congruence with selected strategies:

- *Succession planning.* Will there be the appropriate leadership through transitions and after?
- *Staffing.* Are the right people in the institution to perform its changing work; if not, where will they come from? How well filled is the pipeline for tomorrow's management?
- *Reward systems.* Does the system attract and contribute to the retention of the key talent needed to manage and operate the institution? Does it encourage employee action producing desired outcomes?
- *Performance assessment, training, and development.* Are there effective systems in place to "value the human resources" of the institution? Are there devices to help

215

individuals develop into the resources needed for the future of the institution? Do people know where they stand?
- *Union organization.* Will employees of the institution feel a need for third-party representation?
- *Employee effectiveness.* Do employees reflect the "image" desired for the pursuit of selected strategies?
- *Compliance.* Are systems in place to help the institution reduce its vulnerability under an increasingly complicated array of benefits and employment-related regulations and guidelines imposed by federal, state, and local governments, and by the changing values of the communities in which we operate?

The "people" issues described here all influence the ability of the institution to pursue its business progress. More and more, these issues demand the time and attention of the CEO and the board.

As a director of a financial institution, it is vitally important for you to include human resource factors in the evaluation of your bank's assets. Clearly it is essential for you to look carefully at the bank's balance sheet, portfolio of investments, and earnings to determine the underlying financial condition of the bank. You will probably want to consider its business strategies, its plans for diversification, and its growth and profit objectives. But steward-ship of the assets and implementation of the business strategy depend on having the right people doing the right job. More than just a casual glance should be taken at the kinds of people top management has entrusted with the implementation of its plans, goals, and objectives.

Increasing Need for Enlightened Human Resource System

Human resource planning and progressive human resource utiliza-tion make more than good sense. They are an absolute necessity, especially with the prospect of continued consolidation and jockey-ing for competitive advantage in the industry. Office automation technology will really require a fundamental rethinking of tradi-tional job families. Bank management will have to begin thinking about the redesign of career paths that have historically been regarded as necessary "stepping stones" to something better.

The classic image of a banker togged in conservative pin-striped suits or plain dresses is a stereotype that represents inaccurately all but a small fraction of the massive numbers of people needed to staff and run a banking institution.

Attention to employee development, an openness to suggestions from workers, and an environment that encourages the free exchange of ideas and feelings in a goal-directed way can allow managers to build jobs, careers, and growth opportunities from among existing underutilized staff. This type of approach, with supervision and with management, will bolster motivation, increase productivity, and improve communication among employees.

As a member of the board of directors it would be unrealistic to expect you to become intimately involved with the minute details of the personnel operation in your bank. You should at least be acquainted, however, with some of the human resource (employee relations) fundamentals shown in Figure 9–1.

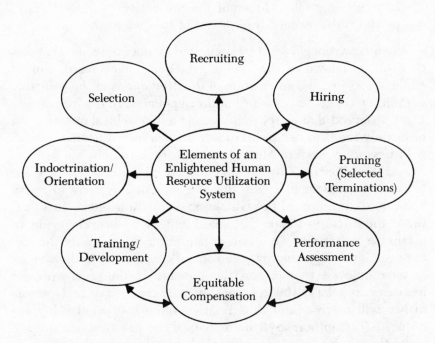

Figure 9–1   The Basic Elements of an Enlightened Human Resource Utilization System.

Management Selection and Succession

The issues of management succession and selection are probably the most difficult and challenging of all the responsibilities entrusted to directors and the top officers of the bank. Members of boards of directors are now accountable for assuring that chief executive officers have made plans for succession. Further, boards must see to it that top management posts in the organization are filled by responsible, talented, and capable people. Although the actual responsibility for selecting high-quality management talent rests with the CEO, the board of directors should be asking the following questions:

- Are there actual successors identified for the key officer positions in the bank? If not, why not, and what are the plans to remedy the situation?
- What is the nature of the management development program?
- What steps are being taken to prepare talented, high-level performers for increasingly responsible positions?
- Is care being taken to avoid the promotion of individuals to positions that exceed their levels of competence?

When Lawrence J. Peter suggested a phenomenon that has come to be known as the "Peter principle," some were amused while others found confirmation of the predictions of the principle in their own organization's promotional policies. In his "principle," Peter observed that every employee in a hierarchical organization ultimately tends to rise to his or her level of incompetence.

Professors Schaefer, Massey, and Hermanson, in an issue of *Across the Board: The Conference Board Magazine*, have attempted to explain just why this phenomenon appears to be an accurate description of behavior in many organizations. In short, these theorists postulate that management is forever trying to maximize the profits within an organization by widening the gap between level of productivity and actual wages paid. In their view, as an employee remains on the job anticipating fairly regular increases in salary, the relationship between salary and performance will narrow, and thus relative value and profitability are reduced. The authors give mathematical and practical examples to make their point, but it is sufficient here to suggest that management will, in fact, promote promising employees to their levels of diminished contribution unless nurturing, enriching, and stretching experiences are carefully, thoughtfully, and regularly provided. The Peter principle cannot gain a strong foothold in a dynamic, progressive organization dedicated to excellence, healthy competition, and innovation. All it takes to deal a death blow to the "principle" is aggressive pruning, a vital management development program, and paying people for their contributions.

Recruiting, Hiring, Selection, and Placement

The quality of the people hired is a critical factor in determining a bank's future. Quality people represent one of the last sources of differentiation between financial institutions. Except for minor differences, banks purchase computers, terminals, proof machines, and other equipment from common vendors. Transactions are usually handled in fairly uniform steps, and the services offered are often quite similar—if not identical. Aside from unique or patented products, the key elements of difference are the people who are processing, servicing, and interacting with customers.

Successful employee selection begins with well-conceived, carefully detailed job specifications. The bank's management should be aware of the importance of job descriptions and the need to carefully delineate the requirements of each opening so that the employment interviewer knows what to look for when conducting screening interviews. The bank should have a clearly identifiable philosophy that sets it apart from the competition. The personnel department should be staffed to respond to employment inquiries in all forms: internal candidates, employee referrals, walk-in traffic, telephone requests, and outside agency referrals. Managers and personnel officers should take great pains to treat applicants with interest, dignity, and concern. It is advisable to see to it that all unsolicited as well as solicited résumés and applications are answered promptly and courteously. The thoughtfully rejected applicant may one day be a loyal depositor or borrower.

The bank should have an attractive, nonthreatening personnel office, designed to allow applicants to be interviewed in privacy. Such a situation is not always easy to create in the open floor plans featured in most financial institutions today. Special care should be taken to produce eye-catching and well-written literature that outlines the policies, benefits, and special advantages of joining "your" bank.

Interviewers should be trained in the fundamentals of in-depth and screening evaluations. Managers, as well as personnel department staff, should be well acquainted with the affirmative action policies of the bank. More will be said about this topic later in the chapter.

From time to time the board should ask management to report on significant hiring statistics such as:

- Average cost per hire.
- Number of applicants interviewed per actual placement.
- Nonvoluntary versus voluntary turnover by department and major job classification.
- Average length of time a position remains open.
- The number of actual promotions from within the bank.
- The number and occupational specialties of new employees above entry level.

These statistics will give some indication of the effectiveness of the personnel operation as well as valuable insights on the cost effectiveness of the staffing in the bank.

The bank might consider creating an internal job-posting system. Posting systems permit better utilization of existing skills and staff and often avoid the expense and delays of looking outside for possible candidates.

In order to avoid confusion and possible embarrassment, the bank should have a formal statement of qualifications (SOQ) or application for employment. This basic employment information document, coupled with an employment requisition process, ensures that the necessary approvals to recruit candidates have been obtained before commitments are made to prospective employees. Few circumstances are more embarrassing than having to "dehire" someone because of miscommunications between the personnel department and a hiring manager as to qualifications, salary, or headcount authorization. Despite the increasing difficulty in securing timely and accurate information from former employers, every effort should be made to do complete and thorough reference checks. A careful reference check prior to an employment decision can save countless headaches, unnecessary costs, and even a lawsuit.

The personnel office should also be prepared to do college

recruiting to fill entry- and higher-level professional openings. It would also be a serious oversight not to consider the financial and community relations gains to be achieved by working with the local staff of Jobs Training Partnership Act (JTPA) offices and actively supporting the programs and policies of the local Private Industry Council (PIC), which provides guidance and counsel to JTPA. If your bank is one of the larger employers of entry-level workers in your community, as a director, you may want to inquire whether the bank is represented on the PIC as one contributing toward solving community problems, vocational training modernization, and employment of relatively unskilled personnel.

The Vocational Education Act of 1984, which mandates the establishment of Vocational Education Commissions in each state, coupled with locally supported training and development programs, makes it possible for a bank to greatly influence the preparation and training that potential employees receive. Your bank might be able to establish funded or partially supported training programs to prepare qualifiable applicants for jobs that might otherwise go unfilled. The benefits of this kind of effort are readily apparent, as are the tax credits that may be added to a bank's bottom line.

Affirmative Action, EEO, and Other Regulations

As a result of executive orders, the 1964 Civil Rights Act and its amendments and subsequent court interpretations, and the amendment to the Age Discrimination and Employment Act of 1978, nearly all corporations are expected to take affirmative actions to increase the number of minorities and women at every level in their work forces. Affirmative action and equal opportunity efforts can mean new or revised company policies that provide expanded opportunities for blacks and other minorities as well as whites, for men and women, and for employees of all ages. In fact, affirmative action can contribute to the creation and growth of an internal climate in which all employees overcome their isolation from and suspicion of other races or religions and the opposite sex.

Alternatively, affirmative action can focus primarily on meeting the demands of compliance agencies. It can mean paper shuffling, forms completion, culminating with an affirmative action plan that is unobtrusively filed away in the personnel office. Affirmative action can pit women and minorities against white males and against each other. Affirmative action can increase anxiety and anger, and reduce employee morale. *But none of this needs to happen.* Bank directors can play an important role in influencing their organization to make affirmative action work for bank employees and for the community.

A bank director and the bank's management should be able to respond positively to these seven questions:

1. Am I as a bank director really interested in more than just meeting the legal requirements of affirmative action?
2. Is bank management committed to equal opportunity and affirmative action?
3. Does the bank include affirmative action and equal opportunity accomplishments in its criteria for rewarding top management and key operating officers?
4. Do bank officers, supervisors, and employees understand the bank's affirmative action program?
5. Are all supervisory personnel capable of intelligently discussing affirmative action with their subordinates?
6. Are managers, supervisors, and employees receiving information and learning more about the history and present dynamics of relations between races, religions, and sexes?
7. Is the bank involving not only management but women, blacks, and other minorities, as well as white male workers, in the development, examination, and review of its equal opportunity efforts?

If the top management of the bank is determined to make progress in this important area, employees at all levels will "get the message," and real problems will be insignificant. Certainly, there will be those who feel threatened by the prospect of women, blacks, or other minorities contending for "their" jobs. Others will be demonstrably in support of affirmative action and equal opportunity programs. However, the largest group of employees in the bank will be more or less on the fence. With real leadership, commitment, and sensitivity, this latter group can be moved in a positive direction. This positive direction will permit your institution to take advantage of the best-qualified talent without the "baggage" that has truly handicapped our nation for too long.

The Threat of Union Organization

Financial institutions in this country historically have not experienced the pressure from unions that we have witnessed in other major industries such as automobile manufacturing, steel, and the building and maintenance trades. This does not mean that a bank's employees might not become the "target" of one or more of a number of unions that are principally focused on clerical and other office workers. Clearly, the best way to prevent unionization is to avoid the conditions in the work place that give rise to employee discontent. Union organizers usually cannot gain a toehold in a company that communicates effectively with its employees. If a financial institution values its human resources and follows as many of the employee relations practices mentioned throughout this chapter as possible, the likelihood of a union winning a representational election will be remote. If, however, a unionization drive is attempted, a bank's management should retain skilled counsel specializing in employee relations and labor law rather than wading into dangerously unfamiliar waters with its fingers crossed.

In targeting a bank for a professional and/or clerical union, union organizers will learn as much about the institution and its activities as they possibly can. They will study the bank's policies, practices, and actions toward its employees. They will search for examples of poor or callous management judgment in the areas of termination, promotion, compensation, and hiring to mention just a few. These data will then be used to convince employees that the bank for which they work is unfair, insensitive, and even autocratic. The organizers will then attempt to convince the bank's employees that a vote in favor of the union is their only salvation.

The conduct of organization campaigns falls under the jurisdiction of the National Labor Relation Board (NLRB), which derives its authority from the Labor-Management Relations Act of 1947. The NLRB will supervise all campaign and election activities undertaken by the bank and the union as the union attempts to gain representation of the bank's employees and the bank tries to stop it. A win by the union is not at all inevitable. Within the past ten years, unions have won only slightly more than half of their unionization drives. Still, unless the bank's management has had considerable experience with handling unionization attempts and winning, again, the very best advice is to seek experienced professional assistance at the first hint of a "signature" campaign.

Reward Systems: Compensation Planning and Administration

Compensation is a subject that generates some amount of discussion at all levels. Most people have an avid interest in how they are paid. Long years of spiraling inflation have created expectations for salary increases that now appear unrealistic as inflationary pressures have largely subsided. While some view pay increases as being unrelated to motivation, most people see them as directly correlated with job satisfaction and the propensity to increase production.

In classical compensation theory, an employee's value and thus compensation are tied almost directly to two factors: increasing productivity and relative purchasing power. Historically, an employee's compensation grows in relation to the perceived value management places on that employee's work output (productivity). Although strict age-related comparisons are no longer legal, length of service and, therefore, age have often been highly correlated with value. Compensation theory posits that it is difficult to satisfy desires for higher wages without somehow obtaining commensurate gains in productivity.

Several sound pay management points should be considered when evaluating a bank management's compensation proposals. Sound pay management can be viewed in terms of four fundamental elements that contribute to making balanced and sensible compensation decisions:

1. The organization's compensation objectives.
2. Tax considerations (local, state, and federal).
3. Environmental constraints and opportunities.
4. Knowledge of the competition's practices.

The Organization's Compensation Objectives

A bank must decide how to position itself in the labor marketplace. Will it pay salaries slightly above the market to attract high-quality people who will tend to remain with the organization, or will it pay salaries that are just adequate, thereby often accepting slightly higher turnover, training, and dislocation costs? Management must decide whether well-compensated employees will in fact yield better service to customers and be more productive for the organization, or whether other factors such as advertising, proprietary products, and creative investment strategies will make up for declining output from the work force.

One of the newer ideas is to link strategy and compensation. This can be accomplished by identifying specific strategic objectives and the very small number of executives who can have significant impact on achieving those objectives. Raises for these executives are made to depend specifically on their success in making progress toward these objectives and eventually reaching them. Singling out certain executives for reward as they move toward strategic success also means untying their salary increases from the usual linkage to short-term corporate or departmental financial performance. A director can legitimately inquire whether new strategies in the course of implementation have been associated with the kinds of specific compensation practices suggested here.

Can technology be relied on to reduce direct labor costs substantially? Possibly, but a problem with this assumption is that employees are less and less willing to perform work that ties them to largely machine-dictated routines. The newer technologies are having a very mixed effect on job content. Artificial intelligence and desktop computers tend to impact the jobs of employees much higher up in the organization than did earlier generations of mainframe computers and their associated systems. The implication of these potentially less interesting jobs needs to be considered in the design of the reward system—both from a financial and nonfinancial standpoint. These kinds of corporate compensation objectives are of paramount importance in the establishment of a sound pay management program.

Tax Considerations

For the most part, salaried or hourly based employees are taxed on the basis of W-2 reported earnings and are not really positioned to take advantage of tax minimization. Indirect compensation is the term applied to benefits or prerequisites that, under existing tax regulations, are not taxed. Presently, such items as parking, subsidized low-cost lunches, medical care, legal aid, and employee assistance programs (EAPs) are not taxable events to the employee. One area of concern with these kinds of benefits or perks is that Congress or the IRS may, at any time, determine them to be income to the employee and, therefore, taxable. Because tax laws and/or interpretations change frequently, tax-favored plans may not be particularly sound investments of an organization's compensation dollars.

In fact, a growing body of evidence suggests that employees often prefer to have the cash anyway—at least to replace benefits that have little advantage to them or to their particular personal or family situations. Satisfying such preferences (so-called "cafeteria" plans) has tended to increase benefit rates and administrative costs. These rising costs are caused by reductions in the size of covered groups and by the need to handle the numerous different coverages that employees select.

Environmental Constraints and Opportunities

There are three forces that no compensation manager can ignore: inflation, demography, and changing societal values. The effects of inflation have begun to abate significantly over the last few years. However, not so long ago average pay raises were ratcheted by inflation. Increases of 8 to 10 percent were commonplace for rank-and-file employees performing at "satisfactory" levels. These increases were being paid, although in most cases job content and productivity remained relatively constant. Merit budgets have become more modest, but reversals in the economy could result in a return to rapid salary escalation fueled by inflation.

Demographic factors are sobering. For the past several years the country's economic rise has been dramatic. Yet, there are growing numbers of unemployed in our nation who do not possess the sophisticated skills that many businesses now demand. At the same time, there are not enough qualified workers in many high-growth fields such as data and word processing and so-called high-technology product design, development, and manufacture. In many cases, jobs go begging because far too many companies and developers locate their plants and office complexes well beyond the reach of public transportation. Often the costs, time, and distances associated with commuting to and from distant suburban locations combine to make these employment opportunities most unattractive. More and more employees balk at the prospects of being transferred to different company locations at the whim of management.

Changing values have begun to have an undeniable impact on pay theory. Workers are less willing to be "good soldiers." Company loyalty is fast diminishing. Employees are placing a greater emphasis on off-the-job interests. More women want meaningful jobs and financially rewarding careers. These environmental and social considerations can be turned into opportunities to better utilize the bank's human resources. Denying the presence of these concerns, however, can lead to higher labor costs, needless turnover, and even reduced levels of service to bank customers. Bank directors should be aware of the extent to which each of the factors affects their banks and what management is doing to take advantage of the situation.

Knowledge of the Competition's Practices

The final element in the quartet of sound pay management factors is the competition's practices. Blindly following the compensation practices of competing financial organizations may be disastrous if the compensation objectives of your organization and theirs are not the same.

The personnel department should be aware of what the competition is doing. It should be equipped and prepared to watch for changes in starting salaries in the area, as well as pay trends and changes in salary structure. If possible, it should participate in local, regional, and even national compensation and benefit surveys for banks and financial and service organizations. Some attention should be given to spot skill shortages that could affect salaries, union contracts, and general increases granted in the area. Extra effort should be taken to review the compensation histories of outstanding performers who leave to take jobs with competitors.

Attractive, competitive, and appropriate compensation programs demand that management:

- Continually assess compensation philosophy and strategies.
- Structure unique pay programs that are attuned to employee needs.
- Where possible, introduce innovative, noncash alternatives that expand the opportunity for "psychological compensation" (e.g., tuition reimbursement programs, job sharing, additional vacation as a reward for reduced loss time for illness, etc.).

- Reward productive employees well for excellent to out-standing performance while deferring raises or weeding out below-standard contributors.

Management cannot forget that it is constantly under the gun to marshall all its creative energies and good judgment in the structuring and administration of the bank's compensation program.

Staff Development

Performance Assessment

Along with compensation, performance assessment is probably one of the most difficult and problematic areas in human resource utilization. Performance assessment serves to help management determine what salary increases to grant, which staff members to promote to higher levels of responsibility, and what training and development opportunities to offer. Performance assessments can also help managers decide how to allocate organizational rewards and recognition such as bonuses, special payments, and other incentives.

Performance assessments can also be used to assist managers in the documentation of poor performers who need more direct supervision or who should possibly be considered for separation from the organization. In addition, timely performance assessments are a powerful mechanism for providing feedback to an organization's employees. Top bank management must instruct the personnel department to see to it that supervisors prepare performance appraisals that accurately reflect employee strengths and shortcomings. In these times of increased employee activism, challenges to traditional employee/employer relationships, affirmative action pressures, and expensive lawsuits, it is essential that a bank have a first-class performance appraisal system. It has to be good if the bank is to avoid difficulties with its staff. Even more important, a really good performance appraisal system becomes a key element in any strategy to make high-quality personnel an explicit factor in maintaining a competitive edge.

Too often performance assessments are flawed because they are treated primarily as a diagnostic tool with virtually no prescription for improvement. Almost none of us enjoys the prospect of facing another person with less than positive observations. Therefore, all too often, supervisors sheepishly handle appraisal sessions in a very general, inexact, and garbled fashion, omitting important shortcomings and work-related problems that might cause the exchange to be "unpleasant." Employees are entitled to an assessment that points out areas that need attention, specific strengths to be developed further, and shortcomings to be overcome. Positive contributions made by employees should be emphasized whenever possible. Employees very much want to hear that their skills are valued and that they have made a significant contribution to their organization. They also usually appreciate learning about those performance areas that really need to be improved.

The performance appraisal process does not stop with the formal annual review. Informal appraisals should be frequent and coincident with performance milestones or shortfalls. After discussing the performance assessment with an employee, the manager or supervisor should follow up to ensure that the employee is taking steps to correct the deficiencies. Real management commitment to thoughtful, accurate, timely, and comprehensive performance assessment will prove to be good for the bank and constructive and positive for bank employees as well.

If your bank is having problems with morale, retention, or recruitment, make sure you inquire how systematically the above principles are actually carried out in performance appraisal practices.

Training and Development

Every organization needs to provide training on some level to its employees. One of the most commonly overlooked and crucial elements of an effective training and development program is a comprehensive employee orientation. Newly hired employees cannot be expected to understand the policies, philosophy, and management perspective of an organization without having them laid out in a careful and professional way.

Management must be cautioned that training cannot be viewed as a quick-fix solution for every employee-related performance issue that arises. Careful attention should be given to providing training only when there is an opportunity for measurable improvement in organizational or individual performance. Of course, a bank may sponsor self-improvement offerings and tuition reimbursement benefits aimed at individual development and personal growth. These programs should be totally voluntary and encouraged only as part of a mutually agreed-upon personal development program that comes as an outgrowth of the comprehensive performance assessment process that was outlined earlier. Employees who believe that management is sincerely interested in their personal growth and their long-term career development will be inclined to link their own aspirations with the bank's growth and profitability goals as well as its longer-term strategic objectives.

There is evidence from the experience of both banks and insurance companies to suggest that computer-integrated financial services delivery systems lead to relative increases in the costs and importance of training programs. When a bank's business strategy is based on technology, a director may want to obtain assurances that effective and timely adjustments in existing orientation, training, and development are in fact being made.

Mergers and Acquisitions

With hundreds of bank mergers and acquisitions completed or underway, it is now safe to say that banking has in no way escaped the human, managerial, and organizational problems associated with corporate mergers in other industries.

As bank directors who must protect the interests of investors and stockholders, you must be prepared to watch more than the financial implications of your growing organization. Both line and human resources managers must grapple with four basic sets of problems in the course of bringing two or more organizations together:

1. Meshing and integrating management systems.
2. Eliminating redundancies and overlaps in functions and people.
3. Resolving career consequences (often for very large numbers of people) to avoid significant longer-term retention problems.
4. Melding possibly quite divergent organization "cultures."

These problem areas can be meaningfully addressed when the business objectives and advantages of the acquisition can be forthrightly stated and dealt with. If combining two or more banks makes economic sense, then it becomes more crucial to turn to these four issues.

Many banks have tried to avoid or delay facing the issues caused by merger by promising autonomy to each new unit as it is added. This seldom works very well from the viewpoint of the acquiring institution, especially since combining the operations of two formerly separate entities rarely, in and of itself, does anything to reduce costs. In fact, the slowed-down pace of decision making and the relative increase in the complexity of decision-making processes may actually result in cost increases. Furthermore, the longer an acquired bank is permitted to operate in seeming isolation, the greater will be the ultimate resentment, disarray, and resistance once integrating efforts finally begin.

People who have experienced a merger appreciate the extent to which the acquired party feels helpless and the acquirers feel vulnerable. It is the predominance of these feelings that makes it important to set up very strong communication channels as soon as possible after the critical merger decision has been made. Without these channels, rumors, hostility, resentment, and unnecessary conflict are likely to win the day. It would be entirely appropriate for you as a director to recommend to your management with firmness that a strong, sensitive, senior, well-funded joint task force or committee be appointed to plan and carry out the process of combining the organizations once the merger has been approved.

The bank director whose institution is in the process of merging should seek answers to questions like the following:

- Has management expressed to the board and to employees a clear and cogent vision about the way the combined banks will operate and what advantages are being sought by combining these institutions?
- Is there a merger plan that makes sense—that actively seeks a future combined operation that will work well and that reflects the present status of both organizations?
- Does the merger plan take specific account of the preexisting management systems and differences between them, of redundancy, of overlapping career plans, and of differences in culture? And is that plan based on detailed knowledge and understanding of each bank involved?
- Is the implementation plan credible? Is it affordable? Does the

schedule for merging functions and systems move along at a sufficiently brisk pace and in a way that can grapple with discordant attitudes and other kinds of interpersonal and interorganizational conflict?

- What assurances are there that the managers are attuned to and capable of solving the human problems that are the real barriers to a successful merger or acquisition?

The "Image" and the Reality

Banking as experienced by its customers is all too often different from its advertising. Imaging messages may tout a bank's claim of being in a "people" business. But it is not really a people business if the motivation of the staff is based on fear and intimidation rather than on a desire to serve its customers well. If career possibilities are rare or nonexistent for all but the so-called fast trackers, the rest of the employees may regard the bank's advertising as hypocritical.

A further gap between image and reality may arise because it is no longer as easy to enforce the service-oriented behavior among employees that customers regard as positive. Standards for meeting the public that used to be inculcated by chief tellers can no longer be taught on the job to many of the employees doing routine tasks but must be the subject of periodic off-line training sessions. This is especially true since the contact that employees have with the public is often no longer from the banking floor but from the telephone. Telephone calls are simply not subject to careful supervisory observation except by methods that seem, to many employees, like spying rather than legitimate supervision.

Understandably, then, a gap can easily develop between the friendliness and service orientation expressed in advertising campaigns and the experiences of the customer in the course of conducting the increasing range of banking and financially related transactions. If bank employees do not feel that they are recognized and rewarded for providing warm and attentively efficient service to customers, they are likely to choose to emphasize something else. The "something else" will be whatever they perceive as what they must do to earn rewards and escape pain under the bank's incentives and punishments systems.

Interestingly, employees who do not feel appropriately treated by their own supervisors often will not—indeed, they almost cannot—treat the bank's customers appropriately. If employees respect their supervisors and managers, they come to accept them as "role models." If they do not respect them, they use perceived mistreatment by the boss as the excuse for actually trying to "do the boss in."

Sound familiar? It should. Nevertheless, these basic conditions and principles are at the heart of the reason why the human resources function is crucial in banking, and why in the bank's business strategy, human resources management has become more and more important. In spite of the massive investment in electronic data processing equipment and automated machines that practically all banks have made over the past 10 to 15 years, people receive and pay out money at the tellers' windows (ATMs—Automated Teller Machines—not withstanding), process loans, issue money orders, open safety deposit boxes, evaluate investment portfolios, check credit references, and proof checks. Bank employees still manually perform a significant proportion of the hundreds, if not thousands, of individual transactions that are the guts and muscle of every financial institution in the nation. Granted, business would probably grind to a screeching halt without computers and other business machines, but removing too much of the human factor too quickly without extra careful thought would be equally as disastrous.

Bank directors, accordingly, are carrying out one of their legitimate functions whenever they ask questions such as the following:

- Are our customers getting the treatment they have been led to expect?
- When a customer calls the bank, what is the real message received? "We are here to serve you" or is it, "Get off the line, I have something more important to do."
- Are personnel policies and practices consistent with the image the bank wants to project?

When you begin to look at the people side of your banking enterprise (or any other business, for that matter), you will discover that the work place is changing dramatically. Turnover in many areas of most banks is staggering. Demands by women and minorities for upward mobility and recognition continue. Individual productivity and performance are declining, while demands by employees for increased flexibility in working hours, expanded benefits and packages, and higher wages go on unabated.

First the futurists and more recently the popular press have concluded that something must be done about the declining productivity and competitiveness of this country in world markets. Article after article has presented powerful evidence that lowered performance, dissatisfaction, apathy, and resentment, coupled with the strong dollar and cheap imports, pose a real threat to our economic vitality. The old values of loyalty and dedication to the job, especially among newer workers, are giving way to a significantly heightened focus on the exploration of outside interests that are embraced more enthusiastically than the so-called work ethic. Clearly, employees have come to expect increased nonwork options that will allow them to enjoy their leisure time. More highly educated employees are looking for increased options, flexible working hours, child care, career training, and other special arrangements.

Employers are often more in the position of having to compete for job candidates who have almost come to take for granted their "right" to a job. These same potential employees are highly sought after (especially those who have the skills and experience to competently perform the jobs that need most to be filled). In spite of significant unemployment in many areas, new job applicants expect regular and frequent pay increases, access to their personnel records and files, cafeteria benefit packages, tuition reimbursement, generous pensions, liberal time-off allowances including flex-time, and even legal and counseling insurance coverage—all this, not to mention a more fundamental and substantial role in actual decision making on the job. These present and future trends focusing on the needs and concerns of the employee fly in the face of almost cutthroat competition for the consumers' dollars among banks, savings and loan associations, savings banks, and other financial service organizations.

Recent legal and regulatory liberalization in the industry is beginning to make the differences between the various types of financial organizations unclear. The general public is faced with a blur of gifts, prizes, and favors by competitive institutions, which only serve to make customers more whimsical in a volatile marketplace. This is especially true when these business markets are maturing.

All of these factors bring a call for increased productivity along with better utilization of the bank's fiscal and human resources in an environment that is regrettably often uncertain and obscure. Can management demand and expect increased productivity without at least considering and ultimately introducing some of the elements that could be expected to lead to more satisfied and productive employees? Let's explore the question, Are increased productivity and worker satisfaction incompatible?

Magazines and papers are full of articles on the office of the future crammed with computers, word processors, high-speed copiers, automatic data entry and retrieval systems, and minicomputers. This fast-moving revolution in office technology gives managers an unparalleled opportunity to attempt to meld dramatically increased productive capability with heightened employee satisfaction.

In an article in the *American Banker,* Phillip Kraft discussed the human opportunity in technology. In his view the new technology will fundamentally alter the way banks deliver financial services in the coming decade. He recounts the growth of the uses of computers and the lost efficiency that has often accompanied the installation of these complicated mammoth systems. It can now be recognized that people were often reduced to acting merely as interfaces to the unyielding demands of the "system." In many ways financial institutions became even more impersonal assembly lines, not at all dissimilar from what might be considered their manufacturing counterparts.

Kraft and others argue, if financial institutions are to stay profitable and responsive to customer needs, management must be willing to redesign work flow and job content as well as procedures and responsibilities to complement the new technologies. The same kinds of thinking that culminated in experiments in job enhancement and work enrichment in manufacturing and automobile assembly plants must also be at least considered for financial organizations.

It is hoped that some of the points discussed in this chapter will convince directors that sound human resource utilization practices make good business sense. Serious reflection on the employee relations policies of the bank leads to an appreciation of the importance that human resources play in achieving greater success and profitability.

Chapter 10

TECHNOLOGY IN BANKING

by Robert E. Moll

Introduction

In years past the director's responsibility relative to the use of technology centered principally on the audit function. Electronic data processing systems were carefully monitored to detect any wrongdoing or tampering with assets and liabilities. That is all changing. The enormity of current and anticipated investments in technology, the growing dependency on outside organizations for the delivery of financial services, and the strategic implications of technological decisions suggest now that the subject of technology is a matter of general concern to all directors.

As Figure 10–1 illustrates, as recently as 1970 the typical bank technological environment consisted of a tightly controlled centralized data processing facility. Access to bank and customer records was limited to a relatively small number of bank employees. During the 1970s, the installation of local and remote automated teller machines (ATMs) grew rapidly, as did the installation of terminals throughout the bank. Data communications networks grew correspondingly fast, providing access to a bank's systems to a much larger number of people.

The trend that developed in the 1970s has grown geometrically in the first half of this decade. As financial institutions seek to position themselves for the future and differentiate themselves in the marketplace, investments in technology-based products are reaching staggering proportions. Today it is common to find many

Time Frame	The New Components	Computing Environment	People with Access
Prior to 1970		• Centralized Computing • Limited number of directly connected terminals	• Limited number of bank personnel
1970 to 1980	• On-premise and off-premise ATMs • Teller and administrative terminals • Cash management services	• Centralized and decentralized computing • Direct connect and dial-up terminals • Proprietary networks	• Large number of bank personnel • Large number of customers
1980 to Present	• Point of Sale systems • Treasurer workstations • Home banking • Clerical workstations	• Distributed processing • Regional and national shared networks • Satellite and radio communications	• Majority of bank personnel • Majority of customers • Many non-customers

Figure 10–1 Technology and Historical Developments Diagram

thousands of people accessing a bank's systems from thousands of locations. Personal computer workstations are widespread and interact regularly with the centralized or decentralized computing facilities. Customers are routinely initiating transactions electronically from often unpredictable locations. This trend will continue.

Now and in the future, bank directors must continue to be concerned with the traditional audit function—that is, safeguarding bank records (assets and liabilities) and those of customers. The rapid proliferation of personal computers and terminals, the magnitude of bank communications networks, the speed with which transactions are processed, and the vast numbers of people and places to contend with make even the traditional audit function a formidable challenge.

In addition to the fiduciary responsibility, bank directors must now be concerned with the fact that the number of opportunities that exist for the exploitation of technology will far exceed the financial resources of most banking institutions. Therefore, bank management will have to select the opportunities most in keeping with the strategic thrust of the company and the risk level the company can sustain. The strategic management of technology and the organizational impact of future developments will present new challenges for bank management and thus are matters of concern for all directors.

Trends in Relevant Technology

The two primary forms of technology utilized in banking are the information processing and communications technologies. These technologies are developing to a point where they no longer are constraints to the financial services we provide nor the manner in which they are delivered. We can compute as fast as we might desire. We can also store as much data as we desire and make it available anywhere in the world we choose. Let us now examine where the technology is headed.

By 1995, electronic components will cost a small fraction of what they do today; they will also be faster. Improvements in components will be devoted to making systems easier to use and more modular, rather than lowering total systems costs. The greater ease of use will decrease the cost of programming and permit more complex forms of customer interaction with the systems. The improved modularity will enable providers of financial services to offer more flexible, custom-tailored networks.

New types of file storage systems will employ greatly improved magnetic and/or optical storage technology. They will be available in many sizes and types of data processing, office automation, and home use and will permit financial systems to be much richer in information content. New "expert" systems, although limited in capability and breadth, will provide an elementary level of financial consulting and guidance to customers.

Terminals will become more modular to support a wider variety of specially tailored services. They will also contain increasing amounts of computing power, storage, and easy-to-use software. In 1995, there will be little distinction between terminals, personal computers, word processors, and TV sets (the most advanced of which will have evolved into "home information centers" containing computers).

The breakup of AT&T will cause rapid and unpredictable changes in the cost and availability of communications services. Local business telephone and leased-line service will cost more, and long-distance and wide-band services will cost less. Local "bypass" communications companies offering cable, satellite, microwave, and fiber optic services as alternatives to telephone service will probably emerge rapidly. New financial services, such as truncation of checks by image transmission and processing, may become feasible, and variations in local regulations may substantially influence the location of financial service provider operations facilities.

During the later 1980s and 1990s, many homes will be equipped with two-way communicating devices that may be used for financial services. These devices will vary according to the consumer's choice of information appliances. More often, the consumer will invest in enhanced entertainment devices derived from the television set rather than in independent computers. By 1990, at least 10 percent of all homes will have such evolved TV sets that cost more than $1,000. At least 40 percent of the higher-income homes in the United States are expected to be equipped with what amounts to two-way terminals by 1990.

The only apparent constraints to the development of new financial services and delivery systems are the human resources dedicated to this activity. While software development productivity is expected to improve in the future, the demand for more advanced systems will continue to outpace the capacity of most organizations. While increasingly adaptable application software packages will appear as a result of joint ventures or investments by major software companies, shortages will continue to limit a bank's activities.

Trends in technology thus present most bankers with a dilemma. On the one hand, virtually anything is possible with technology. On the other hand, human and financial resources have limits. This dilemma is compounded by the fact that the development of electronic delivery systems is increasingly complex and costly. As such, in the future banks must carefully prioritize investments in technology-based products. In order to do that, management must first target the market the bank seeks to serve and correspondingly target the products the bank will provide. New insights into the market forces that affect the evolution of technology-based products will be required.

Market Forces Driving Technology-Based Products

Many forces interacting with each other will shape the evolution of financial service products. Deregulation is often credited as having the greatest impact on the financial services industry at the present time. While deregulation will certainly influence the basis of competition and structure of the industry in future years, its impact on the evolution of financial service products and how they will be delivered is less pronounced.

The pace with which deregulation proceeds will somewhat impact the ease with which financial service products will evolve, but technology is and will continue to be used as a means of bridging regulatory barriers. For example, communications and computer systems can be used to link the product offerings of banks and insurance companies and present a single-product package to the marketplace. Where required, third-party organizations are being used as product integrator, as illustrated by the recent joint venture announcement of Chemical Bank, Bank of America, AT&T, and Time, Inc. for the delivery of home banking services.

While deregulation may lead to changes in the basis of competition, competition itself will alter the evolution of financial service products and delivery mechanisms. As financial institutions seek to differentiate themselves in the marketplace, they are constantly searching for ways to broaden their product offering. Diversification attempts into related financial services and in some cases unrelated services have become commonplace—for example, the entry of banks into the discount brokerage business, the real estate management business, and the selling of life insurance. Some bankers are seeking to carve out market niches that they can serve in a unique way. Others are attempting to create product packages that have a greater appeal in the marketplace.

Pricing practices are also appearing that attempt to attract particular classes of customers or in some cases alter the customer behavior pattern. Citibank, for example, experimented with special charges for transactions performed by human tellers. Girard Bank (now part of Mellon Bank) provided financial incentives for customers to perform transactions electronically in an apparent attempt to alter their behavior pattern toward less costly mechanisms.

Some people believe that it is technology that is shaping the evolution of financial services. The introduction of ATMs, the invention of the "Smart" card, and the use of debit- or credit-card-activated gasoline pumps are cited as examples of technology looking for a problem to be solved. While some of this is certainly true, it is more appropriate to view technology as a tool that is now available to product development people for use as a competitive weapon. Technology and technologists should be solicited for input to the product planning process and not be allowed to operate in a vacuum. The advancement of technology to this state intensifies the need for a proper *balance* between the business side of banking and the traditional operations side of the business.

Because technological skills are now required in many functions of banking, the roles and responsibilities of individuals are in some institutions becoming blurred and need to be clarified. Technology itself should be viewed as a secondary force or tool to be used and not the principal driving force. Technology needs to be managed.

The principal force that must ultimately be given credit for the evolution of financial service products is the marketplace. It is the customer or potential customer who ultimately determines if a particular service, packaging, and price combination is sufficiently attractive to warrant consideration. And the customer is becoming much more discerning as the options expand. In assessing the attractiveness of *technology-based products,* customers of both the consumer and corporate sector will consider four interrelated factors beyond the traditional demand for stability of the parties involved.

The first of these factors is *convenience* and is measured in terms of accessibility and simplicity. The rapid acceptance of ATMs and cash management services is clear evidence of the role convenience will play. Home banking and the increasing use of on-site terminal or personal computer delivery systems in corporations are a continuation of the attempt to make banking more accessible. The delivery of financial services remotely and on a self-service basis requires a level of self-sufficiency on the part of the customer. No longer is the banker present to provide guidance in the selection of options or completion of forms. As a result, for these services to be truly convenient, they must be simple to use. The need for simplicity as it relates to convenience suggests that the services must be finely tuned to the needs of the particular customer and uncluttered by superfluous capabilities.

The second factor that will determine the level of acceptability of a particular technology-based service is the degree to which the service is *tailored to a particular market segment*. This factor has two important aspects to it when we consider services delivered electronically on a self-service basis. The first is that the product must be designed with the buyer in mind. For example, if a bank is interested in the indirect automobile loan market and wants to deliver lending services electronically at the point of sale (dealer location), it must deliver a product that truly benefits the dealer as well as the consumer. To benefit both requires that the service facilitate the purchase and sale of an automobile. As such, the service must address the insurance and registration requirements of the transaction in addition to the granting of credit. It may further necessitate that the buyer be given a facility to do comparative shopping regarding loan interest rates as well as insurance premiums and coverage. Thus, the deliverer of such a service must view the delivery as a business unto itself—a fee-based service that is measured on a stand-alone basis. The success of the loan component of the product will depend on the rate, terms, and convenience associated with it.

The second aspect of the need for electronically delivered services to be tailored to the particular market segment is an outgrowth of the first. If we are to deliver services at the point of sale that satisfy the unique requirements of the environment and we are to deliver them simply and uncluttered with attributes that do not relate to this environment, the number of market segments we must consider will grow significantly. In the future, we must look at market segments more discreetly than we have in the past. The requirements for a product targeted to the automobile market will be different in at least some respects from a product targeted, for example, to the appliances or boat market.

The third factor affecting the success of technology-based products in the future will be the *economic* considerations for both the customer and provider of the service. The rapid movement of funds from depository institutions to the money market funds several years ago was clear evidence of the desire of consumers to seek a higher yield. It also weakened the traditional significance placed on institutional loyalty. In the future, the consumer, as well as the corporate customer, will continue to be influenced heavily by both the yield on investments and the price paid for services.

In order to provide competitively priced services in the future, and to provide them profitably, banks will find increasing pressure to know and to reduce the cost of delivery. This issue will be exacerbated by the previously described need to tailor products to more discreet market segments and to satisfy a broader range of the needs of the particular delivery environment. The costs for the creation of products and delivery systems will increase significantly. This will necessitate more selectivity on the part of bankers regarding the market segments they serve, the products they provide, and the role they play in the delivery process. Few, if any, financial institutions will find it possible to serve all needs of all markets. In the future, we will see more modularization of banking products and their support systems with low-cost modules packaged or repackaged for unique market segments—in other words, a disintegration of product components and reintegration at the time and place of delivery.

The fourth factor affecting the success of future technology-based products is the *information component* of the product itself. This will express itself in two forms. First, the customers need information that will enable them to select and perform the proper service for their particular needs. This class of information is educational or tutorial in nature. Information of this type is necessary not only for the customer, but also in some cases for the agent of the financial institution. Take, for example, the difficulty for a property/casualty insurance agent to construct a portfolio of coverage that is closely aligned and priced to the unique needs of a particular corporation. Or consider the interaction required to administer employee benefits on a cafeteria basis. We will shortly see, therefore, the use of artificial intelligence—knowledge-based or expert systems incorporated into products to assist the customer or the institution's agent in the delivery or execution of services.

The second form in which information is becoming a component of financial services is that banks and others are involved in processing data that are extraneous or superfluous to the financial transaction itself. Take, for example, the movement of invoice data between the buyer and seller of goods or services (home banking or electronic data interchange). Most of the data that are processed are for the benefit of the customer and are not needed directly for the debiting or crediting of the bank account. This, too, will impact the economics of services banks choose to provide or the role that they elect to play.

The forces interacting to shape the evolution of financial services, the factors that are becoming important in the marketplace, and the cost to maintain or gain a competitive advantage require significant senior management involvement and director awareness. Financial institutions cannot be all things to all people. Selecting the markets they will serve, the products they will provide, and the role they will play in their delivery will have strategic and financial implications of major significance.

Product Implications

When we examine the market forces driving the evolution of technology-based products and consider the potential of the technology itself, we can gain some insight into how financial service products are likely to evolve in the future. The likely evolution of financial service products is marked by two distinct characteristics that have broad management implications. The first is the extensive use of electronic delivery mechanisms that will be utilized. The second is that financial service products will be highly customized for specific market segments. Let us examine these characteristics in more detail and identify the management implications of each.

The use of electronic delivery systems for such services as home banking, cash management, indirect lending, and others implies the use of a communications network. If we are to package our services with the services of others, such as insurance companies, publishers, or retailers, it may also imply the use of outside organizations to assist in the product packaging process. In both cases, third parties, often unregulated third parties, may be involved in the distribution of our financial service products. An organization needs to consider the security, legal liability, and image implications of these decisions. It also suggests that a bank must decide on the role that it will play—will it manufacture the service, distribute the service, or market the service to the end user. The decision to utilize or involve third parties may also vary for particular market segments or particular classes of products. The bank may elect to play all roles for a certain market niche and only market a range of services for another market segment.

The second characteristic identified for products of the future is that they may be highly customized for specific market segments. For example, if a bank delivers services electronically to physicians, products will need to be tailored to the unique needs of the physician and the environment in which the physician functions. This will increase the cost of product development and narrow the market that will be expected to absorb the development expense. This suggests that in the future banks must be more discerning regarding the markets they serve—particularly the markets served electronically.

Electronically delivered services to any market also increase the geographical limits of the marketplace and place new burdens or opportunities on the organization. At the same time, electronically delivered services dramatically increase the number of institutions that potentially compete in the traditional marketplace.

Organizational Implications

The most significant impact of technology and technology-based products on a banking institution will be the necessity for the organization to become market driven. In the past the products offered and the markets served were largely dictated by the regulatory barriers that were in place and the geographical positioning of a branch network. As such, bankers would devise products and promote those products to a local market. The organization structure of most banks reflects this product orientation (lending, trust, etc.).

As the regulatory barriers diminish, as technology is used to package products that cross institutional boundaries, and as electronic delivery systems enable banks and their competitors to enter new market areas, choices will be necessary. Because most institutions cannot afford to be all things to all people, each bank must be selective.

Essentially, technology and other factors allow management to create and deliver any product to any market. But, human and financial resources are not infinite. Therefore, the bank must answer these questions: What markets do we want to serve? and What products do we want to offer those markets?

The banker who chooses to deliver services electronically must be more sensitive to the overall needs of the environment in which the service is being delivered (the physician). Therefore, the bank must look at our market segments more discretely than in the past and analyze the needs of each market segment in more detail. Banks must also be more conscious of the economics of providing a particular market with a range of products. The number of alluring opportunities and the increased cost of developing technology-based products necessitates deliberate financial analysis before the fact and quality cost accounting after the fact.

The transition from being a product-driven to a market-driven company is difficult. It is a cultural change that will impact the organization structure, the management skills, and the entire decision-making process. Yet, those organizations that recognize and address the need will become the leaders of technology in banking.

Chapter 11

THE BANK ENVIRONMENT OF THE FUTURE

by Martin L. Ernst

Introduction

The previous ten chapters examined many of the far-ranging and often unique aspects of the banking environment that raise matters of concern to directors. This final chapter summarizes the more important of these features but in the context of describing the social background, problems, issues, and opportunities that we believe are central to determining how banks will operate in the future. This futures approach leads to only limited review of many of the short-term questions that occupy most of the time at directors' meetings. However, it does focus on the many interrelated forces that are acting to establish what banks will need to be successful in the future and how directors can contribute to the process of meeting these needs.

The First Half of the Decade

To improve our sense of the turmoil and pace of change that banks have been experiencing, it is useful to review what happened in the first half of the 1980s.

249

Economic Environment

During this period, inflation rates climbed far above any level that had been forecast and thereafter declined to a generally acceptable rate. These events demonstrate that we have adequate measures to maintain low inflation rates. However, the political and economic price for doing so is sufficiently serious that confidence in maintaining the 1985 level is at best tenuous, with resulting impacts on the availability and cost of long-term debt. Interest rates followed a similar pattern, but their dropoff left them high relative to inflation for a number of interrelated reasons, the primary ones being the federal budget deficit and concern about an increase in inflation. Interest rates were very volatile for the early years of the decade. By mid-decade, they became more stable, but any conviction that this would continue was weak. All of these events placed pressures on our depository institutions, with particularly damaging results on thrift institutions.

Regulation

The trend toward deregulation of banks started in 1980; it was fueled by competitive initiatives, technological changes, and high inflation and interest rates. If the banking industry had been forced to continue operating within the old constraints, its very survival would have been in question. For this reason certain political moves were made in the direction of equalizing the ability of banks to compete with other types of financial institutions. It is important to note, however, that most deregulation was of a type that encourages more effective competition rather than loosening the special responsibilities that our society considers appropriate for banks.

With greater competitive opportunities available, the pace of deregulation slowed. In the middle of the decade, however, banks were threatened with reregulation if a sufficient number of them (or their holding companies) demonstrated that they were using their greater freedom unwisely. Regulation that concerns financial safety and soundness and consumer rights was never eased; rather it tended to increase in coverage and complexity for many types of banking operations.

Competition

Competition in the first half of the 1980s clearly increased throughout the financial services industry. The growth of giant organizations offering a full range of financial services began before 1980, but at the start of the decade it was only in embryonic form. By 1985, integrated financial services organizations had become active on a more complete scale, although whether the "financial supermarket" concept makes economic sense and whether such organizations could command continuing customer loyalties continued to be debatable issues. In many cases, the financial conglomerates ran into management difficulties when they tried to combine financial activities that involved widely differing sets of attitudes and practices. However, the resources behind the larger organizations were extensive so the debate went on. Meanwhile, the general competitive level increased during the 1980s among banks on both a national and local scale, and between banks and a wide variety of nonbank organizations. International competition among banks also grew.

Financial Instruments

The variety of financial instruments available to meet requirements for both borrowing and saving continued to multiply in almost bewildering fashion. It became difficult to find a form of debt that could not be repackaged and marketed to increase its fungibility. Similarly, means for hedging against almost any type of future financial requirement became widely available in many different forms. Many of the new instruments were not legally available for banks to employ, even though some of these instruments competed with traditional bank services.

Technology

Applications of technology continued to spread, although the process was more an exercise in consolidation than in the development of new concepts. ATMs proliferated, and credit cards became more sophisticated in an effort to combat counterfeiting. Debit cards began to be used for payment at the "point-of-sale" but made only limited market penetration. And "Smart" cards that can provide a substitute for cash came under intensive development by the large credit card organizations.

Banking-at-home had been technologically feasible for some time, but made little progress in the marketplace in the early 1980s. It continued to be weak until a number of conditions could be met. The number of home computers had to grow significantly, suitable relationships between individuals' banks and billing organizations had to be worked out, and a pricing system acceptable to consumers had to be developed.

In many respects, the most dramatic accomplishment of technology was a very quiet one—demonstration of the ability to develop the computer and telecommunication systems needed to provide transaction processing support for a wide range of new products, such as individual asset management systems, in a reliable and economic fashion.

Customers

The sophistication and information resources of bank customers grew dramatically in the first half of the 1980s. On the wholesale side, this process had been under way for many years as better-trained financial officers began to make effective use of computers and of the growing flow of all types of financial information to improve the cash management practices of their firms. As part of the process, it became routine for them to shop among banks for the one that best could meet their requirements. A bigger change, however, took place in the retail market, where consumers acquired a painful education from the impacts of inflation and high interest rates. Here, too, individuals benefited from improved education, computer and hand calculator assistance in evaluating alternatives, and a wide range of information concerning advisory and direct financial services. The individual asset management account is a prime example of this change in how individuals handle their personal financial affairs.

International

Global interactivity continued to grow in the early 1980s, with new major financial centers emerging, more complex international production arrangements being entered into by both transnational and other businesses, and some of the financial instruments that were developed in the United States spreading into world markets. With active money and security markets operating in major world centers 24 hours a day, it seemed likely that the next decade would see more types of banking operations being conducted on a similar basis by more large banks.

In the first half of the 1980s, a number of developing countries encountered major debt problems, with serious implications for many large U.S. banks. Although the international banking system demonstrated a great deal of flexibility in dealing with the debt situations of individual countries, the underlying problems had not been solved in some of the important cases; a threat remained that was viewed as likely to require strong government intervention if the worst scenario arose.

General Industry Restructuring

The general restructuring of U.S. industry continued as the country moved increasingly to a service and information orientation. Many important industries that once were major customers of banks weakened in the process. A decline in oil prices and an extensive oversupply of shipping, in particular, had major impacts on many U.S. banks. U.S. agriculture moved to a near disaster state. And analyses of future world agricultural production suggested that it was unlikely that its past strength ever could be completely regained.

Uncertainty about general U.S. international competitiveness continued, even though many of the surviving manufacturing companies had greatly improved their efficiency. Meanwhile, some aspects of the restructuring—such as hostile takeovers and leveraged buy-outs—offered profitable opportunities for banks and other financial institutions. Restructuring also provided opportunities for questioning and criticizing the process and the use of credit resources for these purposes.

Financial Industry Restructuring

The factors just described, in combination, were instrumental in bringing about a major restructuring of the financial services industries. Financial services conglomerates eventually emerged. Bank holding companies proliferated and gained strength, although participation in the newly authorized activities did not

necessarily provide them with a significant fraction of total revenues. Competition and unwise lending led to a rapid rise in bank
failures to a level higher in 1984 and 1985 than any since the Great
Depression. Key legislative measures permitting banks to compete with other organizations on a broader basis seemed increasingly less likely to be passed by Congress. This left unresolved the
key question of whether and how the activities of different types of
financial services organizations would be differentiated—if at all.

Banks in the early 1980s did find more opportunities to circumvent many of their traditional barriers, especially those related to
interstate banking. Changes in state laws, use of computers and
telecommunications to support loan generation and various processing activities remote from the home state, and participation in
"rescue" operations to save failing banks and thrift institutions
worked to make nationwide banking more of a reality.

Bank Directors

In the midst of all this change, the role of bank directors became
more complex, more important, and more dangerous. To perform
their function well, directors had to deal with a far wider variety of
issues than in the past. In addition, they needed greater knowledge of many of the details of their bank's operations. The guidance that directors can furnish became increasingly valuable as
even those banks with the most professionally competent managers found themselves moving into relatively uncharted waters.
And the legal liability of directors became far more explicit; it was
enforced by court decisions to an extent that led to greatly
increased liability insurance rates. In some cases, it even made
such insurance quite difficult to obtain.

Not surprisingly, the many changes described here tended to
appear as gradual ones when they arose; it is only from the
perspective of a period of years that their pace and magnitude can
be fully appreciated. Since we still face many uncertainties and
unresolved issues, there is no reason to expect the rate of change to
slacken. Central to the process will be a critical question as yet
unanswered: What does this nation want of its banking system?

Over the years, banks have been given a variety of social
responsibilities and standards with regard to their expected conduct. These were mostly expressed in terms of constraints on their
operations. Simultaneously banks were granted a number of privileges and forms of protection from nonbank competition. While

many key constraints have been removed or weakened, it is at least questionable whether these compensate for the losses in protection from nonbank institutions in the post-1985 environment. If banks have a social responsibility to offer mortgages in all parts of their operating territories, will they be able to compete effectively with organizations that do not face such a requirement? If higher bank capital ratios are imposed in an effort to assure greater financial integrity, will the requirements for the profitability needed to achieve socially desirable growth lead to banks accepting greater risks in their lending operations, thereby defeating the intent of the capital requirement? Dozens of similar questions can be raised.

In a sense, the problem is one of identity. It seems unlikely that Congress envisions banks operating in a way that is undifferentiated from other types of financial services institutions. However, a direct response to competition would suggest moving in just that direction. Given this state of affairs, perhaps the more meaningful question to raise is, What can bankers, themselves, propose to establish and support a socially valuable, clearly differentiated, profitable role in serving their community and society generally. Answering this question calls for vision. Fortunately, the history of banking is full of examples of vision.

One clearly important role for directors, although not one normally ascribed, is to encourage and support appropriate vision on the part of bank management as the underlying basis for establishing objectives and building strategy. A starting point for directors is a clear understanding of where banks are now—their strengths and weaknesses relative to other financial service organizations—and a similar sense of the economic and social needs among the bank's constituencies that the bank validly can serve as a business organization.

Competitive Strengths of Banks

In spite of regulatory constraints that both limit the range of activities in which banks can compete and place a variety of restrictions on their operations, banks have some formidable and often unique sources of strength. These include federally insured deposits, participation in the Federal Reserve settlement system, a wide range of credit services, cooperative skills, integrity, and local identity.

Federally Insured Deposits

Among financial services organizations, only depository institutions have this form of insurance. Furthermore, the coverage of the insurance will in at least some situations be interpreted quite broadly, as was evidenced in the case of Continental Illinois. Other types of financial services organizations often offer some form of insurance to their customers, arranged through an association or obtained from private insurance sources. However, this coverage lacks the credibility, as well as the underlying strength of that available to banks. Experiences in 1985 with state-insured thrifts tend to confirm the view of many depositors that there is no substitute for insurance backed by the federal government.

Transaction Settlement

Only banks and thrift institutions can participate in the settlement system operated by the Federal Reserve System. This fact tends to give banks an extremely strong position whenever rapid transaction completion is required, even though this position may be bypassed if a nonbanking organization owns a limited service bank. Alternatively, nonbank organizations can achieve a nearly equivalent capability by using appropriate technology to support cooperative arrangements for a specific bank to handle the transaction settlement portion of a nonbank product offering.

Variety of Credit Services

Relative to the range of credit services offered by banks, other types of financial service institutions basically serve a set of niche markets. Some of these are very important niches and ones that can disintermediate traditional bank markets. Nevertheless, without a participating bank, many opportunities that nonbank corporations would like to exploit are limited or closed off.

Cooperative Skills

More than most types of organizations, banks have had to learn how to cooperate with one another, even when competing fiercely. The nature of our national banking system requires such cooperation. The entire check processing system, for example, would be inoperative without the cooperative establishment of many types of standards; it would be less efficient if not supplemented by local and regional cooperative arrangements. Similarly, the variety of services available at most banks would be limited if correspondent relationships had not been widely developed. Banks increasingly have developed cooperative arrangements with nonbank organizations such as publishers, communications organizations, and others, to offer services that they are not permitted to provide but that have a significant banking component. Similarly, use of franchises has grown as a means for smaller banks to acquire capabilities they could not afford by themselves. These cooperative skills have great potential for building a strong competitive position for banks.

Integrity

Part of the payoff banks receive for undergoing FDIC examinations is a degree of credibility that few other financial institutions can acquire. Painful though it may be on occasion, this examination by outside parties that have no financial relationship whatever with the bank being examined has very significant benefits in terms of the trust that is created. Coupled with local identity (described next), it provides banks with a type of reputation others cannot equal. This trust in banks relative to other financial institutions has been demonstrated repeatedly in consumer surveys.

Local Identity

Even though large banks are growing and effective interstate banking is spreading, banks have been able to maintain a considerable degree of local identity. We are still a nation of relatively small banks; the local bank is considered to be a part of the community in a way that the branch office of a national financial services institution cannot match. This applies even in cases where these local banks are making use of correspondent relationships to move a portion of their funds to areas where loan demand is greater. The growth of new banks in many states[1] tends to confirm a widely held

---

[1]For example, in 1983, 69 new banks were chartered in California (which had 387 banks at the start of the year), while only 15 banks were acquired or gave up their charters. If California can be regarded as representative of the United States as a whole, then with complete interstate banking we will still have well over 4,000 banks—a sharp contrast to the far more concentrated situation found in most parts of the world.

opinion that a really well run local bank can compete very effectively with larger, more remote banks, as well as with other types of financial institutions, as long as the local economy remains relatively healthy.

Weaknesses of Banks

Against these strengths, banks also suffer from disadvantages, most of which have been discussed earlier. Regulatory constraints are the most obvious, even though the constraints that deal with consumer and depositor protection also contribute to bank strengths. Vulnerability to disintermediation flows from the regulatory constraints. Some forms of disintermediation, such as business use of commercial paper, are likely to continue indefinitely, since the fundamental economics favor brokerage over lending in many situations. Other forms, such as the development of money market funds, may decline in importance if interest rates stay relatively stable.

There are, however, a number of by-products of regulatory constraints that are less obvious but extremely important. First, the existence of regulation tends to limit innovation by banks. This is not to say that banks cannot be innovative, because many of them have been, but rather that the form of possible innovation is restricted. One reason for this is the great extent to which an innovation in banking becomes effective only if or when it is used by most or all banks. With geographical restrictions on banking, most protectable proprietary concepts usually will have only a limited market if confined to use by a single bank—the creative bank can exploit its innovation only by sharing with others and giving away a portion of the profit. In addition, limitations on permissible bank activities make some product or service concepts impractical except through association with nonbank organizations. While not stopping innovation, these factors limit the benefits in an inhibiting way.

Somewhat closely associated with the restrictions on innovation is the fact that banks only recently have come to recognize the importance of marketing and have started to develop the skills necessary to identify particular customer segments and build products of value for them. Bank marketing was not as critical a function when only relatively limited and standard products were available and when banks often possessed strong local and unchallenged positions. In the current world, marketing skills are vital; while banks have made major progress, they still have a way to go before they fully utilize their competitive strengths.

The Future Environment

Our review of the first half of the decade suggests that many of the features critical to future operations of banks cannot be forecast with any useful degree of accuracy and reliability; too many changes can arise from a complex interaction of economic conditions, legislation, events taking place outside the United States, and actions by the banking industry itself. There are, however, some areas in which we can be reasonably secure, and these provide a natural starting point for examining future possibilities.

Demographics

Short of national catastrophe, many demographic factors can be estimated with a high degree of accuracy for at least the next ten years. Among these are the aging of our population and smaller families.

As is widely recognized, we are an aging society. This arises from both a decrease in the number of children being born per adult and an increase in average lifespan. During the period 1970–1980, there was an increase in life expectancy of almost one-third of a year per calendar year, and this trend is likely to continue as medical technology improves. One result is that during 1986–2000, we must anticipate an increase in the population over 65 years of age at a rate of about 1.3 percent per year. Due to growth in the working population during much of this period, the severity of the situation will be limited until after the year 2000. However, the political strength of the elderly certainly will increase, as will their ability to bring pressures to bear on the problems they will be facing.

The declining birth rate obviously implies smaller families, and this itself will have an impact on the care of the elderly. The large family home into which grandparents could move at what amounts to marginal costs for room and food is vanishing, making the post-retirement period increasingly expensive. Efforts to have the government take over a larger proportion of this burden through Social Security, health care support, and other forms of contributions are being cut back as the costs of such programs are examined and found unacceptable. This makes pension plans increasingly important, but less than half of the labor force is covered by pensions. The net result is that more of the support requirements are being placed on individuals themselves, with all the financial information and service requirements this involves.

The problems raised by a growing elderly population, particularly in the housing and health care areas, are far from answered. New creative ways for assisting the elderly in the liquidation of a portion of their assets for the sake of gaining security during their last years will become more and more important. Many of the steps that could be taken to assure adequate housing are best designed and planned at a local level and are of a type where banks can have a significant role. This can provide banks with business opportunities, while simultaneously making an important contribution to meeting social needs.

Other aspects of demographics—for example, growth in numbers of working women, in complex household arrangements and in multiple worker families; a decline in new entrants into the job market; and the segmentation of markets by affluence and living styles—have already received much attention from banks and other financial institutions. All of these trends offer well-recognized opportunities for creative actions by banks.

Technology

Chapter 10 on technology emphasized the facilitative nature of technical applications. This view, while fundamentally sound, does not provide a complete picture, since some aspects of technology have the nature of a driving force. This arises for two reasons. First, the technologies of greatest importance for banks are almost all very broad ones, of importance not only to industry, but also to government, defense, education, and home life. These enormous markets provide great incentives for technological advance, assuring that improved technologies will arise whether or not banks choose to employ them.

Second, although a good argument can be made that the new technologies have not improved the productivity of financial service institutions as much as anticipated, technology used as a competitive weapon has been of enormous importance to some individual banks that took the leadership in developing and implementing new applications. Not all pioneers were successful, but some of the leaders that chose the proper timing achieved great gains. This pattern has the effect of forcing other banks to follow in the use of successful new applications, almost regardless of their preference in the matter.

In many areas of technology, such as computer speeds and memory, quite accurate forecasts can be made. In others, such as artificial intelligence (AI) techniques, the situation is less certain. Nevertheless, two important trends are underway that seem almost certain to continue well into the future: First, we are going to become increasingly capable at automatically building information out of data and knowledge out of information. This is the primary objective of AI knowledge-based and expert systems. Note that no reference is made to building wisdom out of information—this domain will continue to belong to humans and will be an important contribution bank directors and management can make to the viability and profitability of their organizations.

Second, unless stopped by law, the pattern of technology-facilitated disintermediation of traditional products that already has impacted the banking community (such as the substitution of commercial paper for what previously would have been loans) will continue. Banks will be disintermediated by other financial service organizations; and banks will be driven to disintermediate or replace their own existing products by substituting new, more efficient mechanisms for meeting customer needs. The latter form of disintermediation is not new—credit card lines of credit as a substitute for individual consumer loans are only one example. Both of these trends appear inevitable; they both pose a threat to banks and again offer opportunities for vision and creativity.

Regulatory Constraints

Special regulatory constraints will continue to be applied to banks, although their form and extent cannot be forecast in any reliable fashion. Deregulation for the sake of improving opportunities for competition in the provision of financial services appears to have peaked in the mid-1980s. In part, this has been the result of failures of both bank and nonbank financial service organizations and the threat that the future will bring more failures affecting even the largest of banks. Socially, we continue to take the view that a bank failure is a special and undesirable event; but we simultaneously tend to set limits on the extent to which government resources should be used to rescue banks that have gotten themselves into difficulties.

Almost by definition, these attitudes make it impossible to have financial services competition that is as free as in other industry sectors. The position appears to be one in which major bank failures always threaten the application of greater restrictions on bank activities. The restrictions can be very selective, such as setting limits concerning the balance among types of loans (e.g., by customer industry or geographical location) that a bank can make, or they can be of a broader type (such as limiting interest rates paid to depositors, but in a more flexible manner than in the past). In the opposite direction, if there are strong indications that regulatory constraints so restrict banks' competitive abilities that their viability is at risk, the result is likely to be either a lowering of existing constraints or the application of restrictions on the activities of nonbank competitors.

Meanwhile, regulation to protect depositors and individual borrowers will continue to increase. Similar measures will be applied more often to protect customers of at least some nonbank competitors, and to the offerings of some newer forms of investment vehicles. The consumerist wave of the 1970s has passed its peak, but the lessons learned by consumer groups during this period have not been forgotten. Also, the litigiousness of our society remains very high. These conditions, when added to the greater sophistication of consumers and their access to larger information resources, position consumerists to continue to challenge financial services practices they regard as inequitable.

The regulatory scene, therefore, is one of great uncertainty; it probably will be more stable than during the early 1980s, but within this general stability there will be many changes of importance to banks.

Industry Structure

As was the case for regulatory constraints, the area of industry structure is characterized by great uncertainty. The trend toward the development of financial conglomerates and agglomerates seems highly likely to continue throughout the last half of the decade. The level of success of these institutions is less certain. The management techniques needed to provide the variety of services offered in a way that produces synergies, while at the same time assuring professionalism, integrity, and an appropriate level of senior management control, are difficult to put in place. This may be an evolutionary problem to be solved through the acquisition of experience and improved use of information resources; or it may be inherent in the efforts to combine activities governed by different philosophies and requiring different business "personalities." For planning purposes, most banks would be wise to assume that the resources behind existing "financial conglomerates" are sufficiently great that their efforts to grow and expand will continue.

The main alternative available to banks—forming partnerships with nonbank organizations for providing specific products and services—may well turn out to be the more sound approach in the long run to the offering of "one-stop" financial services. The partnership concept avoids many of the management difficulties of the conglomerate and has the potential to offer very equivalent services. Advanced information technologies make many arrangements of this type feasible in a way that will be almost transparent to the consumer. The one trend that seems clear is that, by one path or another, mechanisms to increase the range of services accessible through a single organization will tend to increase.

Products

Products and product lines are likely to continue to increase in number and complexity during the next decade. The types of products that will be most successful depend critically on both the economic environment and the tax codes; both of these are likely to continue to change in significant ways. However, a major lesson of the early 1980s is the recognition that product opportunities are limited only by the creativity of their designers. Every environmental change can establish new needs, and these needs lead to new service opportunities. The list of possibilities is almost endless.

As they try to exploit perceived opportunities, financial service organizations will learn, as manufacturers have, that new product failure rates can be high, and that careful experimentation and market testing is necessary if one wishes to be a pioneer. However, the payoff from truly successful innovative products can be very high, so entrepreneurial efforts will continue within and outside the banking system.

What is important to the individual bank is not that it be able to provide all products directly, but that it can provide its customers with access to a good range of such products in a transparent manner. While this relieves the banks of the responsibility of developing a full range of products, it does not relieve them of the need to train their own personnel so that they can discuss the products intelligently with customers.

International Banking

As indicated earlier, financial markets of significant strength are growing throughout the world. This trend will continue, and it will force those nations that maintain a very conservative posture into opening up their systems if they wish to be effective participants.

The larger the bank, the greater its need to be able to participate directly or indirectly in transnational money market activities. Given the size distribution of U.S. banks, it seems likely that most of them will not participate directly in the international markets. However, the entire world financial community is to some extent moving into unknown territory. When markets operate 24 hours a day, there no longer exist "buffering" periods when activity is closed down, accounts are settled, and uncertainties resolved before the markets open again. There may well be sources of instability in this much more dynamic environment. If there are such instabilities, all banks may feel their effects until the instabilities and their causes are identified and means are found to attenuate them on a global basis.

As can be seen, expectations for the future suggest a continuing pattern of the types of changes we have experienced in the recent past, modified mainly to reflect the extent to which past trends seem likely to have peaked or grown. Since we now have acquired considerable experience in living through a period of rapid change, some of the lessons from that experience can be useful guides for surviving in the future.

What Your Bank Can Do

In a period of change, there are no simple rules for survival. Flexibility and a capability for fast response to external events are, of course, important, but are not in themselves sufficient. Most of the required actions simply represent good management practices, based not only on traditional banking principles, but also on skills developed in industries characterized by greater volatility than most banks had to face until the late 1970s. The major areas we believe you will find important in the future concern internal operations at the bank and a bank's external relationships.

Internal Operations at the Bank

Professionalism. Part of the basis for trust in banks on the part of consumers is their sense that banks are among the more professional of the financial service organizations. It is important that this image be maintained in an environment where demand for a wider range of skills will grow. This factor should be central to the human resource policies of your bank. The growing number of products banks will have to provide will require greater personnel training and a careful understanding by your staff of all aspects of the products for which they are responsible and the best means to rapidly access or direct a customer to sources of information on products about which they have less knowledge. Considerable cross-training in products will become important. Fortunately, this whole process can be assisted by careful application of some of the artificial intelligence techniques that will be growing in capability.

If a bank has the goal of developing new products, it will have to acquire the relevant skills. These include market analyses and product design, experimentation, the conduct of appropriate trials, and the scale-up of the new operation, all under careful management control. If one chooses not to be a developer, it will be important not to get lost in "following the leader." Most of the banks that jumped too quickly into new areas where dramatic successes appeared to be arising (such as REIT's, financing of tankers, developing country loans, etc.) paid for this speed if the move was into fields they did not fully understand. The key to professionalism remains the basic rules of good banking, and these must apply now in a world too often characterized by hopes of rapid rather than steady success.

Costs. Central to intelligent management of operations is a good understanding of the costs associated with bank products and services. Establishing such costs is difficult in the bank environment because of the large number of activities that share resources. One way or another, however, it is critical to develop at least good estimates of such costs, so that management control and decisions can be made, not on the basis of functional department costs alone, but on the basis of specific activities and products with which bank costs are associated.

Pricing. Changes in pricing policies must be anticipated in the future. Banks traditionally have underpriced their transaction processing activities for the sake of gaining deposits and, in some cases, float advantages. Failure to charge properly for transactions has permitted other types of organizations to capture many of the deposits and much of the float, while leaving to banks the under-priced transaction process component of their activities.

A number of banks have sought to correct this situation by imposing transaction charges more closely related to costs. Unfortunately, they have tended not to succeed due to competition and, in some cases, failure to offer enough benefits to the consumers and businesses they were trying to get to accept the new and higher cost structure. We expect this situation will continue, but that more rational pricing will slowly emerge.

A certain amount of "price warfare" will continue to exist in the bank world, even occasionally reaching a level of destructive competition. With good understanding of costs, however, banks can make adjustments that will mitigate requirements to occasionally face competitors whose prices may reflect their lack of understanding of their own costs.

Information Resources. Although automation has not increased bank productivity to the extent that was anticipated, it will continue to be a critical area for most banks. The scope and the importance of having good information resources will continue to grow. Careful attention to the availability and the management of both internal and external information is a prerequisite for efficient operations and a necessary tool for intelligent marketing and product development.

Marketing. As indicated earlier, banks need to hone their marketing skills. This is not purely a matter of segmenting the market and producing products appealing to desirable segments; it also includes developing sensitivity and awareness of the needs, interests, likes, and dislikes of customers who use only relatively routine and traditional services. The problem will become more complicated as even these conservative customers begin to use more services—whether traditional (such as more types of accounts at a single bank) or those involving newer and more complex offerings.

Personnel Management. With decreasing numbers of young people entering the work force, personnel problems may become more severe. Combined with the professionalism requirement mentioned earlier, personnel policies and careful attention to the human aspects of operations will become a greater need. Banks generally have offered very desirable working conditions, but much of the work that must be done is relatively routine and clerical in nature. Maintenance of morale, a sense of quality, and ability to relate well to customers under difficult situations require management recognition of the dignity and importance of all its staff, and especially those in routine contact with customers.

External Relationships

In the area of external relationships, perhaps the primary requirement is to develop capabilities for cooperative arrangements that will enable each individual bank to be effective against the particular type of competition it faces. Obviously, when a bank has the resources to compete directly, this is likely to be the preferred course. For most banks in the United States, however, cooperation in one form or another is likely to be necessary in an environment where large organizations are growing and nonbank organizations continue to selectively invade areas previously dominated by banks.

Underlying successful application of management efforts in all of the above areas is the need for the form of vision described earlier—to provide the guidance that will enable all the staff of the bank to sense the direction in which they should move and the style and attitudes they should be expressing to the outer world. Directors can do a great deal, both to help develop this vision and to encourage management in the development of appropriate practices to support the bank's vision and its strategy.

GLOSSARY

Account Analysis A comparison of the cost of service provided to support a checking account and the earnings on the balances in the account during the month. The excess of cost over earnings is assessed as a charge against the account.

Asset/Liability Management The process of deciding on the characteristics of the financial assets and liabilities the bank will own or owe at any particular time, in particular the yield, maturity, and risk characteristics.

Assets The financial instruments (loans, leases, bonds, notes, currency) and real property (buildings, computers, furnishings) owned by the bank.

Audit Committee A committee of the board responsible for arranging for an independent organization to examine the records of the bank for accuracy, completeness, and compliance with regulatory requirements and generally accepted accounting principles. The committee reports the results of this examination to the board and shareholders. The committee also works closely with the bank's internal auditor and regulatory agencies.

Automated Clearing House/Electronic Clearing House A facility that performs intermember (financial institutions) clearing of paperless entries between such institutions. Most ACHs are operated by the Federal Reserve and use rules, procedures, and programs developed on a local basis by their participating financial institutions under the general direction of the National Automated Clearing House Association.

Automated Customer Services The computerized non-banking transaction, reporting, and record keeping functions performed by the bank for customers. The term is also used to describe the automated services that one bank sells to another.

Automated Teller Machines (ATMs) Computer-controlled terminals, located on the premises of financial institutions or elsewhere, through which customers may make deposits, withdrawals, or other transactions as they would through a bank teller. Groups of banks sometimes share ATM networks located throughout a region of the country that may include portions of several states.

Bank-at-Home The use of telephones, personal computers, and/or television sets by consumers in their homes to complete banking transactions. Being tested in a variety of forms.

Bankers Acceptance Bankers acceptances are negotiable time drafts or bills of exchange that have been accepted by a bank which, by accepting, assumes the obligation to pay the holder of the draft the face amount of the instrument on the maturity date specified. They are used primarily to finance the export, import, shipment, or storage of goods.

269

Bank Examination   The review of operating and financial affairs of the bank by state or federal bank supervisory personnel to determine that the bank is financially sound and operating in compliance with banking law and regulations.

Bank Holding Company   A corporation owning one or more banks, which may also own certain non-bank businesses if approved by the Federal Reserve Board.

Book Value   The value at which a security is carried on the bank's balance sheet. Book value is often acquisition cost, plus or minus accretion or amortization, which can differ from market value significantly.

Branch Banking   The right of banks headquartered in some states to take deposits, cash checks, and make loans at more than one location (branch) in the state. Where branch banking is not allowed, "unit banking" prevails.

Business Unit   A part of a bank managed and accounted for as a self-contained, independent business, serving customers outside the bank and/or other business units in the bank. These units are encouraged to innovate and contribute to corporate profits, while remaining consistent with corporate policies and objectives.

Capital   The bank's funds, resulting from sale of stock, bonds, or notes issued by the bank, and retained earnings.

Capital Adequacy   The degree to which a bank's capital is considered by regulators, investors, or other observers to be sufficient to insure the financial health and soundness of the bank. The common measure is the ratio of capital to assets.

Cash Management   The process by which a corporate financial officer optimizes the use of short-term corporate funds through prompt collection of funds due, profitable investment of corporate balances, and conservative timing of disbursements.

Cease-and-Desist Order   An order issued after notice and opportunity for hearing, requiring a depository institution, a holding company, or a depository institution official to terminate unlawful, unsafe, or unsound banking practices. Cease-and-desist orders are issued by the appropriate federal regulatory agencies under the Financial Institutions Supervisory Act and can be enforced directly by the courts.

Certificate of Deposit ("CD")   A contract representing a bank's promise to repay, with interest, funds left on deposit for a fixed period of time. Small CDs (under $100,000) are not negotiable, since the bank will pay only the original depositor. Larger CDs are frequently negotiable.

Chain Banking   Control of more than one bank by the same group of individual owners. Chain banking is most commonly encountered in unit banking states and in states that limit or prohibit holding companies.

Charter   The legal authorization to establish a bank, granted by a state or by the federal government in the case of a national bank.

Check Clearing   The movement of checks from the banks or other depository institutions where they are deposited back to those on which they are written, and funds movement in the opposite direction. This process results in credits to accounts at the institutions of deposit and corresponding debits to the accounts at the paying institutions. The Federal Reserve participates in check clearing through its nationwide facilities, though many checks are cleared by private sector arrangements.

Check Truncation   The practice of retaining checks at a bank and providing the customer with only a listing (by check number) of the checks received. The objective is to lower the cost of providing account services to customers.

Clearinghouse   An institution where mutual claims are settled between accounts of member depository institutions. Clearinghouses among banks have traditionally been organized for check-clearing purposes, but more recently have cleared other types of settlements, including electronic fund transfers.

Commercial Paper   A contract representing a corporation's promise to repay, with interest, funds paid to the corporation for a fixed (usually short) period of time. The contract is negotiable, since the corporation will pay the current owner at the date of maturity.

Community Reinvestment Act   A 1977 federal law that encourages investment in the immediate communities served by depository institutions.

Comptroller of the Currency   The senior administrative officer of the office in the Department of the Treasury responsible for the chartering and supervision of national banks. The agency is known as the Office of the Comptroller of the Currency, or OCC.

Consumer Group   As used in this book, the collection of bank units directed at serving the needs of the individual. The units which might be included are branch administration, branches, small business loan servicing, and consumer loan servicing.

Core Deposits   Deposits, either demand or time, which remain with the institution regardless of the level of interest rates. "Hot" deposits, on the other hand, move to higher interest rate vehicles when an opportunity exists (disintermediation).

Correspondent Banking   The network of relationships among commercial banks through which banks assist each other with lending and operating services.

Covering Contracts   Contracts intended to reduce the risk of a price change on a foreign currency or other asset by hedging.

Credit Card   Any card, plate, or coupon book that may be used repeatedly to borrow money or buy goods and services on credit.

Credit History   A record of how a person has borrowed and repaid debts.

Credit Risk   The possibility of non-payment associated with a loan.

Credit Scoring System   A statistical system used to determine whether or not to grant credit by assigning numerical scores to various characteristics related to creditworthiness.

Debit Card   A card issued by a bank to an individual account holder, used to identify the customer at merchant or banking locations for withdrawal, deposit, or payment services.

Demand Deposits   A deposit payable on demand, or a time deposit with a maturity period or required notice period of less than 14 days, on which the depository institution does not reserve the right to require at least 14 days written notice of intended withdrawal. Commonly takes the form of a checking account.

Demand Loan   A loan that the bank may request payment of at any time, in contrast to a term loan, which has a specified repayment schedule.

Depository Institutions Deregulation and Monetary Control Act of 1980   Among its major provisions, this act applied uniform reserve requirements to all depository institutions with certain types of accounts and required reports from these depository institutions. It also extended access to the Federal Reserve discount window and to other Federal Reserve services in step with the implementation of a fee schedule. It authorized NOW accounts and the phase-out of ceilings on interest paid on deposits.

Direct Deposit   The process whereby a check's issuer delivers the check directly to the payee's bank for credit to his or her account. The term is often used to refer to the Federal Government's direct deposit program for Social Security checks. It is also used for military and civilian salary payments, Civil Service and Railroad Retirement annuity payments, and Veterans Administration compensation and pension payments.

Discount Broker   A broker who provides execution services for buyers or sellers of securities, as agent, but does not provide advice to customers.

Discount Rate   The interest rate at which eligible depository institutions may borrow funds, usually for short periods, directly from the Federal Reserve Banks. The law requires the board of directors of each Reserve Bank to establish the discount rate every 14 days subject to the approval of the Board of Governors.

Discount Window   The facility at a Federal Reserve Bank through which an eligible institution can borrow from the Federal Reserve Bank at the "discount rate." Any institution holding demand deposits or balances in negotiable order for withdrawal (NOW) accounts is eligible.

Double Counting of Balances   A customer may get services from a number of areas of the bank without paying a fee because of substantial deposit balances. The term "double counting of balances" is often used to describe the situation when the deposits, while adequate to pay for some services, are inadequate to pay for all services received.

Douglas Amendment   An amendment to the Bank Holding Company Act of 1956 which allows a holding company owning a bank chartered in one state to acquire a bank chartered in another state only if permitted by the law of the second state.

Edge Act Corporation   An organization chartered by the Federal Reserve to engage in international banking operations. The Board acts upon applications by U.S. and foreign banking organizations to establish Edge corporations. It also examines Edge corporations and their subsidiaries. The Edge corporation gets its name from Senator Walter Edge of New Jersey, the sponsor of the original legislation to permit formation of such organizations.

Equity Capital   Funds invested in the bank by stockholders plus retained earnings.

Eurodollars   Deposits denominated in U.S. dollars at banks and other financial institutions outside the United States. Although this name originated because of the large amounts of such deposits held at banks in Western Europe, similar deposits in other parts of the world are also called Eurodollars.

Factoring   The sale of accounts receivable by a non-financial business to a bank or other financial business, which then collects from the debtors. The receivables are sold by a non-financial business at a discount to obtain earlier use of the funds.

Federal Deposit Insurance Corporation (FDIC)   Agency of the federal government that insures accounts at most commercial banks and savings banks. The FDIC also has primary federal supervisory authority over insured state banks that are not members of the Federal Reserve System.

Federal Funds   Reserve balances that depository institutions lend each other, usually on an overnight basis. In addition, federal funds include certain other kinds of borrowings by depository institutions from each other and from federal agencies.

Federal Home Loan Bank Board (FHLBB)   The agency of the federal government that supervises all federal savings and loan associations and federally insured state-chartered savings and loan associations. The FHLBB also operates the Federal Savings and Loan Insurance Corporation, which insures accounts at federal savings banks and savings and loan associations that apply and are accepted. In addition, the FHLBB directs the Federal Home Loan Bank System, which provides a flexible credit facility for member savings institutions to promote the availability of home financing. The FHL Banks also own the Federal Home Loan Mortgage Corporation, established in 1970 to promote secondary markets for mortgages.

Federal Open Market Committee   A 12-member committee consisting of the seven members of the Federal Reserve Board and five of the twelve Federal Reserve Bank presidents. The president of the Federal Reserve Bank of New York is a permanent member, while the other Federal Reserve presidents serve on a rotating basis. The Committee sets objectives for the growth of money and credit that are implemented through purchases and sales of U.S. government securities in the open market. The FOMC also establishes policy relating to System operations in the foreign exchange markets.

Federal Reserve System   The central bank of the United States, created by Congress, consists of a seven-member Board of Governors in Washington, D.C., 12 regional Reserve Banks, and depository institutions that are subject to reserve requirements. All national banks are members; state chartered banks may elect to become members, and state members are supervised by the Board of Governors and the Reserve Banks. Reserve requirements established by the Federal Reserve Board apply to nonmember depository institutions as well as member banks. Both classes of institutions have access to Federal Reserve discount borrowing privileges and Federal Reserve services on an equal basis.

Fiduciary Responsibility   The legal power to act on behalf of another, with the attendant obligation to act within the law, in that party's best interest.

Fixed Rate   A traditional approach to determining the finance charge payable on an extension of credit. A predetermined and certain rate of interest is applied to the principal.

Fixed-Rate Long-Term Assets   Contracts owned by a bank under which a borrower is committed to repay funds in the relatively distant future (more than 10 years) and to pay a stated, unchanging rate of interest on the debt in the meantime. Bonds and mortgages with maturities more than ten years in the future are examples.

Flagship Bank   The largest bank in a multi-bank holding company; also referred to as the lead bank.

Functional Organization   The arrangement of a bank's personnel into groups with responsibility for carrying out specialized functions in the bank, such as operations, investments, commercial lending, and branch administration.

Garn-St Germain Depository Institutions Act of 1982   Legislation providing for the phase-out of differentials in interest rates paid by banks and thrifts on deposits, authorizing money market accounts, approving new powers for thrift institutions, and granting regulators new authority to deal with failing institutions.

Glass-Steagall Act   A portion of the Banking Act of 1933, the Glass-Steagall Act forbids commercial banks from engaging in investment banking.

Grandfathered Activities   Nonbank activities, some of which would normally not be permissible for bank holding companies and foreign banks in the United States, but which were acquired or engaged in before a particular date. Such activities may be continued under the "grandfather" clauses of the Bank Holding Company Act and the International Banking Act.

Interest Rate Risk   The possibility that a change in the prevailing level of interest rates during the life of a fixed-rate loan will lower (or increase) the income to the bank, arising out of the difference between the rate paid by the bank for funds and the (fixed) rate received on the loan.

Interlocking Directorates   The presence of several persons on the boards of more than one corporation, giving them the opportunity to influence decisions in each corporation for the benefit of the other(s).

Investment Group   As used in this book, the collection of bank units whose activities involve managing the bank's portfolio and operating the money desk, which handles the sale of repurchase agreements, large certificates of deposit, treasury issues, and municipal securities to the public.

IRA/Keogh   A tax deferment product offered not only by banks (where it is a term deposit product) but also by insurance underwriters, securities brokers, consumer finance companies, mortgage bankers, and others. These offerors provide trustee services under IRA and Keogh plans.

Item Processing   The internal receiving, recording, and perhaps redistribution of checks, drafts, or other debit and credit items written by customers of an institution or deposited by its customers and drawn on another institution. This includes posting or recording of the check in the individual customer's account and the microfilming and balancing of all such items received.

Letters of Credit   Letters of credit (LCs) are evidence of a financial institution's willingness to underwrite the dealings of its customers in arrangements where the customer is unknown to the seller of the product or in countries where the extension of trade credit to foreigners is forbidden (e.g., Japan).

Leverage   The ratio of total assets to the equity capital of a bank or any organization using a mix of invested and borrowed funds.

Liabilities   The financial obligations of a bank or other business to others. Deposits and purchased funds are the primary liabilities of a commercial bank.

Liquidity Risk   The risk that a new loan (asset) can be funded only by acquiring deposits or other funds (liabilities) at a rate above the yield of the loan or by liquidating securities (assets) below book value.

Margin Account   An account with a broker in which the customer holds nominal ownership of securities for which funds were borrowed to finance the purchase. The margin is the fraction of the purchase price paid by the purchaser from his own funds.

Market Organization   The arrangement of a bank's personnel into groups with responsibility for serving the needs of all customers in a particular category, such as small businesses, wealthy individuals, and international corporations.

Matched Book   If the distribution of the maturities of a bank's assets equals that of its liabilities, the bank is said to be "running a matched book." The term is commonly used in connection with the Euromarket.

Maturity Profile   The distribution of the total amount of an asset or liability balance sheet item into categories based upon maturity.

McFadden Act   A 1927 Act of Congress which establishes some basic rules for national banks. Specifically, this act subjects the nationally chartered banks headquartered in a state to the same restrictions on branching that the state's law applies to state chartered banks.

Member Banks   A depository institution that is a member of the Federal Reserve. All national banks are required to be System members, and state-chartered commercial banks and mutual savings banks may elect to become members. Member banks own stock in Federal Reserve Banks and elect some of the Reserve Bank directors.

Money Market Funds   A mutualized, non-insured form of investment providing prevailing interest rates paid on large (over $100,000) certificates of deposit or commercial paper instruments to investors of as little as $1,000.

Money Stock:

   M1—   The sum of currency held by the public, plus travelers' checks, plus demand deposits, plus other checkable deposits (i.e., negotiable order of withdrawal [NOW] accounts, automatic transfer service [ATS] accounts, and credit union share drafts).

   M2—M1   plus savings accounts and small-denomination time deposits, plus shares in money market mutual funds (other than those restricted to institutional investors), plus overnight Eurodollars and repurchase agreements.

   M3—M2   plus large-denomination time deposits at all depository institutions, large-denomination term repurchase agreements, and shares on money market mutual funds restricted to institutional investors.

Mortgage Banking   The process of acting as an intermediary between the loan origination and funding systems. Generally, the mortgage banker will be equipped with the origination system and will tap national secondary markets for funding. Three common secondary marketmakers exist: Federal National Mortgage Association, Government National Mortgage Association, and Federal Home Loan Mortgage Corporation.

Mortgage Lending   The extension of credit secured by a lien on real property. At one point, the insurance industry was the single largest component of the home mortgage market. Today, that is not the case. Insurance companies are opting to concentrate on the large commercial property market because of increasing real estate values and opportunities to earn additional interest by participating in increases in rents as well as the secondary mortgage market. Others participate in the mortgage market by purchasing individual mortgages or packages of mortgages assembled and marketed by such organizations as the Federal Home Loan Mortgage Corporation (FREDDIE MAC) in secondary markets.

Mutual Capital Certificates   A special purpose financial instrument authorized by a 1980 Act of Congress for use by mutual institutions to raise capital funds. The certificates carry no ownership rights in the institution and are not deposit instruments. They yield dividends and have first claim on the bank's earnings, comparable to a preferred stock.

Negotiable Order of Withdrawal (NOW) Account   An interest-earning account on which checks may be drawn. Withdrawals from NOW accounts may be subject to a 14-day or more notice requirement, although such is rarely imposed. NOW accounts may be offered by commercial banks, savings banks, and savings and loan associations, and may be owned only by individuals and certain nonprofit organizations and governmental units.

Net Income   The difference between total receipts and total expenses for a specific period of time, for the bank or an operating unit within the bank.

Net Interest Income   The difference between the interest earned in a specific period of time on loans and investments made by the bank and the amount paid out in interest on the funds used to make these loans and investments, expressed in dollars.

Net Interest Margin ("Spread")   The difference between interest earned and interest paid by a bank during a specific period, expressed as a percentage rate.

Net Worth   The difference between total assets and total liabilities on the bank's Statement of Condition. Net worth results from the retention of earnings and proceeds from the sale of stock in the bank.

Nonbank Bank   A new type of financial institution which takes deposits *or* makes commercial loans, but not both, in order to avoid fulfilling the legal definition of a bank. (A bank takes deposits *and* makes commercial loans.) Such an institution could be used to circumvent the Bank Holding Company Act, if the courts (or Congress) provide legal sanction for it.

Open Market Operations   Purchases and sales of government and certain other securities in the open market by the New York Federal Reserve Bank as directed by the FOMC in order to influence the volume of money and credit in the economy. Purchases inject reserves into the depository system and foster expansion in money and credit; sales have the opposite effect.

Options/Futures   Options are a tradeable right to buy or sell securities. Futures contracts are legally binding agreements that call for the purchase or sale of a real or hypothetical commodity at a stated price and future point in time.

Overdraft Checking Account   A checking account associated with a line of credit that allows a person to write checks for more than the actual balance in the account, with a finance charge on the overdraft.

Pay-by-Phone   A payment system based on telephone instructions for payments to third parties. Usually associated with monthly payments, pay-by-phone systems enable a consumer to avoid checks, postage, and delays in the mail.

Performance Assessment   Monitoring and evaluating the work of the bank's managers, primarily through financial results achieved.

Personal Trust   Services wherein financial institutions manage the assets of others for a fee. Wholesaling aspects involve correspondent relationships and trust companies as agents for financial institutions without the necessary infrastructure to support the activity.

Point-of-Sale Programs   Programs or systems established by banks, merchants, and others to facilitate customer payments at the point of sale of goods and services. In different parts of the country, POS systems have been established to verify or guarantee checks, to process credit card transactions, and in a few instances to process on-line debits against consumer transaction accounts.

Points   Finance charges paid by the borrower at the beginning of a loan in addition to monthly interest; each point equals one percent of the loan amount.

Portfolio of a Bank   The securities owned by the bank. Sometimes the term "portfolio" is also applied to other categories of assets, such as the "loan portfolio" or the "mortgage portfolio."

Prime Rate   The rate charged by a bank on loans to its most creditworthy corporate borrowers.

Rate Sensitivity   The amount that the net interest margin changes for a given change in overall interest rate levels.

Regulation Q   The regulation of the Federal Reserve Board that established legal ceilings on the interest rates payable on deposits. Regulation Q is statutorily scheduled to be phased out by 1986.

Repurchase Agreement   An investment offering based on government securities. The investor purchases the security subject to the agreement of the bank to buy it back at a set price and time.

Reserves   Funds set aside by depository institutions to meet reserve requirements. For member banks, reserve requirements are satisfied with holdings of vault cash and/or balances at the Federal Reserve Banks. Depository institutions that are not members of the Federal Reserve System may hold their reserves in the same manner, or they may pass the reserve balances through a correspondent institution to the Federal Reserve Banks.

Revolving Line of Credit   Generally a consumer product that enables an individual to borrow and repay loans under a predetermined and approved limit, this product is often wholesaled by banks to NDFIs (nondepository financial institutions) and retailed with the latters' other product lines (money market account, annuity, debit card).

Short-Term Liabilities   Obligations of the bank to repay the holder at a stated time, generally between 30 and 180 days after issue. For some purposes, however, the short term can be a period of up to one year.

Statement of Condition   The balance sheet of a bank, showing assets, liabilities, and net worth.

Subordinated Notes and Debentures   Debentures are bonds secured only by the general credit of the issuer, while notes are issues with a relatively short original maturity. When these are subordinated, their claims against the corporation rank after those of holders of various other unsecured debts of the issuer.

Syndicated Loans   Loans involving multiple banks and nondepository financial institutions in cases where the overall credit involved is in excess of each bank's comfort or legal lending limit. One bank usually acts as agent for the others, thereby earning a fee for its efforts (and therefore becoming a transaction product provider).

Thrift Institutions   Depository institutions other than commercial banks—that is, savings banks, savings and loan associations, and credit unions. Originally conceived as exclusively serving the retail sector (and thereby promoting thrift), the equalization of powers among the different types of depository institution is breaking down many of the historic distinctions.

Time Deposits   Funds in accounts of the bank that can be withdrawn by the account holder only on request and, in some cases, only after they have been on deposit for a certain minimum length of time (without penalty for early withdrawal). Neither checks nor NOW drafts can be written on time deposits.

Trading Account   The inventory of securities held by the bank primarily for resale to customers. The bank is acting as dealer in securities.

Transaction Account   This is a new term in banking parlance, used to describe an account like checking or NOW. Established for paying transactions, its primary value is to permit differentiation from savings or investment oriented accounts.

Treasury Bills   Short-term U.S. Treasury securities issued in minimum denominations of $10,000 and usually having original maturities of 3, 6, or 12 months. Investors purchase bills at prices lower than the face value of the bills; the return to the investor is the difference between the price paid for the bills and the amount received when the bills are sold or when they mature. Treasury bills are the type of security used most frequently in open market operations.

Treasury Bonds   Long-term U.S. Treasury securities usually having initial maturities of more than 10 years and issued in denominations of $1,000 or more, depending on the specific issue. Bonds pay interest semiannually, with principal payable at maturity.

Treasury Notes   Intermediate-term coupon-bearing U.S. Treasury securities having initial maturities from 1 to 10 years and issued in denominations of $1,000 or more, depending on the maturity of the issue. Notes pay interest semiannually, and the principal is payable at maturity.

Trust Group   As used in this book, the collection of bank units serving the trust-related needs of both high net worth individual and corporate customers. The units that might be included are personal trust, corporate trust (pension, profit sharing), transfer agent, and custodian.

Unit Bank   A bank with only one office—i.e., a bank with no branches.

Variable Rate   A variable rate agreement, as distinguished from a fixed rate agreement, calls for an interest rate that may fluctuate over the life of the loan. The rate is often tied to an index that reflects changes in market rates of interest. A fluctuation in the rate causes changes in either the payments or the length of the loan term. Limits are often placed on the degree to which the interest rate or the payments can vary.

Velocity   The rate at which money balances turn over in a period for expenditures on goods and services (often measured as the ratio of GNP to the money stock). A larger velocity means that a given quantity of money is associated with a greater dollar volume of transactions.

Wholesale Banks   Banks with most or all of their customer relationships concentrated in the business sector of the economy.

Wholesale Group   As used in this book, the collection of bank units directed at serving primarily the borrowing needs of corporate customers. The units that might be included are commercial lending, collateral lending, leasing, mortgage banking, real estate lending, commercial finance and factoring, loan servicing, and loan review.

Wholesale/Retail Lockbox   Also known as remote item processing or remittance processing. A banking service provided for the rapid collection of a customer's receivables and rapid credit to the customer's account. The service provided by the bank includes collecting mail from the company's post office box; sorting, totaling, and recording the payments; processing the items; and making the necessary bank deposit or forwarding the funds to another depository.

Wire Transfer   The process of moving customer money from one place to another without the transfer of paper documents by means of telecommunication between financial institutions. Larger banks have access to Federal Reserve facilities, while smaller institutions rely on their correspondent banks to perform the task. The important characteristics of wire transfer are speed and the secured nature of transmission.

INDEX